Secret Violences

Secret Violences

The Political Cinema of Michelangelo Antonioni, 1960–1975

Sławomir Masłoń

BLOOMSBURY ACADEMIC
NEW YORK • LONDON • OXFORD • NEW DELHI • SYDNEY

BLOOMSBURY ACADEMIC
Bloomsbury Publishing Inc
1385 Broadway, New York, NY 10018, USA
50 Bedford Square, London, WC1B 3DP, UK
29 Earlsfort Terrace, Dublin 2, Ireland

BLOOMSBURY, BLOOMSBURY ACADEMIC and the Diana logo
are trademarks of Bloomsbury Publishing Plc

First published in the United States of America 2023
Paperback edition published 2024

Copyright © Sławomir Masłoń, 2023, 2025

Cover design: Eleanor Rose
Cover image: Michelangelo Antonioni, Zabriskie Point, 1970
© Allstar Picture Library Limited / Alamy

All rights reserved. No part of this publication may be reproduced or transmitted in any form or by any means, electronic or mechanical, including photocopying, recording, or any information storage or retrieval system, without prior permission in writing from the publishers.

Bloomsbury Publishing Inc does not have any control over, or responsibility for, any third-party websites referred to or in this book. All internet addresses given in this book were correct at the time of going to press. The author and publisher regret any inconvenience caused if addresses have changed or sites have ceased to exist, but can accept no responsibility for any such changes.

Library of Congress Cataloging-in-Publication Data
Names: Masłoń, Sławomir, author.
Title: Secret violences : the political cinema of Michelangelo Antonioni, 1960-1975 / Sławomir Masłoń.
Description: New York : Bloomsbury Academic, 2023. |
Includes bibliographical references and index. |
Summary: "A reinterpretation of Antonioni's most important films as political cinema, engaged with issues which are still crucial in the 21st century"– Provided by publisher.
Identifiers: LCCN 2022043146 (print) | LCCN 2022043147 (ebook) |
ISBN 9781501398230 (hardback) | ISBN 9781501398278 (paperback) |
ISBN 9781501398247 (epub) | ISBN 9781501398254 (pdf) |
ISBN 9781501398261 (ebook other)
Subjects: LCSH: Antonioni, Michelangelo–Criticism and interpretation. |
Motion pictures–Political aspects.
Classification: LCC PN1998.3.A58 M285 2023 (print) | LCC PN1998.3.A58 (ebook) |
DDC 791.4302/33092–dc23/eng/20221121
LC record available at https://lccn.loc.gov/2022043146
LC ebook record available at https://lccn.loc.gov/2022043147

ISBN:	HB:	978-1-5013-9823-0
	PB:	978-1-5013-9827-8
	ePDF:	978-1-5013-9825-4
	eBook:	978-1-5013-9824-7

Typeset by Integra Software Services Pvt. Ltd.

To find out more about our authors and books visit www.bloomsbury.com and sign up for our newsletters.

Robertson: Beautiful. [...] Doesn't the desert have the same effect on you?
Locke: No. I prefer men to landscapes.
Robertson: There are men who live in the desert.
The Passenger

Nothing appears as it should in a world where nothing is certain. The only thing certain is the existence of a secret violence that makes everything uncertain.
Lucretius quoted by Antonioni

Contents

Introduction		1
1	*L'avventura* (1960)	11
2	*La notte* (1961)	41
3	*L'eclisse* (1962)	71
4	*Red Desert* (1964)	93
5	*Blow-Up* (1966)	115
6	*Zabriskie Point* (1970)	133
7	*The Passenger* (1975)	161
Bibliography		177
Filmography		181
Index		183

Introduction

Although Michelangelo Antonioni gained international fame, first in the art cinema world with *L'avventura* (1960) and then with the commercial success of *Blow-Up* (1966), and thus became one of the icons of "modernist" cinema, his position in the pantheon of great directors has never been quite secure. Unlike his famous contemporaries, like Ingmar Bergman or Luchino Visconti, who might be criticized for this or that, but whose essential contribution to the art of cinema is hardly ever questioned, Antonioni's work has been repeatedly denigrated from many angles for both aesthetic and political reasons. Though the historical importance of some of Antonioni's films as an incarnation of certain attitudes and problems characteristic of the 1960s and '70s is not denied, they are often considered passé, artificial, and boring.

On the one hand, as far as their subject matter is concerned, it was a critical fashion while Antonioni was making his major films to discuss them philosophically in the existentialist context of post-war alienation (from Monica Vitti's characters who are interpreted as being in the grip of anxiety to David Locke in *The Passenger* seeming to be tired of his social roles and searching for authentic existence) and moralistically (rather than politically) as showing the crisis of traditional middle-class values brought about by the quick modernization and "Americanization" of Italy in the 1950s. On the other hand, there was Antonioni's notorious style (his predilection for abstract forms, for shots in which nothing happens in conventional narrative terms, etc.), which differed conspicuously from both the language of mainstream cinema and the new post-neorealist arthouse orthodoxies. The style is obviously "artificial"—if one compares it to the supposedly more "natural," that is, unobtrusive, narrative conventions of some other famous *auteurs* (again Bergman and Visconti are good points of comparison)—so it has often been taken to be a liability, which can be exemplified by Pier Paolo Pasolini's derogatory remark that Antonioni's vision "is delirious with estheticism,"[1] that is, too arty for its own good. In relation to this, Antonioni has also been accused of not being professional enough. This was straightforwardly formulated by Bergman:

> Antonioni never completely learned his job. ... If, for example, he found a certain street for *The Red Desert*, he would have the houses of the damned street repainted. This is the shortcoming of the aesthete. He concentrated on the individual shot but couldn't understand that a film is a rhythmic flow of images, a breathing, a moving process. To him, by contrast, everything depended upon this shot, and then that one, and then another one.[2]

This accusation has also at times taken a more convoluted and surprising form: that Antonioni's cinema is *too literary*, which seems strange considering that his major films are visually stunning, narratively "thin," and in most cases rely quite little on spoken dialogue. But when one reflects on the context of these accusations, it becomes clear that what is meant by "too literary" is that his films are not cinematic enough, because they stretch their language to include the discourses of other arts (painting, architecture, literature) and their modes of experimentation. Because these modes are purportedly foreign to the art of cinema, Antonioni's work is held to be "impure."[3] But what might "pure" mean in the context of a bastard art form such as cinema is (an impure inmixture of visuals, sound, and narrative) and in the case of a director who tends to desubstantialize plots, thus diminishing the "literary" (narrative) content of his films in order better to expose their visual and aural inventiveness? One would expect that this is precisely a movement toward "pure" cinema, but apparently it is not. If imports from other discourses (if they are imports) that tend to undermine the narrative and make it of secondary importance are somehow polluting, what is the real thing that is supposedly being polluted? It seems that what constitutes "pure" cinema for Antonioni's critics is a seamless integration of the multiple

---

[1] Pier Paolo Pasolini, "The Cinema of Poetry," in *Movies and Methods, Volume I*, ed. Bill Nichols (Berkeley: University of California Press, 1976), 553.

[2] Ingmar Bergman, *Interviews*, ed. Raphael Shargel (Jackson: University Press of Mississippi, 2007), 192.

[3] "Antonioni does approach cinema like a painter, which is to say that, despite the stylishness of the surface of his images, his cinema is impure—it is derived from a variety of artistic and cultural sources and intervenes not only in the history of cinema, but in the history of aesthetic modernism. ... Antonioni's cinema takes itself too seriously, and the problem of its doing so extends from its desire to want to be something other than cinema—not more than cinema, just not cinema on its own or *purely* on its own terms." Laura Rascaroli and John David Rhodes, "Interstitial, Pretentious, Dead: Antonioni at 100," in *Antonioni: Centenary Essays*, ed. Laura Rascaroli and John David Rhodes (Basingstoke: BFI/Palgrave Macmillan, 2011), 6.

aspects of film for a reason (Bergman's images are characteristically organic: "a breathing, a moving process"). And because to blend visuals, sound, and narrative "organically" means that they cannot be even relatively autonomous (their autonomization would result in emphasizing the impure status of their inmixture), one aspect of cinema, under this view, has to subordinate the others. In other words, what is supposed to govern "a rhythmic flow of images," in which the organization of particular shots is of secondary importance, is a narrative purpose. Both Bergman and Visconti are again good examples here; it turns out that "pure" cinema is surprisingly literary. But need this kind of overwhelming and imperative *Gesamtkunstwerk* machine, sure of its effects (and the professional rules by means of which they can be achieved), which were created to subdue the viewer, be taken as the only proper incarnation of cinema?

Antonioni came of age as a director precisely when the narrative machine was coming to be questioned by Italian neorealism, which wanted the multifaceted reality of ambiguous facts to spill into the cinematic spectacle, so that the latter could render the former's material truth. And neorealism believed in the solidity of this truth: three-dimensional reality and the substantiality of bodies (both human beings and things in their relations) are at the center of attention, presented in long shots and rendered by the depth-of-field photography, which give the material world a heightened presence in which human agents struggle to carve out their routes. The neorealist universe is one in which the essential events take place outside and in which what matters is how the bodies relate to themselves within a given constellation. Although Antonioni had a role at the origin of the Italian neorealism (working in the 1940s with both Visconti and Fellini), his own early efforts in feature film aimed at taking the "neo-reality" in directions it seemed unlikely to go.[4] His basic intuition was that the solidity neorealist reality offers is reductive, that something more than objective material order is needed in order to render reality more fully.

One can say that at this point his inspirations might indeed have been literary—Antonioni argued for the psychologization of the neorealist insight:

> And is neorealism over? Not exactly. It is more correct to say that neorealism is evolving, because whenever a movement or a current ends, it gives life to what comes after it. ... Today, once the problem with the bicycle [in De Sica's *Bicycle Thieves*] has been eliminated ... it is important to see what is inside this man

---

[4] Though, as many critics have noted, there are affinities between Antonioni's Italian feature films and Roberto Rossellini's films with Ingrid Bergman, especially *Journey to Italy* (*Viaggio in Italia*, 1954).

whose bicycle was stolen, what are his thoughts, what are his feelings, how much is left inside of him of his past experiences, of the war, of the period after the war, of everything that has happened to our country, a country which, like so many others, has just come out of such an important and serious experience.[5]

Although this proposition sounds quite traditional—almost as if Antonioni wanted to write a Stendhal novel—it should of course be taken in the context of modernist literary experimentation (Antonioni's acknowledged literary influences range from Joseph Conrad to F. S. Fitzgerald and T. S. Eliot), which desubstantialized reality by turning attention from the object to its impression in the human mind, in order to represent the world in more subtle ways and be able to tell different kinds of stories (or truths) than those in which causes and effects predominate.

However, when one examines Antonioni's early efforts in feature film, it turns out that psychological analysis of the characters is of only tertiary importance in them. The only exception is *The Girl Friends* (*Le Amiche*, 1955), a story adapted from a psychological novella by Cesare Pavese, in which relationships between a number of female protagonists (some male characters are also involved) are analyzed by presenting them as different psychological types. This, however, results in a film close to the Italian cinematic mainstream of the time, into which traces of Antonioni's distinctive style are quite smoothly integrated. On the other hand, if we consider *Story of a Love Affair* (*Cronaca di un amore*, 1950) or *The Lady without Camellias* (*La signora senza camelie*, 1953), these films offer completely depsychologized characters, due to the narrative conventions used. Because *Story of a Love Affair* is a noir narrative involving blind instinct, guilt, and planned murder and *The Lady without Camellias* is a melodramatic story of male oppression and betrayal and of female sacrifice and suffering, the characters' behavior cannot be analyzed psychologically the way it is possible in *The Girl Friends*, because the protagonists are only genre ciphers and thus they follow the conventions of their genres rather than precepts of any credible "psychology."[6] What stands out, however, in these films is Antonioni's innovative

---

[5] Michelangelo Antonioni, *The Architecture of Vision: Writings and Interviews on Cinema*, ed. Carlo Di Carlo and Giorgio Tinazzi, American edition by Marga Cottino-Jones (Chicago: Chicago University Press, 2007), 7–8.

[6] *The Vanquished* (*I Vinti*, 1952) is a weird affair consisting of three separate episodes shot in three different countries (Italy, France, and England) and in three different languages, supposedly dealing with the pathologies of disillusioned and materialistically oriented youth. Though the film obviously possesses some features of Antonioni's style, the dominance of the didactic subject matter thoroughly contravenes his methods. This is perhaps most visible in the English episode, which is uncharacteristically conventionally comic (though dealing with a murder).

style, which does not really fit the familiar subject matter, and thus, in a sense, undermines the genre conventions by focusing on matters which are external and therefore indifferent to them. For instance, by disjoining the spoken word from the image, that is, eliminating narratively important on-screen action, Antonioni frees the camera to engage in an interplay with the actors moving out of and into the frame, constantly displacing the film's spatial coordinates by skillful manipulation of the relationship between the on-screen and off-screen space, often relying on false point-of-view shots and breaks in spatial continuity.[7] Although these gestures do not contribute to the narrative, they cause it to be infused with a certain surplus, the effect of which is quite surprising: presenting more than is strictly necessary according to the mainstream cinematic conventions of "realism" does not make the cinematic reality more solid. With the overdose of details and points of view the convention becomes undermined and the result is desubstantialization of the reality in question. Paradoxically, these "superfluous" elements—whose significance in the context of the narrative is obscure—derealize the story, making it somehow oneiric and tenuous (or perhaps even uncanny), while for instance the conventional "illustrative" and "symbolic" use of objects and landscapes (so literary in their origin) reinforces the reality effect.

So what Antonioni seems to have found out was the wrong-headedness of his plea for psychologization in order to desubstantialize the cinematic reality, because, unlike in literature, in cinema psychologization means the opposite of desubstantialization: concentration on human psychology and human relations in given circumstances solidifies the world represented, because the author cannot allow too much decontextualized detail to blur the analysis, which has to be conducted by externalizing the interiority of a character into its relations to other people and things. One can turn to the world and start experimenting with its presentation only when one can forget about the psychological credibility of one's characters. But this presents an obvious problem for a filmmaker: without changing the role of the character in his or her films, he or she is faced with an alternative of pursuing either conventional integration (whether it is more or less psychological does not matter) or depsychologized experimentation.

In this context Antonioni's next work, *The Cry* (*Il Grido*, 1957), is a telling example. This movie is usually taken as an explicit forerunner of Antonioni's

---

[7] An analysis of these features of Antonioni's early style on the example of *Story of a Love Affair* can be found in Noël Burch, *Theory of Film Practice*, trans. Helen R. Lane (Princeton: Princeton University Press, 1973), 75–80.

later films with Monica Vitti, and one can understand why. If one considers the four following works as films focusing on alienation and anxiety, this is precisely what *The Cry* seems to be about: an inarticulate, emotionally wounded man wanders aimlessly about the Po valley against a landscape of mud, rain, and fog, unable to rediscover his place in the society. But this film seems to be a sign of a stalemate rather than of progress: the contradiction between psychological analysis and experimentation with the representation of reality is overcome only superficially. Although the film is not a representative of any obvious genre (though it can be treated as a kind of the road movie) and focuses on an unhappy protagonist, he is psychologically a blank. Aldo's world crumbles at the beginning of the film when the woman around whom he has built his identity abandons him for another. So we have a traumatized character whose psychological "interiority" has been emptied out into the "desperate" landscape of the film (the dreary landscape is throughout illustrative of Aldo's state but only in a vague, non-specific way), which allows Antonioni to forget about the psychology of the wanderer and concentrate on the wandering, that is, to experiment with non-narrative structuring of the movie reality. That Antonioni is not interested here in any narrative or psychological development is certified by his abandonment of any pretense to resolving the plot. Needing some ending, Antonioni has Aldo, for no apparent reason, return to where he started and die. *The Cry* is ultimately a mood piece whose main interest lies not in psychological analysis or even representation but in its visual inventiveness (expansion), which, however, uses as its support a story of diminishment (contraction) and desperation. This contradiction is a sign that Antonioni has not solved his problem yet: what should be the purpose of the desubstantialization of reality and what role should a character serve in these circumstances?

Antonioni found a solution in his films with Vitti by adding a crucial political dimension to his works. Contrary to widespread opinion, these are not psychological films, because in them Antonioni is not really interested in what individualizes his characters. Instead he pays close attention to supraindividual discourses that speak through them, so in this sense his characters are still depsychologized. But now they are not just ciphers for cinematic conventions (a woman has to sacrifice herself in a melodrama, etc.) but mouthpieces of the dominant ideologies. We usually learn nothing psychologically important about the protagonists (about their background, their previous lives, etc.)—what makes them who they are for us are the discourses they are "plugged into," and because the "middle" Antonioni's plots are about couples, this is mostly the discourse of patriarchy.⁸ Such an approach makes the characters quite uninteresting on the dramatic level (their love affairs, their "anxiety," etc.), because they are puppets (both men and women) of their patriarchal scripts. Their interest lies in the roles they are assigned as figures in Antonioni's eccentric style, which, rather than reinforce the melodramatic narrative (cut to the measure of the patriarchal ideology voiced by the characters⁹), interrupts it. Antonionian hiatuses during which the camera abandons the plot not only prevent us from settling into the smooth melodramatic groove, but demonstrate that this patriarchal discourse is secreted by the material context (as material and spectral as Antonioni's abstract images), which in the case of the middle Antonioni is Italian modernization and the building boom of the late 1950s, whose excess is displayed in "weird" industrial and architectural landscapes so characteristic for this director.

But unlike the mainstream cinema, in which the symbolic use of the mise-en-scène solidifies both the conventional narrative line and the substantiality of the characters, Antonioni movies are based on desubstantialization of both. We have already mentioned the way Antonioni's style derealizes cinematic reality, and his problems with integrating his style with the narrative and psychology of the characters. In his middle films depsychologization is no longer gratuitous—it plays a crucial role: in the narrative hiatuses the characters are consistently shown as emanations of a spectral materiality characteristic of modern capitalism.¹⁰ Thus, the way in which characters become engendered by their world out of the virtual reality of capital, which is materialized as meaningless patterns (exquisitely rendered by Antonioni's "abstract" style), becomes the primary (non-narrative) focus of these films and makes the semi-melodramatic plots secondary. (Patriarchy is just one of the discourses in which the spectral substance of capital speaks.) Therefore, what Pasolini took for Antonioni's retrograde "ecstatic estheticism" turns out to be much more insightful and politically penetrating than Pasolini's own contemporaneous melancholic elegizing about the last pockets of pre-capitalist life being erased from the face of Italy (as in *Accattone*, 1961).

---

[8] I use the term "middle Antonioni" to refer to his films with Vitti: from *L'avventura* to *Red Desert*.
[9] The ideal couple is formed by a superficially independent male and a superficially independent female. In fact, Antonioni's men turn out to be aggressively conformist and the women pathologically submissive.
[10] Perhaps the most extreme example is Valentina in *La notte*, who is shown as a spectral presence haunting an emblematic modernist glass-filled villa built by her stocky and down-to-earth industrialist father.

In fact, the devaluation of the patriarchal plot takes place also on the level of the narrative itself—what we have taken for the narrative structure is exploded at the end of each film. Although in *L'avventura* (1960) the final image of the blank wall and Mount Etna (two modalities of the same thing as I argue below) blocks any path forward for the paired protagonists, this is precisely the moment in which the absent Anna, who stands for the beyond of patriarchy, haunts the scene most forcefully (even on the most basic narrative level: the audience realizes that the enigma of her disappearance will not be solved). In other words, the provisional narrative structure (the search) gets exploded precisely by the surplus, which has so far sealed it (the audience has been waiting for the resolution of the mystery) and in the process gestures to a beyond which the patriarchal plot has suppressed. In *La notte* (1961) the outside of the patriarchal discourse is at first investigated by Lidia but when patriarchy reasserts itself with a vengeance in melodramatic guise, it is undermined by being brought to such a feverish level of intensity that it collapses under its own weight, culminating in the ridiculously "symbolic" image of an impasse—a couple squirming silently in a sandtrap—from which the camera characteristically turns away as if to contextualize it as meaningless. And *L'eclisse* (1962) finally abandons its main characters as being completely futile, and shifts its attention to what has thus far been the indifferent background to their relation. When the controlling, patriarchal script disappears, the cityscape can finally gather up the small interruptions it has introduced into the plot and open itself up to a different (utopian) dimension.[11]

Thus it begins to become clear that a successful film by Antonioni is the opposite of the integrative machine that Bergman and Antonioni's other critics claim cinema "naturally" is. In his work the narratively meaningless moments (interruptions) are so distributed that in the end they make possible the prizing open and devaluation of the morally and politically constrictive ("organic") narrative structures, and with it the overthrowing of the primacy of character and plot, on the one hand, by showing them to be emanations of the spectral materiality of capital, and, on the other hand, by allowing for an opening, a reaching forth beyond meaning into the utopian dimension, implying engagement in the rethinking of our attachments to the world. In

---

[11] *Red Desert* (*Il deserto rosso*, 1964) is a special case, because it focuses on a traumatized character, Giuliana (a female version of Aldo, in a sense). Although both patriarchy and capitalism feature in this film, it is not organized like the ones mentioned above, in which the tentative narratives get exploded toward the end by what they have suppressed.

other words, creative disintegration, not integration, is Antonioni's *forte*. One might temperamentally prefer the narrative machinery (identification with the characters, etc.), but criticizing Antonioni for sabotaging it on the grounds that "organic" narrative makes for pure cinema is to mistake his technique and purpose.

Antonioni's three films for Metro-Goldwyn-Mayer—*Blow-Up* (1966), *Zabriskie Point* (1970), and *The Passenger* (1975)—take him out of his native Italy and into different social and political circumstances. He abandons the couple as the center of his attention and with it his concentration on the relation between patriarchy and capitalism. While in his later Italian works he analyzed patriarchal symbolic (or sometimes not so symbolic) violence, his "international" films become more explicitly political and deal with violence in a more straightforward sense (there are corpses in all of these movies). But the main focus remains the same: the violence shown—although it might look, or be, extreme, and therefore unconnected to the everyday life of ordinary people in the Western world—always turns out to be rooted in the mainstream ideology and the supposedly harmless fantasies it gives rise to.

Antonioni's political cinema, at least in the form this book tries to analyze, ended with *The Passenger* and with hindsight it is tempting to imagine that the famous penultimate shot in which the camera disengages from the main protagonist, David Locke, and leaves his corpse behind can be taken for an unintentional farewell to fully engaged cinema by the director. His following film, *The Mystery of Oberwald* (*Il mistero de Oberwald*, 1980), was an experiment in TV technology facilitated by an exaggerated melodramatic plot, and therefore a kind of throwback to his early Italian period. *Identification of a Woman* (*Identificazione di una donna*, 1982) reemploys the search motive but in exactly the opposite way to that in *The Passenger*. Although the plot engages obliquely with the politics of the contemporary Italy (at the beginning of the film violence in the form of the terrorist threat hovers in the air), the film ultimately turns inwards as the story of a director's search for inspiration, which becomes an investigation of his obsessions (and Antonioni's mannerism and motifs) rather than a search for what haunts the ruling discourses.

Perhaps *Identification of a Woman* was only an example of a transitory crisis, which augured a creative change, as plans for the film provisionally entitled *The Crew*, based on Antonioni's story "Four Men at Sea," suggested[12]—a film that

---

[12] Sam Rohdie, *Antonioni* (London: British Film Institute, 1990), 1.

might possibly have been very different from what one would expect from the director. But a stroke Antonioni suffered in 1985, which left him partly paralyzed and unable to speak, destroyed this possibility forever. Antonioni's final films,[13] although they must have been of great importance to this broken but resilient man, for whom making films was life,[14] no longer hunt for specters of violence. They are themselves but specters of his former brilliance.

The aim of this book is to conjure this brilliance once again and pay respect to it.

***

An earlier version of the chapter on *Blow-Up* was published as "All Eyes in Swinging London: Antonioni's *Blow-Up* and the Maze of Violence," in *Urban Amazement*, ed. Monika Kowalczyk-Piaseczna and Marta Mamet-Michalkiewicz (Katowice: Wydawnictwo Uniwersytetu Śląskiego, 2015), 75–95. An abridged version of the chapter on *La notte* was published as "Looking for Something New: Antonioni's *La notte* and Spectres of Femininity," in *Camera Obscura* 37, no. 1 (May 2022): 115–47.

I would like to thank David Schauffler for helping me prepare the final version of this book.

---

[13] *Beyond the Clouds* (*Al di là delle nuvole*, 1995), directed with Wim Wenders, and *The Dangerous Thread of Things* (*Il filo pericoloso delle cose*), an episode in an omnibus film *Eros* (2004).

[14] "Fare un film è per me vivere" is the title of an article Antonioni published in 1959.

1

L'avventura (1960)

During the first screening of *L'avventura* at the Cannes Film Festival on May 15, 1960, the audience hissed, booed, and laughed. This event provoked Antonioni to come forth with a statement concerning the film during a press conference the following day. Because the statement is a comment on the director's intentions (though a rather oblique one) and was made, moreover, in a moment of crisis (which, however, catapulted Antonioni to international fame), critics almost inevitably fall back on quotations from this text as their guide to the meaning of the film. The most popular of these remarks is probably: "But Eros is sick."[1] Taking into consideration that the vicissitudes of a relationship between a man and a woman are the thematic center of *L'avventura*, the choice is not surprising. What may be worth examining, however, is the way the larger meaning of the sickness of Eros is constructed in virtually all interpretations of the film, in which "an overwhelming erotic impulse," as Antonioni calls it,[2] is usually inscribed into the familiar "existentialist" problematic of modern alienation of the individual, the impossibility of communication, the superficiality of human relationships, etc.

But is the impossibility of communication between two human beings and their alienation really a major theme of *L'avventura*? The film seems to begin on this note by presenting to us Anna (Lea Massari), a character who is introduced by a conversation with her father (Renzo Ricci), which is an example of intentional non-communication, a verbal exchange in which both sides keep undermining the other's claims. Moreover, we soon learn that Anna's "alienation" also concerns her relationship with her fiancé, Sandro (Gabriele Ferzetti).[3] But

---

[1] Michelangelo Antonioni, "A Talk with Michelangelo Antonioni on His Work: Students and Faculty at the Centro Sperimentale di Cinematografia in Rome," in *L'Avventura: A Film by Michelangelo Antonioni*, ed. George Amberg and Robert Hughes (New York: Grove Press, 1969), 222.
[2] Ibid.
[3] Whom she explicitly confronts later in the film with a rhetorical question: "[A]re you convinced that even between us we're unable to understand one another?" Unless otherwise noted, all translations are from the DVD of *L'avventura* released by the Criterion Collection in 2001.

can Anna's exasperation with Sandro and her father be called "alienation" in any other sense than a literal one, that is, estrangement? And is there anything "existential" about it? This seems unlikely if we take into consideration the background against which Anna's subsequent behavior is set against, namely, a rich party's cruise to the Aeolian Islands in which Anna and Sandro take part.

Firstly, throughout the cruise Anna is shown to be "alienated" from everybody—she treats all the characters around her the way she treats Sandro and her father. There is, however, one exception, Claudia (Monica Vitti), who is Anna's friend and who has not previously met other participants of the cruise. She is the only person Anna treats "nicely." Anna has only bitter or scathing words for everybody else, which culminates in her spiteful attempt to scare the party (she cries "Shark!" while they are swimming around the yacht in the Tyrrhenian Sea). But not only does she show affection for Claudia, she tells her that the shark was only a "joke," in order to reinforce their mutual bond. This "opening up" of Anna to Claudia is emphasized by Antonioni in a scene in which he places both women together in a cramped space belowdecks, where they are almost touching and almost naked (are undressing to change their wet swimming suits).[4] In other words, there is no sign of alienation in this particular human relation—in intimate circumstances with Claudia, Anna inexplicably turns into an unalienated character. Secondly, the moment Anna disappears from the action, all alienation and impossibility to communicate disappear with her—the cruising leisure party is quickly reconstituted as an amiable company on the terrace of the palace of the Montaldos,[5] where Anna's disappearance is turned into a joke ("Maybe he's done away with her," says Princess Montaldo about Sandro). And when Sandro and Claudia (who leaves the Montaldos to join Sandro) finally meet the party (or what remains of it) at the end of the film, everything is nice again, as if Anna had never existed, until Claudia, in a fit of panic, brings up her name.[6] Moreover, although at first Anna's aggressive attitude

---

[4] The intimacy is so obvious that a number of critics, beginning with George Amberg ("But Eros Is Sick," in *L'Avventura*, ed. Amberg and Hughes, 248), have suggested a homoerotic attraction, which perhaps cannot be excluded out of hand but which is not substantiated by anything else in the film.

[5] Apart from Claudia and Sandro, who remain in the vicinity of Lisca Bianca, where Anna disappeared, to check some clues, the rest of the party repairs to the mainland to wait for them in the villa of the Montaldos, the placing of which is unspecified in the film but which was shot in Villa Niscemi in Palermo (Tomasso Chiaretti, "The Adventure of *L'Avventura*," in *L'Avventura*, ed. Amberg and Hughes, 202).

[6] In fact, the characters in the film, and this pertains to Claudia and Sandro especially, understand each other rather too well, which is one of the reasons why their love story is a conventional one (excepting the manner in which it is shown): from pretended hostility, which masks attraction, on Lisca Bianca, to submission, guilt, and reconciliation.

to everybody except Claudia, and the others' indifference to Anna, may seem rather strange, in due course we are given a piece of information that should explain Anna's weird behavior: toward the end of the film, when Claudia and Sandro arrive at a luxurious hotel in Taormina, we learn that Claudia does not belong to the moneyed class whose life we have been witnessing throughout the film. In this light, Anna's alienation does not look so existential after all; it seems that the source of her troubled state is simply her estrangement from her own class, which is represented by her diplomat father in the first sequence of the film and for the rest of it by rich real estate brokers and their wives or partners.

Furthermore, the "Eros is sick" motive is only of secondary importance in Antonioni's Cannes statement. Most of the text is devoted to a discrepancy which rarely finds its way into critical discussions of the film, the discrepancy between the future and the past, or, to be more precise, between the modern man whose main mode of existence is science, which "has never been more humble and less dogmatic than it is today," and "the present moral standards we live by, these myths, these conventions" which "are old and obsolete." This man "reacts, he loves, he hates, he suffers under the sway of moral forces and myths which today, when we are at the threshold of reaching the moon, should not be the same as those that prevailed at the time of Homer, but nevertheless are."[7] In fact, for Antonioni the situation is more than merely a discrepancy—it is a full-blown crisis which he compares to the Copernican fall of man from the grace of Ptolemaic fullness: "Then man discovered that his world was Copernican, an extremely limited world in an unknown universe. And today a new man is being born, fraught with all the fears and terrors and stammerings that are associated with a period of gestation."[8] The gestation of the modern man is stifled because rather than confront "the moral unknown,"[9] he carries on with the moralistic business as usual. Do such problematics translate into an essentially conventional moralistic story, which *L'avventura* is usually taken to be, of an innocent (Claudia) and a weakling (Sandro) brought low by being contaminated by the corruption of a modern world devoid of values, which is represented by the fashionable world of the Italian economic boom? If anything can be said about that scenario, it is that it incarnates "the moral known" in its most boring and worn-out form.

---

[7] Antonioni, "A Talk," 221.
[8] Ibid., 221.
[9] Ibid., 223.

There is another quotation which is often mentioned in connection with *L'avventura*, because Antonioni himself used it a couple of times in this context and in the context of "middle-class problems." It comes from Lucretius: "Nothing appears as it should in a world where nothing is certain. The only thing certain is the existence of a secret violence that makes everything uncertain."[10] Can such violence be conceived, as it often is in the critical literature on Antonioni, on the moralistic level, as, for instance, misdirected drives, which—unable to attach themselves to traditional objects like "*paese*, church and family"—get frustrated and turn into the aforementioned "overwhelming erotic impulse"? Or, if this moralistic interpretation seems rather flat-footed, perhaps the matter should be taken to the proper existentialist level of human "thrownness" or *Geworfenheit* and be seen as "the eruption into tangible, visible presence of the secret violence, the storm of reality and mystery, which it is the purpose of all our drugs and games to conceal."[11] After all, we seem to start off from the bare rocks of the Aeolian Islands (one may recall the already-quoted Homer reference in Antonioni's Cannes statement), which the pleasure-seekers have to unwillingly confront in the storm. But may not this tragic or pathetic opposition of the self-satisfied superficial glitter of the rich (or a more ordinary one of drugs and games) to the darkness of the profound mystery of existence be yet another moralistic charade, only this time clad in a pseudo-philosophical garb? Rather than scaling the heights of the human condition, where the air is rather thin, I propose we start with the specifics, that is, with some intertextual clues whose presence in *L'avventura* is quite evident.

After the "prelude" in Rome, to which we will return, the film cuts to the Aeolian Islands, or, to be more precise, to an extreme long shot of a sailing yacht shown against the island of Stromboli on the horizon. This is not a gratuitous shot. Although most of the action in this sequence will take place on an islet called Lisca Bianca (White Fishbone), the conical shape of Stromboli, one of the three active volcanoes in Italy, will accompany the characters from afar in crucial moments. And Stromboli is not an innocent background—it has a prominent place in the history of Italian cinema as the setting of Roberto Rossellini's *Stromboli, Land of God* (*Stromboli, terra di Dio*, 1950). Moreover, although *Stromboli* is strongly neorealist and *L'avventura* is nothing of the

---

[10] For instance in ibid., 227.
[11] Both points made in William Arrowsmith, *Antonioni: The Poet of Images*, ed. Ted Perry (New York: Oxford University Press, 1995), 34, 36, but similar interpretations are quite common.

sort, there are strange parallels between the films, and both of them feature a woman who, in a sense, disappears.

Stromboli, Rossellini's first film with Ingrid Bergman, tells the story of Karin, a displaced Lithuanian who, in order to escape an internment camp, marries a native of Stromboli and moves there with him. There she finds herself living in harsh conditions and in a closely knit traditional Catholic patriarchal society which is hostile to her "worldly" habits. Although her husband, Antonio (Mario Vitale), supposedly loves her, her unselfconscious behavior makes him a fool and a cuckold in the eyes of the community—so a need arises to show Karin the woman's place in a "traditional" wife-beating way. In the film, the "natural" patriarchal order is explicitly connected with the image of the volcano in both formal[12] and symbolic ways, and through the image of the volcano (the power of nature) to the power and majesty of God.[13] Like the God-given power of the patriarch Antonio, the power of God/volcano/nature has to be submitted to, because its beauty and majesty, and the subsistence it gives, are the signs of God's love. As Rossellini shows it, Antonio is in a sense morally forced by others to beat his wife in order to assert his position and show Karin the place assigned to her in the Stromboli community; therefore, the beating is his symbolic duty—he beats her in spite of or even perhaps because of his love. But of course even a wife-beating represented in such a way is much more than a symbolic act—although it wears the mask of a reluctantly performed duty, it obviously has its own surplus and yields unacknowledged pleasures. The volcano shows the same two faces: it is the support (even literally) of the community, but from time to time it has to assert its "majesty" by erupting. That is, apart from its "balanced" symbolic incarnation as the "natural" laws of the community, the volcano has also another, enigmatic dimension which has to be presented to the faithful as violent excess.

Not surprisingly, her life on Stromboli becomes more and more painful for Karin (she has also become pregnant), until she cannot stand it any longer and flees the village. But in order to reach the port to leave Stromboli, she has to get to the other side of the island by climbing the slopes of the volcano. On

---

[12] To give just one example: "[A]fter Antonio's assertion of the male prerogative, ... [t]he camera, echoing their feelings, cuts quickly to an extreme long shot that pins them in their forlorn isolation against the harshness of rock and sea. Karin walks away, leaving Antonio standing there. The camera begins suddenly to move in the opposite direction, panning up the hill past the pitiful town to the top of the volcano, that theophallic symbol of the ordering power of authority." Peter Brunette, *Roberto Rossellini* (Berkeley: University of California Press, 1996), 118.

[13] Ibid., 124.

the way she becomes more and more intoxicated by the volcano's fumes, under whose influence she gradually loses the possessions she had taken from the village (she abandons her suitcase, her overcoat, her handbag, etc.). Finally she collapses and, looking up, sees the starry sky above (the fumes have dissipated). When she wakes up it is a sunny morning and she looks around and says to herself: "What mystery … How beautiful."[14] In "confronting" the volcano, Karin has gone through "the night of the world" during which she has been gradually divested of all that has belonged to her also in the symbolic sense, freed of her symbolic attachments both to the "wider world," from which she had come, and to the village. In other words, she has ceased to be the same person through the experience of what Hegel calls "abstract negativity," which constitutes the empty core of the subject and which is the ultimate site of its freedom, because it makes possible the relinquishment of the image one has had of oneself.[15] Although Rossellini explicitly links Karin's symbolic "rebirth" with the name of God (Karin exclaims, "God! My God! Help me! Give me strength, the understanding and the courage!" [sic]), so that we seem to be returning to subjection to the patriarchal power, the director in fact is lifting this burden from Karin's shoulders—this is the point when she realizes that she is "morally" free to go in any direction: forward to the port or back to the village. And this is how the film ends—just before the moment of decision.[16]

Although in one interview Antonioni called *L'avventura* a "giallo alla rovescia,"[17] it could, perhaps more justifiably, be called "*Stromboli* alla rovescia." Whereas in *Stromboli* we have the depiction of a community whose life involves everyday confrontations with deprivation and death, which is set against the portrait of Karin, a former representative of the leisure class, *L'avventura* features a cruise by rich people who are accompanied by one fascinated outsider, Claudia. However, although the rich are on a pleasure cruise, they seem to experience

---

[14] "Che mistero … Come bello." Translated as "How strange … It's so beautiful" on the BFI Blu-ray disk with the film (2015), which is not the best of translations.

[15] Slavoj Žižek, *Enjoy Your Symptom! Jacques Lacan in Hollywood and Out* (London: Routledge, 1992), 43. This interpretation of the end of *Stromboli* is Žižek's.

[16] This is Rossellini's ending. In the version released in the United States, cut and changed by the RKO studio, the experience of freedom is completely obliterated—a voiceover (never previously used in the film) tells us: "Out of her terror and her suffering, Karin had found a great need for God. And she knew now that only in her return to the village could she hope for peace." Quoted in Brunette, *Rossellini*, 125.

[17] A yellow inside out, in reverse. "Yellows" are Italian murder-mysteries. Seymour Chatman, "All the Adventures," in *L'avventura*, ed. Seymour Chatman and Guido Fink (New Brunswick, NJ: Rutgers University Press, 1989), 9.

their life of pleasure as excruciating, which is explicitly voiced by one of them, Raimondo (Lelio Luttazzi)—when he is asked, just before he jumps into the sea, whether he likes scuba diving, he answers: "I simply loathe it, but I must conform, what can I do?" And it is not only Raimondo whose "good time" distresses him—all members of the cruise seem to feel that way. Patrizia (Esmeralda Ruspoli) experiences nothing but boredom; Corrado (James Addams), picking all the time on his girlfriend Giulia (Dominique Blanchar), turns her life and his own into purgatory; and Sandro is constantly made miserable by the behavior of Anna, whose state of "alienation" we have already noted. In other words, the activities of the rich, which pass for having a good time, are painfully loathsome; yet, they have to be performed. Like the life of the poor fishermen of Stromboli, the "diversions" of the fashionable society consist of painful obligatory rituals (back-breaking work in the case of the poor) and conformity to the rules of the community. Only Claudia seems to enjoy herself during the cruise, but only because it is not *her* way of life that she is experiencing—as we have already noted, toward the end of the film we learn that she is a kind of gatecrasher at the party of the rich.

Furthermore, against this "reverse" or "back-to-front" background (the life of leisure taking the place of a life of bare necessities), we also have the figure of a girl who wants to disappear, and does. In *Stromboli* it is Karin whose trip across the volcano (the symbol of patriarchy) does away with all her symbolic ties. In *L'avventura* it is Anna who also seems to be going through "the night of the world"—she is dissolving her attachments to the patriarchal order. As we have already noted, she behaves aggressively toward the members of her own class (making Claudia comment: "I don't need to know why you behave this way"), which is epitomized in her cry "Shark!" when most of the company are having a swim. Moreover, we are shown that Anna refuses the symbolic roles that pin her to her place in the patriarchal order. In the first scene of the film she refuses the role of the good daughter to the father whose main concern is to put her in another "proper" place for a woman ("That guy [Sandro]—he'll never marry you," he warns Anna). Later, on Lisca Bianca, she refuses to become Sandro's wife.[18]

---

[18] Anna's "counterpatriarchal" stance is noted by Peter Brunette: "She is looking for what in 1960 would have been termed an 'authentic existence,' an identity apart from her husband's (and her father's), but in this society that is impossible, so she merely disappears, both from the society and from the film, which thirty-five years ago, would have been equally incapable of suggesting solutions for her dissatisfaction." *The Films of Michelangelo Antonioni* (Cambridge: Cambridge University Press, 1998), 34.

The refusal of these two attachments is explicitly stated in the film, but there is yet another one whose dissolution is not so obvious, and has to be reconstructed from its visible traces. Not surprisingly, *Stromboli* might be of some help also here. The refusal of the roles of the daughter and the wife (mother to be) is not enough to effect Anna's complete withdrawal from the patriarchal order—her role is fixed not only by the male gaze of father/husband (two modalities of the same master). To work properly, the gaze has to be individually, but also socially, incorporated by the object of the gaze, that is, by women themselves. Therefore in a crucial scene in *Stromboli*, in which the community's gaze unequivocally condemns Karin's behavior (she is playing/flirting on the beach with another man, a lighthouse keeper), the gaze is not male[19]—it is the women of the village who gather at the scene to silently and disapprovingly look on. Correspondingly, the last link that has to be dissolved in Anna's case takes the form of the gaze of a female other which fixes her to patriarchy, which in the constellation of *L'avventura* is clearly Claudia's.

How is this "fixing" relation represented in the film? We have already noted that Anna treats Claudia differently than she does the others. But how does this relationship look in reverse? Claudia supposedly loves Anna and asserts this to Sandro after Anna's disappearance ("You love Anna very much." "Yes, very"), but what does she love about her? It seems obvious that Claudia is in a transferential relationship with Anna as a representative of the life of the class with which Claudia is fascinated. In other words, Claudia is in love with Anna as her own ideal image, what Claudia would like to be or become, and thus Claudia's gaze is yet another one which fixes Anna to the place she wants to withdraw from. This relation becomes more clearly visible only later in the film, after the Lisca Bianca episode, in a sequence that takes place, after Anna's disappearance, in the villa of the Montaldos, when Claudia looks at herself in the mirror wearing a black wig (Claudia is a blonde, Anna was a brunette). First, Patrizia, a "rightful" member of the moneyed class, wearing a blond wig, is shown by the camera directly and then as a reflection in the mirror. "How do I look?" she asks Claudia. "Divine," the latter answers, confirming an identity between the person and her image in the mirror. With Claudia, who is a stranger among the rich, the procedure is reversed—she is first shown as a black-wigged reflection and only then directly. Patrizia's reaction to Claudia's perusal of her own ideal image is telling: "You

---

[19] The male part of the community expresses their disapproval in a more "carnivalesque" way and *verbally*—they sing obscene songs that place Karin's husband, Antonio, in the position of a cuckold.

look like somebody else."[20] Additionally, already during the cruise sequence there is a hint of Anna's awareness of her role in Claudia's imaginary theater and her intention to resolve this relation. As if she knew what will happen in the film, she offers Claudia a blouse that Claudia likes,[21] the blouse Claudia will wear at the moment she replaces Anna in Sandro's affections.

Therefore, having dissolved all attachments to her class and the patriarchal order as such, Anna has no choice but to disappear from the film,[22] because this lack of choice is also Antonioni's. This is precisely a point he makes in his Cannes statement:

> The present moral standards we live by, these myths, these conventions are old and obsolete ... but we have not been capable of finding new ones. We have not been able to make any headway whatsoever toward a solution of this problem, of this ever-increasing split between moral man [the man of obsolete morality] and scientific man [who should be willing to face "the moral unknown"], a split which is becoming more and more serious and more and more accentuated. Naturally, I don't care to, nor can I, resolve it myself; I am not a moralist, and my film is neither a denunciation nor a sermon.[23]

In other words, Antonioni can represent an impatience with or a loathing for the old and obsolete conventions, and even a withdrawal from them, but what is beyond "the night of the world" by means of which one frees oneself from

---

[20] This ideal identification, however, does not exhaust the interest of the scene, which we will therefore return to.

[21] When Anna asks Claudia "Which shall I wear?" showing her two blouses, Claudia does not hesitate: "This one. This one is divine." Anna then puts on the other one and clandestinely tucks the "divine" one into Claudia's bag. As we can see, almost anything encountered in the world of the rich is "divine" for Claudia.

[22] What is interesting is that Anna does not disappear completely without a trace—she leaves a textual trace or, in fact, two of them: in Anna's bag Claudia finds copies of the Bible and *Tender Is the Night* by F. Scott Fitzgerald. Although the kind of critic who sees homoerotic attraction between Anna and Claudia would be able to find even more attractive "material" in Fitzgerald's narrative (a rich girl who is "troubled" because she was sexually abused by her father), one can also note that it is a novel about a brilliant man, Dick Diver, who is ultimately broken by his association with the fashionable world of the rich. The appearance of the Bible in relation to Anna is also quite intriguing. Although her father takes its presence in her bag as a sign of her faith and therefore a proof that her disappearance is not due to suicide, his belief must be considered deluded. In the context of Antonioni's words in his Cannes statement concerning the necessity of confronting the moral unknown and our interpretation of Anna as a protagonist of *L'avventura* who is closest to this attitude, the presence of the Bible among Anna's belongings can only be taken, to use Kierkegaard's distinctions, not as indicating the suspension of the aesthetical by the ethical (tired of the repetitive and exhausting world of pleasure Anna nostalgically reconsiders the moral known, that is, Christian norms), but as a handbook of the suspension of the ethical by the religious, that is, by the moral unknown (the scandalous subversion of the Judaic moral known that Christ performed).

[23] Antonioni, "A Talk," 221–2.

one's patriarchy-determined ego is anybody's guess—this is the area the film gestures toward but cannot represent.[24] What *does* it represent, then? Although after Anna's disappearance the plot proceeds forward in time, logically it takes us backward, that is, what happens in *L'avventura* after Anna is gone presents us with the reasons for her disappearance. Therefore the jeers of the Cannes audience were unjustified even on the most superficial level: the explanation of Anna's disappearance was there for all to see, but what the viewers demanded was the resolution of a *giallo*, a mystery plot: they demanded to be shown what happened to her.

So what are these "moral forces and myths which today, when we are at the threshold of reaching the moon, should not be the same as those that prevailed at the time of Homer, but nevertheless are?" We have already used the fateful word many times: patriarchy. Its rule in the primitive world of *Stromboli* (in many ways harking back to the times of Homer, though the film takes place in the Italy of the late 1940s[25]) is evident and complete, but what about the Italian hyper-modern ruling capitalist class which is the subject of *L'avventura*?

One thing which can be noted initially is that after Anna's disappearance the patriarchal order reconstitutes itself almost immediately. What is more, it reconstitutes itself in two modalities, as it were. After Anna disappears, her "night of the world" turns into a real dark and stormy night, full of recriminations and tumultuous feelings,[26] for those of her companions who remain on the islet in case she reappears (Claudia, Sandro, and Corrado). Into this "serious" constellation a *comic* figure intervenes—on the island, which they had taken to be deserted, all of a sudden appears the inhabitant of the hut in which they take shelter from the rain. He is a family man (he shows his surprised audience photographs of members of his family who live in Australia, where, as he says, he spent thirty years[27]) and a shepherd subsisting in this world of bare rock and desolation ("Do you call five in the morning early?" he asks Sandro, who is suspicious of his early rising)—a kind of thirty-year-older version of Antonio

---

[24] However, Antonioni will be returning to this theme of cutting ties to one's previous life and becoming somebody else in *Zabriskie Point* and, even more obviously, in *The Passenger*, though these films feature male protagonists, which is, in a sense, an easier option.

[25] The "Homeric" parallel is perhaps most evident in the two most celebrated neorealist sequences of the film: the slaughtering of tuna fish and the boat evacuation of the village during the eruption of the volcano. Such scenes may not have looked much different in Homer's times.

[26] Claudia and Sandro begin to accuse each other and quarrel about Anna's disappearance.

[27] One remembers that another paternal figure, Anna's father, claimed to have been a diplomat for thirty years.

from *Stromboli* who has come back home from Australia to die. In fact, we do encounter such aged former emigrants who have come back to the native island precisely as comic figures in *Stromboli*,[28] but the comic appeal of the shepherd in *L'avventura* has a different origin—although he is obviously both a remainder and a reminder of the "sublime" patriarchy of back-breaking toil and scarcity (the real image of the Aeolian Islands we otherwise never see in the film),[29] in the "alla rovescia" world of *L'avventura* he can only be relegated to the comic level. But this is only the beginning.

After the turmoil of the night,[30] the main protagonists, Claudia and Sandro, wake up chastened to a beautiful clear morning (it is five o'clock, as the shepherd claims)—like Karin on the slopes of Stromboli—and start a wistful conversation about Anna, in which Sandro evinces subtle feelings and a vulnerable side by expressing yearning for his beloved, yet simultaneously fixing her into her proper place in the patriarchal scheme of things by complaining that "she acted as though our love, yours [Claudia's], her father's, mine, in a manner of speaking, meant nothing to her."[31] And Claudia joins in this patriarchal song of love and positioning: "Sometimes I wonder what it is I could have done … to prevent all of this from happening." Therefore it does not seem surprising at all that one element which serves as a background to this duet is the image of Stromboli itself, which throughout their conversation appears between the characters as if offering them its benediction. Because what is happening in this scene is the constitution of an ideal patriarchal relation by the coming together of two loves (Sandro's and Claudia's for Anna) and the disappearance of the middle term. On the one hand, Claudia finds herself in the idealized symbolic place: Claudia's love

---

[28] The old men who are hired (or perhaps just asked) by Antonio to renovate his house say they have come back to their native island from Brooklyn where they spent most of their lives.

[29] But even this comic figure obeys the double logic of patriarchy we encountered in *Stomboli*. Although when we meet him he is introduced as a paternal figure representing family ties and hard labor (the Law of the symbolic father), the following day, after the police arrive and start to search for Anna, he is shown exchanging meaningful looks with one of the marshals when a suspicious-looking boat is mentioned (it turns out to be a smuggler's boat), which results in the marshal's uneasiness that we see displayed in a close-up on his face. In other words, there is more to this father than just his official "castrated" side.

[30] Both natural and "symbolic." As in *Stromboli* two sides of nature (a volcano: earth and fire) represent the calm and the wrathful sides of the ultimate patriarch (God), in *L'avventura* the same power is indicated *alla rovescia* by water and air: the calm water of the sea in which one may take a leisured swim, and the water made dangerous by the wind (generally a storm, but Antonioni takes particular care to show the conjunction of water and air by filming a waterspout). And one should not forget that all the turmoil (both natural and "symbolic") is, somewhat "miraculously," initiated by Anna's scream: "Pescecane!" ("Shark!").

[31] As we have noted, these are precisely three relations (father, husband, fellow woman) which fix Anna as an object of patriarchy.

for Anna is founded not only on her fascination with Anna's glamorous image, but even more importantly on her fascination with her place in the patriarchal structure, that is, her position in the network of (primary patriarchal) relations, of which her relationship with a man like Sandro is the most important.[32] On the other hand, Sandro, after all his "problems" with Anna, finds himself in the position of an idealized wished-for partner (later in the film Claudia tells him "I only want what you want"). No wonder that from this moment on he follows in Claudia's footsteps like a dog and his yearning for this new object is even emphasized by the appearance of extra-diegetic music.

Interestingly enough the pathetic scene between Claudia and Sandro including Stromboli's blessing has a comic equivalent in the film. While they are on the train from Milazzo to the Montaldos, they overhear a conversation in an adjoining compartment (they have moved to the corridor), which makes Claudia laugh. But one wonders if this laugh is not hysterical, because the scene on the train basically repeats in a comic register the "morning scene" between Claudia and Sandro. In the conversation a man informs a woman that he has heard about her through his acquaintance[33] (he is probably making this up) who has said that she is "a well-brought-up girl" who minds her business,[34] and then brings love into the conversation:

Man: Which comes first for you? Music or love?
Woman: Music of course. A fiancée [sic] you've gotta look for, but a radio can be bought.
Man: Oh no, love for me. I am a man and I know about this kind of thing. Love first, then music.

---

[32] In other words, being in a transferential relation to Anna (fascinated with her), Claudia is always already in a transferential relation to Sandro (a major part of the fascination is a fascination with Anna's ability to attract men like Sandro). We have already mentioned that Claudia wears Anna's blouse in the "morning scene." It can also be added that in the very first scene of *L'avventura*, taking place in front of Anna's father's house, at the very moment when the father tells Anna that Sandro will never marry her, we see Claudia appearing behind him—this is her first appearance in the film.

[33] Sandro and Claudia meet for the first time only in the second scene of the film, in which Anna and Claudia reach Sandro's apartment in Rome, but because Claudia is Anna's good friend, Sandro must have heard about Claudia from Anna before meeting her in person.

[34] While they are on the train, Claudia too is trying to be a well-brought-up girl who minds her business—she tries to persuade Sandro to stick to his symbolic/patriarchal duties (e.g., that you don't flirt with your fiancée's best friend, especially not the very day after the fiancée disappears). In other words, she is trying to keep up the idealized configuration established in the "morning scene": herself as a true friend, Sandro as an honest, although frustrated, lover. This is not the first time she tries to do this. Earlier, on Lisca Bianca, when Patrizia expressed her surprise at Sandro's calm behavior after Anna's disappearance ("Sandro really astonishes me. He seems so self-possessed"), Claudia jumps to his defense (to rescue his ideal image) by "bending" the facts: "Self-possessed? I don't think so ... He was up all night."

As we have noted, Claudio also knows how things should have stood with love (but did not: "she acted as though our love, yours, her father's, mine, in a manner of speaking, meant nothing to her"), while the conjunction of love and music seems to constitute a kind of meta-joke on Antonioni's part: after Claudia takes Anna's place in Sandro's affections in the "morning scene" we hear extra-diegetic music ("Love first, then music"). Though some critics are of the opinion that the comic scenes in *L'avventura*, and especially the one on the train, strike a false note because they are "out of tone,"[35] one should consider that this is precisely their role and therefore that such critics are wrong for the right reason. The comic scenes do undermine the "serious" register in which the characters prefer to imagine their situation, but precisely for this reason they are crucial, because they explicitly show that the main plot might just as well be perceived as comic and that stories like that are two a penny. In fact, what can be better comic material than Sandro, whose "fate"[36] is determined by "something mechanical encrusted on the living," which is exactly Bergson's definition of comedy?[37] Isn't it his penis—as "something mechanical," which is alien to him as a "psychological" person—that makes Sandro do its bidding and whose enjoyment ruins Sandro's life as an autonomous (and "spiritual") individual, including his self-esteem? Moreover, although the "serious" plot about the impossibility of communication does not seem to tolerate well the comic scenes that interrupt it, perhaps there is another—and more interesting—theme in *L'avventura* which is able to accommodate them quite easily.

What happens in the film to the images of patriarchy when its "natural" symbolic support (bare rocks, the volcano, the struggle for survival) disappears? We have already noted that on Stromboli the "primitive" patriarchal master, whether husband or God, comes in two incarnations: the master of contracts, of the laws of the community, who is supposed to be dead as far as enjoyment is concerned, that is, one who is just and impartial, giving the impression of not enjoying his power; and the opposite of that, a figure hiding in the cracks of the

---

[35] Gene Youngblood in the audio commentary to the Criterion DVD of *L'avventura* is characteristic. First, he claims that in the comic scene on the train Antonioni aims at presenting the impossibility of communication "in a folkloric way" (this is enough for one's jaw to drop) and then he says: "There is something about these scenes that has always struck me as a little problematic … They seem out of tone and out of place in the seriousness of the whole meditation that he [Antonioni] is doing."

[36] Claudia: It's absurd./Sandro: Great. And all the better if it is absurd. It means we can't do anything about it.

[37] Henri Bergson, *Laughter: An Essay on the Meaning of the Comic*, trans. Cloudesley Brereton and Fred Rothwell (Copenhagen and Los Angeles: Green Integer Books, 1999), 39.

Law, the master who thoroughly enjoys his eruptions of violence. But this is also precisely the way the capitalist master is constituted in *L'avventura*. Although the film starts with an image of the supposedly impotent and "obsolete" father (helpless to influence his daughter and hemmed in by sprawling modernity), and then of powerless Sandro who does not know how to deal with Anna, this impression is gradually corrected by the appearance of the double figure of the paradigmatic modern Italian master of the time (the film was released in 1960), the real estate developer. What is interesting is that his two incarnations are shown to us in the inversion of the usual order of appearance. Normally, as in *Stromboli*, we first get to see the visage of the balanced guardian of the Law (for instance, a good husband) and only then the cracks in it appear, which allows us to see its enjoying/violent reverse. In *L'avventura* we first encounter Corrado, a man whose main aim in life seems to be the humiliation of his (much younger) girlfriend, Giulia, from which he seems to derive all his satisfaction. But we do not have to wait too long for this master of enjoyment to be paired with the master of symbolic contracts, Corrado's business partner Ettore, a reliable, "castrated" man who does not even share his wife's bed (as we see in the hotel in Taormina) and "would forgive you anything, as long as you admit he's the better driver" (his wife says).[38] What is really important, however, is not so much the individual (or double-individual) characteristics of the real estate masters but the way these characteristics become incarnated in the real estate itself. In other words, as the "primitive" master of *Stromboli* was incarnated in both the neutral laws and the wrathful excess (symbolized in the double figures of good/violent husband and good earth/violent volcano), the modern mastery is displayed in both the laws and the excess of "the second nature" (as Walter Benjamin used to call it): in our case, real estate capital.

---

[38] In fact, the characterization of these two faces of the capitalist master is a bit more convoluted, because it involves both couples, Corrado-Giulia and Ettore-Patrizia, in each of which the master's relationship to the other is reflected back to him. Therefore the excess experienced by Corrado in humiliating his partner (for instance: "It's better if you sleep. You say: 'How beautiful,' no matter what you're looking at: the sea, a child, a cat. Your sensitive little heart races at nothing") is returned to him in the excess "produced" by Giulia through her seduction of the "artistic" princeling Goffredo at the Montaldos ("If Corrado looks for me, you can tell him I'm here. And tell him that my little heart is racing, racing"). So when Corrado, looking at Giulia with Goffredo, characterizes her with the words, "Giulia is like Oscar Wilde. Give her the extras ["di più"—excess], and she'll do without necessities" (translation modified), he is actually describing himself, too. The same pertains to the other couple, in which Ettore is literally the man of (developer's) contracts (he pesters Sandro with demands for delayed cost estimations, so that he can fulfill his obligations) and Patrizia is a bored lady who spends her time solving jigsaw puzzles, claiming that she loves nobody and that people's vitality irritates her.

The usual take on the meaning of architecture in critical discussions of *L'avventura* relies on a rather sentimental opposition ("old and obsolete," one is tempted to repeat after Antonioni) between modern buildings, the fruit of the Italian building boom of the late 1950s and early 60s, and the Sicilian Baroque, which is featured prominently in the film. This unproblematic critical attitude, however, seems rather strange, because it simply adopts an opinion which is expressed in the film by its most unreliable protagonist, Sandro. When Sandro and Claudia, pretending (mostly to themselves) that they are looking for Anna, arrive in Noto, Sandro, an architect, takes Claudia to the top of one of the churches to view the town—a quintessential collection of Sicilian Baroque architectural designs—from above. At first he is overwhelmed by what he sees: "What imagination! Look at all the movement ... They were interested in the stage effects. Extraordinary freedom."[39] This leads him to a reflection on himself: "I must make up my mind, decide once and for all to stop working for Ettore. I'd like to get back to drawing up plans ['fare dei progetti'—making projects] again. I had some ideas, you know?"[40] Claudia's reaction is the expected "I am convinced you could make really beautiful things." What we encounter here is, of course, a repetition of the scene we have already witnessed on Lisca Bianca, the "morning scene" in which Sandro exposed the depth of his soul to Claudia,[41] that is, projected for her his ideal image that has kept Claudia in thrall ever since, and by parading which he can assert his patriarchal dominion. No wonder, therefore, that Claudio's train of thought sparked by the architecture of Noto ends with an offer: "Shall we get married?" It is surely not accidental that Sandro can come up with this proposal only having recharged the glitter of his patriarchal image by identification with the symbolic position of an architect—and not just any architect (nominally, he is an architect after all), but a "true" architect with a "higher calling." Moreover, he reinforces this identification by concocting a sort of "tragic" narrative. First, he claims that he turned into a cost estimator because he could not stand the stupid requests of the rich ("Because it's not easy to admit that a red floor looks nice in a room when ... when you're convinced that it doesn't. But the lady wants it red. Because there is always some lady, or some gentleman"), and then "universalizes" his predicament as the general state of the

---

[39] The DVD translation modified in accordance with the translation published in *L'avventura*, ed. Chatman and Fink, 125-6.
[40] Translation modified in accordance with *L'avventura*, ed. Chatman and Fink, 126.
[41] It was his exquisite sensibility displayed as love for Anna on Lisca Bianca; it is his sensibility displayed as love for architecture now.

(capitalist and architectural) world: "And what good are beautiful things now, Claudia? Once they had centuries of life ahead of them [like the buildings of Noto]. Now—ten, twenty years at the most ... and then ... well ..." One can note, however, that such a "tragic" narrative does not sit very well with Sandro's ordinary behavior. Tragic plots demand heroic actions or at least resistance and perseverance, but Sandro's "life tactics" are to follow the line of the least resistance (which fits much better into a comic plot, as we have noted): he throws himself at Claudia in the yacht's cabin the day after Anna's disappearance, and, when Claudia runs away, he dogs her footsteps and complains that he does not want to sacrifice himself ("Sacrifice! I have no intention of sacrificing myself—it's idiocy sacrificing oneself ... "). Therefore, it is not accidental that in order to take up the position of the symbolic (and fascinating) master again, Sandro has to wipe out as much as possible of his own image as a master of enjoyment, and perhaps especially because he has just scored a success in the latter role: on the way to Noto he and Claudia have had their first sexual encounter.[42] Thus it is really strange that Sandro's opinions expressed in the attempt to "recharge" his symbolic position are so easily taken up by the critics who, like Claudia, adopt Sandro as their guide and construct an opposition with an obvious moralistic meaning (we have already quoted Antonioni from the Cannes statement: "I am not a moralist, and my film is neither a denunciation nor a sermon"): the Sicilian Baroque is supposed to stand for the humanist freedom of the spirit and joy of life, whereas modern buildings are supposed to represent an "alienated" existence which is functionalistically ugly, ephemeral and badly "staged."

The claim for such an opposition in the film is usually additionally supported by reference to the first sequence of *L'avventura* in which, during a conversation

---

[42] The encounter takes place outside of an abandoned village, next to a railroad. After a prolonged sexual scene (in which we mostly see Claudia's face in close-up), the film cuts to an extreme long shot of a seashore landscape with a train going leftward along the shore and distant Mount Etna (an active volcano, like Stromboli) almost invisible on the horizon (the train disappears screen left). In the next shot, a medium close-up, we see Claudia and Sandro lying on the grass and after a few seconds the train passes them a few feet away, moving from left to right. Witnessing a quick coupling in a barren landscape, we are very distant from the "sublime" scenario which was evoked against the image of another volcano in the "morning scene" on Lisca Bianca. Thus a train, on which the "morning scene" was repeated in the comic register and in which Sandro complained that it was idiotic to sacrifice oneself, reappears to remind us of the "indecent" (and therefore also comic) side of what we are seeing (the film in which the most famous cinematic example of sexual innuendo involving a train occurs, Hitchcock's *North by Northwest*, was released in 1959, less than a year before *L'avventura*). When Sandro is in his element, the "sublime" symbolic phallus withdraws into virtual invisibility (the volcano) and a mechanical one (the train), "encrusted upon the living," appears to enjoy in its place, subverting the principles (the laws) according to which reality is put together in an orderly manner, including the cinematic rules of continuity editing which Antonioni blatantly breaks in this scene.

between Anna and her father in front of his house (he is a *pater* and a *dominus*), the dome of St. Peter's basilica, visible on the horizon, seems to contrast with the sprawling modern apartment development that hems in the retired diplomat's villa. Of course, the looming dome as a background to a couple (though a father and a daughter this time) brings to mind once again the "morning scene" on Lisca Bianca where, in the circumstances of primeval nature and with the patriarchal blessing of the cone of Stromboli on the horizon, Claudia "naturally" submits to the glitter of Sandro's idealized image. St. Peter's (obviously not a random specimen of the second nature) seems to serve the same function at the beginning of the film—it reinforces the symbolic paternal authority displayed in the foreground, only this time the trick does *not* work. But why doesn't it? Is it because the Italian patriarchal authority the dome symbolizes (in many dimensions: religious, political, aesthetic) is being undermined by the modern architectural slime (symbolizing "alienation," for instance), which is the support for the attitude of a dissolute daughter? One may have serious doubts about this, especially because the father figure, when examined closely, does not represent a contrast but a *continuity* between the old and the new: he himself admits to having been a diplomat for the past thirty years (that is, from around 1930), which nicely illustrates the institutional continuity between fascist Italy and the Italy of the Christian Democrats, so often remarked on by historians of the country.[43] Therefore the new houses that crowd the villa of Anna's father cannot be taken as a modern faceless force at odds with the old and conservative values represented by him ("We are in the hands of God" is how he sums up her disappearance) precisely because he himself, as a functionary of both these regimes (the fascist and the Christian Democrats), is responsible for creating and perpetuating that force. The houses under construction are here a representation of the ascendancy of the dynamic new generation of the ruling class of which Anna's father is a member and a retired functionary—three of the five male protagonists of the film who are individualized enough to be given names (Sandro, Ettore, Corrado) are, or are associated with, developers and land speculators responsible for the Italian building boom.[44] And although at first sight St. Peter's dome may not seem to have much to do with that modern

---

[43] Also by P. Adams Sitney, *Vital Crises in Italian Cinema: Iconography, Stylistics, Politics* (Oxford: Oxford University Press, 2013), 129. The continuity between the old and the new is also picked up later in the film when Sandro tells Claudia: "Do you know that as a boy I wanted to be a diplomat?"

[44] The remaining two are Raimondo, a long-suffering admirer of Patrizia (Ettore's wife) during the cruise, and Goffredo, a Sicilan princeling turned painter.

constellation, it does not seem to flash its patriarchal message gratuitously: the backing of the Christian Democrats, the political party that uninterruptedly ruled Italy from 1944 to the 1980s, by the Vatican is an important part of the socio-political landscape of the boom.

Like the dome of St. Peter's, the baroque architecture of Noto seems to offer a contrast to modern nondescriptness and this is the reason Sandro enthuses about it so much, as we have noted. However, *before* we are transported to the top of the church to feast our eyes on an architectural staging of the ideal order (of feudal-hierarchical Sicily—and its "extraordinary freedom") with Sandro and Claudia, we are given a clear indication of its mundane content: when Sandro visits the Trinacria Hotel, in order to check whether he can find any information about Anna, and Claudia is left in the street to wait for him, she is lasciviously ogled by a crowd of local men who circle around her in ever greater numbers, so that their prurient gazes almost stifle her.[45] In other words, what for the man at the top of a tower (and at the peak of his intoxication with the idea of the patriarchal "higher calling") will look like an incarnation of extraordinary freedom, for the woman at street level feels like extraordinary harassment.[46] But in fact, it is not even necessary to descend from the tower in order to notice the obscene enjoyment that is the patriarchal substance of the Sicilian Baroque, because the style flaunts it for everybody to see—the buildings in question (and the Sicilian Baroque in general) are the very images of excess displayed in their characteristic flamboyant flourishes and overabundant decorations.[47] As has often been remarked, these are buildings which look like elaborate wedding cakes topped with ornaments looking like icing sugar—an appropriate incarnation of the *jouissance* of the Sicilian feudal patriarchal order founded on the mortification of the living flesh (and not excluding the soul either) that belonged to the world of peasant scarcity and toil.

---

[45] This is a companion scene to the one we have noted in *Stromboli*: the community's symbolic gaze is incarnated in the gaze of women (who want to mortify Karin's enjoyment), while the obscene master's gaze finds its representatives in men who ogle Claudia.

[46] Like all important "serious" scenes of *L'avventura*, this one too has a comic equivalent, to which we'll return: in Messina a "dissolute" woman, Gloria Perkins, causes a riot of men, who swarm around her completely beside themselves.

[47] Anthony Blunt describes these decorations as "either fascinating or repulsive" (this is exactly what one may say about enjoyment) and adds, "but however the individual spectator may react to it, this style is a characteristic manifestation of Sicilian exuberance, and must be classed amongst the most important and original creations of Baroque art on the island." *Sicilian Baroque* (London: Weidenfeld & Nicolson, 1968), 10.

It is interesting that in spite of his initial intoxication with the panorama of Noto, Sandro seems to become finally aware of the reverse side of its "extraordinary freedom." While Claudia stays in the Trinacria Hotel, Sandro goes out to visit a church, and when he finds it closed,[48] in the street he encounters a small folding table with an unfinished sketch of an architectural detail, which has just been drawn by a young man who is conversing with somebody else nearby. Sandro scrutinizes the sketch carefully and then intentionally overturns the ink bottle, so that the sketch is destroyed by a big stain of black ink. This scene is usually interpreted as the expression of Sandro's envy of the young man's idealistic engagement with architecture, which inspires Sandro's aggression because he already knows he will not break up with Ettore and become a "true" architect. But there seems to be much more than envy in Sandro's gesture. Having descended from his elevated stance at the top of the church to the level of the street, Sandro returns to "reality"; he realizes that his identification with his ideal symbolic mandate was only a dream caused by his intoxication with the panorama of Noto, and therefore the ideal image that caused this intoxication (Noto's orderly architectural design, of which the sketch of the town's architectural detail is a synecdoche) must be destroyed by a black formless smear, which materializes the imageless substance of enjoyment that disfigures Sandro's life and wrecks the image of himself he would like to maintain. But, of course, the substance of enjoyment is not only Sandro's—it is the dissimulated content of the ideal image of the patriarchal social order itself. If one looks at the "symbolic" representation of that order (e.g., the panorama of Noto as expressive of "extraordinary freedom") from an appropriate angle, one sees enjoyment seeping through the cracks that appear in it, or, more precisely, the very black ink lines with which the ideal image is sketched are the cracks through which the black substance of enjoyment overflows. Thus, after Sandro's brief altercation with the furious drawer of the sketch, the formless black stain of enjoyment is visually reconfigured and takes the "social" form of a group of black-dressed boys who spill out of a nearby church (the same church Sandro wanted to visit earlier) overseen by priests and

---

[48] The episode in which the sublime symbolic master was encountered (and identified with) by Sandro while viewing the panorama of Noto is (typically for the film) doubled by a comic one. A coachman Sandro accosts and complains to about the closed church, which should be open to tourists, answers, "Tourists? What tourists? Last year we got a few French, they went to the beach to swim with the 'jeep.'" Sandro corrects him, "With the *slip* [bikini]! And so?" "We let them know that they'd better move on, leave … " After this Sandro even looks up at the towering façade of the closed church (complete with bells and a balcony at the top, like the one he visited earlier with Claudia), as if referring what the coachman has said to his earlier elation.

whom Sandro, in a sense, joins—he follows them down the steps descending from the church.[49] In this way, the "institutional" excess Noto exudes finds yet another image and, as in the previous case (from the tower the excess presented itself as a controlled movement of stage effects), the enjoyment asserts itself in its "opposite determination" as restraint enforced on the boys.[50]

Overwhelmed by the suffocating blackness of enjoyment, there is nothing Sandro can do but to succumb to it—he returns to Claudia and tries to force himself on her in a completely joyless manner, as if something mechanical (encrusted upon the living) guided him. One can clearly see here the nature of *jouissance*: Sandro is not enjoying what he is doing, but *something* does, *something* is enjoying itself. For Claudia this is a sobering experience—she is no longer overwhelmed by Sandro's phallic appearance (a romantic lover, an architect with a calling who could make very beautiful things, etc.), but is traumatized by something she is not able to recognize: "I feel as if I don't know you," she says, panicking. Answering which, Sandro puts things in a new perspective by finding the something that enjoys on Claudia, too—"And you're not happy? You have a new adventure!"[51]

This omnipresence of such painful enjoyment in Noto should take us back to the deserted village whose uncanny emptiness is usually contrasted by the critics with the beauty of the baroque town. But is this modern-looking (no baroque icing sugar here) village really the architectural equivalent of modern "death," that is, the incarnation of the alienated spirit that has built it? Claudia calls it a cemetery, but something strange happens when, spooked by the desolation, the couple decides to leave. When the film cuts to a long shot of the car they are getting into (the car is parked in a piazza in front of the church toward which leads a little cobbled street where the camera is placed), their anxiety seems to find a cause: the camera starts slowly tracking toward them as if, in spite of appearances, something were alive in the village. So what is the origin of all this strangeness? Sandro gives expression to his astonishment by saying, "I wonder why they built it at all," but he, as a building cost estimator, is precisely in the position to know this: so that he (or someone like him) could have estimated its

---

[49] John Simon also connects the black ink-stain with "a phalanx of little seminarians in black garb." "Thoughts on *L'avventura*," in *L'avventura*, ed. Amberg and Hughes, 268.

[50] By "joining" the boys Sandro is also infantilized. One may recall what Patrizia said about Raimondo (a *jousseur*, like Sandro, though a rather melancholic one) during the cruise: that in spite of superficial corruption he is like a baby.

[51] Translation modified.

costs. In other words, the village was built so that certain people (like Ettore and Corrado) could make a profit, although it serves no purpose.

Thus the mysterious existence of the abandoned village is not so mysterious after all. In fact, its haunting presence nicely illustrates the collusion between at least two far-from-mysterious politico-economic forces at work in the Italy of the 1950s: the Christian Democracy (Democrazia Cristiana, DC) and the real estate business and speculation in the building sector.[52] In the late 1940s, in order to neutralize the peasant mobilization inspired by the Communist Party, which resulted in protests and land occupations (especially in the South, including Sicily, where land occupations continued well into the 1950s[53]), the DC embarked on a program of agrarian reform whose results turned out to be rather modest for the targeted groups of smallholders who lived near the subsistence level and landless laborers,[54] but not so meager for the DC officials, the party's important supporters and the construction business connected with it. For the former two the party could offer positions in the new government agencies: ERAS, set up to deal with the land reform in the South, and the Cassa per il Mezzogiorno, the state fund for the South.[55] For the latter it offered big governmental contracts, which did not necessarily have primarily the interests of the impoverished population on their agenda.

The story of Schisina (the name of the abandoned village we see in the film[56]) is a good illustration of the way in which these agencies operated. Why was the village abandoned? The land reform confiscated and redistributed only a limited amount of unimproved land which was hard or impossible to cultivate because of its location (we can see that the abandoned village is in the mountains) or/and because of the lack of irrigation.[57] But perhaps more importantly the failure

---

[52] The subject of a famous 1963 film by Francesco Rosi, *Hands over the City* (*Le mani sulla città*).
[53] Paul Ginsborg, *A History of Contemporary Italy: Society and Politics 1943–1988* (London: Penguin, 1990), 136.
[54] The problem was especially acute in the South and especially in Sicily, where most of the land was in possession of a handful of absentee landowners.
[55] "Not surprisingly, one third of ERAS's budget in the first eight years of its activity went on administrative costs. Other reform boards were not as bad, but all were valuable sources of local patronage for the DC." Ginsborg, *A History of Contemporary Italy*, 136.
[56] Rosalind Galt, "On *L'avventura* and the Picturesque," in *Antonioni*, ed. Rascaroli and Rhodes, 147. To be more precise, what we see in the film is one of the seven small hamlets (another one of them is also seen in the distance by the characters in one of the shots) which went to make up Schisina, as explained in Rossella Scalia, "Schisina Ghost Villages, Sicily," accessed February 19, 2018, https://vimeo.com/126946161.
[57] "Grandiose irrigation plans were announced, but by 1966 only 150 of the small earth-dammed hill lakes had been completed, out of the more than 5,000 originally planned." Ginsborg, *A History of Contemporary Italy*, 136.

of villages like Schisina was caused by completely disregarding both the needs of the peasants and even the basic demands of "reality" (for instance, the location in the mountains) by the functionaries of ERAS or the Cassa. In effect, the agencies were spending money on construction of unhabitable villages by which only the contractors profited:

> With no electricity nor running water in the house and only two rooms—a kitchen and a bedroom—next to a small animal stall, the seven villages have never been thought of as an opportunity, but rather as a sacrifice for those who had chosen to live them. ... The surrounding area also needed a land amelioration in order to be suitable for farming; the cold winter months that piled the snow on the flat roofs of the houses—mistakenly designed for a Mediterranean climate thus unsuitable for mountain weather conditions—encouraged the brave survivors to leave en masse the hamlets and never come back.[58]

Therefore the abandoned village is not a sign of some mysterious death wish that has grabbed the Italian spirit which has been ravaged by godless modernity. In fact, the opposite is the case: Schisina is a useless excrescence produced by the shameless excesses of a political institution, the DC, that preaches decorum and restraint in the form of conservative Christian values ("*paese*, church and family").

This institutional DC logic operating in the rural South has also a metropolitan incarnation, which we see in the modern buildings under construction in the first sequence of *L'avventura* which takes place in Rome. The effects of this attitude are described by Paul Ginsborg thus: "The thirty years between 1950 and 1980 (the peak of the DC power) saw a catastrophic change in the landscape and cityscape of the Italian peninsula. Many of the historic centres of the Italian cities and towns were modified irreversibly, and their suburbs grew as unplanned jungles of cement."[59] This state of affairs was the result of the DC governments' turning a blind eye to the excesses of developers and speculators in the building sector, and their collusion with corrupt municipal authorities. But it is not only the case that the sprawling modern constructions on the outskirts of Rome in the first scene of *L'avventura* are the outcome of the same patriarchal logic as the buildings of the abandoned village in Sicilia, that is, they are the ugly excrescences of enjoyment of the Christian Democratic master (literally present

---

[58] Scalia, *Schisina*.
[59] Ginsborg, *A History of Contemporary Italy*, 246.

in the scene as embodied by Anna's father). What is much more interesting is the modern buildings' most emphatically non-antagonistic relation to the ultimate patriarchal image looming on the horizon in the shape of the dome of St. Peter's:

> Throughout the great building boom of 1953–63, there was often open collusion between the municipal authorities and the building speculators. The "sack" of Rome, as it came to be called, was dramatic testimony to this. Property developers like the giant Societa Generale Immobiliari, *whose principal shareholder is the Vatican*, were allowed to fill up every available space in the city itself, and then to cover the periphery with apartment blocks of poor construction and ever poorer aesthetics. … It was not surprising that by 1970 one house in every six in Rome was "abusive," i.e. it had been built without any proper permit, and that 400,000 people were living in habitations which officially did not exist.[60]

Thus the black substance of "feudal" enjoyment that Sandro found in Noto in the form of baroque excess and humble seminarians turns out not to be so feudal after all—its updated versions (like Societa Generale Immobiliari) sweep over modernity with a vengeance, spawning men who build unhabitable villages in Sicily, "abusive" buildings in Rome, and who riot at the appearance of Gloria Perkins (Dorothy De Poliolo) in Messina. Although this last scene—in which a crowd of "sex-mad" men chases after Gloria who displays to them a bit of her sexy thigh visible through a burst seam on a side of her dress—is usually taken as the supreme image of the modern "sickness of Eros" in *L'avventura*, one may have serious doubts about its modern provenance. Despite the fact that the scene looks superficially modern by incorporating a recent (in 1960) phenomenon of mass adulation of pop stars (Gloria, protected by the police, blows kisses and waves to the crowd of men who swarm around her), in the eyes of the male population of Sicily (it is said that she caused a similar riot in Palermo[61]), she is not a pop star at all—Zuria, a journalist Sandro has been looking for in Messina, explicitly "exposes" her as the Whore.[62] And this is obviously what the character "mythically" is—a comic incarnation of the ages-old antifeminist male fantasy of feminine enjoyment: an entirely sexualized creature, which undermines the patriarchal order from within. In the carnivalesque world of the Messina episode, Zuria's epithet is even comically (and obscenely) literalized by a "slit"

---

[60] Ibid., 247; emphasis added.
[61] "Exactly the same thing happened in Palermo," says Zuria.
[62] "Fifty thousand! Why all of this racket then? It's all a ruse to be noticed. … Ah well, if fifty thou weren't a month's worth of my wages, that's one of those whims I would have indulged, I assure you."

(a burst seam of her dress along a thigh),[63] which Gloria displays to the world to make men crazy. To them she is nothing but a "hole"; that hole, however, destabilizes the whole—because of it, the Sicilian patriarchal order comically plunges into chaos.

The riot Gloria causes in Messina is also a comic (and thus exaggerated) version of what will happen to Claudia later in the film in the streets of Noto, where she will be lewdly ogled and encircled by a crowd of men. Yet there is nothing modern about the men of Noto—in fact, we are in "backward" Sicily and what they display is the most "archaic" (and aggressive) patriarchal attitude to an unaccompanied woman in the street (Sandro has left Claudia only for a few minutes). Moreover, when the deceptive "modernizing" pop-cultural context we encountered in Messina disappears, it is not difficult to realize that the men in the street who grin obscenely at Claudia are not exactly the modern "hollow men" who have forsaken the ideals of "*paese*, church and family." In fact, the opposite seems to be the case—they are just grown-up versions of the priest-ridden boys in black garb we later see spilling out of the church: the men whose patriarchal mentality (and sexuality) is founded on the traditional catholic splitting of the image of the woman into the Madonna/Mother and the Whore.[64]

Gloria, however, has yet another role to play in *L'avventura*. She appears again in the hotel for the rich in Taormina, in which Claudia and Sandro are also staying, and although this role of hers is less carnivalesque than the previous one, her presence is a clear indication that what is going on in the hotel is just a glamorized version of the same chaos we have encountered in the streets of Messina. In fact, the pretenses of the cultured order are immediately undermined by an ironic association of Gloria with a certain charitable character. Just when she is noticed by Sandro in the hotel, the film immediately cuts to a shot of a baroque painting of a young woman breastfeeding an old man, an image of the so-called Roman Charity, in which Pero surreptitiously feeds her father, Cimon, who was sentenced to the death by starvation in prison.[65] This is obviously yet another of the double images we have encountered in the film: like the panorama of Noto, the Roman Charity tells a symbolic story (this time of filial love); yet, enjoyment seeps through its cracks. Even leaving aside the incestuous

---

[63] So much for Antonioni's lack of humor, high seriousness, and anxiety-mongering—when it suits his purpose, he can even be obscene.

[64] A famous contemporary comic "analysis" of which occurs in 8½ by Federico Fellini (1963).

[65] Simon, "Thoughts on *L'avventura*," 271; Seymour Chatman, "Notes on the Continuity Script," in *L'avventura*, ed. Chatman and Fink, 163.

undertones of a picture of this kind, one may be reminded that, as in the case of the Renaissance and Baroque images of Greek goddesses, the symbolic content here is to a large extent just a pretext to show a beautiful woman exposing her bare breast for all (or rather for a male buyer) to see and salivate over.[66] In other words, a painting like that is just a "gentrification" of what was earlier represented as Gloria's "slit," which is dissimulated both by the symbolic narrative associated with it (Pero and Cimon) and by its status as a refined aesthetic object. Thus the half-naked Roman Charity hanging on the wall of a luxurious hotel (the incongruity in itself is ironic) pretends to partake in the ordered universe of ideal values (filial love, aesthetic principles),[67] in contrast to the street-walking Gloria whose body causes chaos in Palermo and Messina. But of course nobody is taken in by such deceptions, which is confirmed by the inviting look Sandro is given by a woman looking at the painting: she has no difficulty recognizing the painting's true message (patriarchal enjoyment) and passing it to Sandro through her eyes.[68]

Waiting for Sandro in their hotel room in the small hours of the morning, Claudia is suddenly overwhelmed by fear that Anna has come back and that this is the reason Sandro has not returned yet ("I'm afraid Anna has come back. I can feel it, that they are together," she tells Patrizia). And although Patrizia answers that this is impossible ("What has gotten into you? We would have had word"), Claudia is, in a sense, right. Unable to calm down, she goes downstairs to look for Sandro and finds him in the arms of Gloria. Thus we witness a stark confrontation between the Madonna and the Whore, which takes place in total silence (nobody says anything), but, as if in compensation, the scene involves a technical "smear," in which the temporal order of events "jams" at the crucial moment of recognition: the moment is repeated twice and shown from two different angles. First, Claudia is shown in medium long shot looking around a

---

[66] The most famous example of this is, of course, Titian's *Venus of Urbino*, an erotically charged painting thought to be a portrait of one of the leading courtesans in Venice, Angela del Moro. Sheila Hale, *Titian: His Life* (New York: HarperCollins, 2012), 340.

[67] It may be amusing to consider that this kind of narrative deterrence can also work on the meta-level of criticism. In his 1985 book on Antonioni, Seymour Chatman had seen "the decadence implicit in that depiction of a patriarch taking refreshment at a lady's breast," but when he later learned about its narrative background (the story of Pero and Cimon) from William Arrowsmith and Svetlana Alpers, Chatman disavowed this remark, calling it erroneous. Seymour Chatman, *Antonioni or, the Surface of the World* (Berkeley: University of California Press, 1985), 100; "Notes on the Continuity Script," 163.

[68] It is not the only scene of this sort in the hotel in Taormina. When Claudia and Sandro arrive at the hotel, she is immediately spotted by an elderly man who asks a concierge: "Who is this little doll?"

huge dining room in search of Sandro; she almost turns back to leave the room but hears some scraping furniture, takes a few more steps, and begins to stare at a couch which is turned away from us. After a while (still in medium long shot) Sandro and Gloria raise their heads, so we can see them over the back of the couch. Then the film cuts to a medium shot, taken from a point just behind Claudia's head,[69] in which we see Sandro and Gloria engaged in lovemaking. After a while Sandro looks up and raises his face to Claudia, followed by Gloria. After this the film cuts to a close-up of Claudia's face looking down on the couple, followed by a close-up of the couple (Gloria's face in the foreground) looking back at Claudia (these are "proper" close-ups, no longer "over-the-shoulder" shots). Therefore it is not very difficult to associate the latter shot—in which Sandro quickly withdraws behind Gloria's back, so only Gloria's face is raised to Claudia's in confrontation, but also as if it were her reflection—with the mirror shot in the villa of the Montaldos in which Claudia wears a black wig (Gloria, like Anna, is a brunette) and Patrizia tells her that she looks "like somebody else." We have already interpreted this scene as a visual confirmation of Claudia's identification with Anna's ideal image as the member of the moneyed class, but there is definitely more to it. In the mirror scene Claudia does not only identify with Anna's "glamorous" image—at the villa of the Montaldos Claudia is waiting impatiently for Sandro to return (in a shot preceding the mirror scene Claudia runs out onto a terrace, hearing a car engine and thinking it is Sandro's car), that is, in her mind she has already taken Anna's position at Sandro's side. But not as the "difficult" partner that Anna was—sporting a black wig in the mirror, Claudia "looks like someone else" in yet another way: she looks like Gloria, because she is offering herself as a willing object of patriarchal enjoyment, the spitting image of which we have just seen in the Messina riot, a sequence which immediately precedes the mirror scene. Thus looking Gloria in the eye (after the over-the-shoulder shot of Sandro and Gloria on the couch we are given three classical eye-line matches: Claudia looking at Gloria–Gloria looking at Claudia–Claudia looking at Gloria), the temporal order "jams" for Claudia and she revisits the earlier mirror shot in its real meaning. In its repetition, however, something uncanny happens: the black smear of enjoyment reappears as if in the mirror, but this time it really does belong to *someone else*. Like a true

---

[69] A typical technique in *L'avventura*, much commented upon, is that we hardly ever have classical point-of-view shots in which the one who looks does not appear—usually we have "over-the-shoulder" shots in which the back of the looking character is visible.

doppelgänger, what used to be Claudia's (idealized) mirror image (Claudia in a black wig seeing herself in the position of Anna) has come alive and taken her place (as in the mirror scene she took Anna's).⁷⁰ In other words, for the first time Claudia sees the content of all her fantasies, both concerning Sandro and, what is more important, herself: she has been a happy servant of patriarchal enjoyment.

Thus there is yet another repetition involved in this scene, because, in fact, it is the second time that Claudia is confronted with the truth of her position. As we have already noted, while in Noto, horrified by Sandro's aggressive sexual advances in the Trinacria Hotel, Claudia exclaims: "What's gotten into you? ... I feel as though I don't know you," despite the fact that earlier on the same day her knowledge of him seemed secure ("I am convinced you could make really beautiful things"). This momentary decomposition of Claudia's ideal image of Sandro is accompanied by a confrontation with an unpleasant insight, which Sandro offers (after all, he has just experienced his own moment of truth in the streets of Noto) regarding her: "And you're not happy? You have a new adventure!" But Claudia is not able to accept this truth at first encounter, and Sandro, sensing this or perhaps seeing panic in her eyes, pretends it was just a joke. So the face-off with the truth has to repeat itself and, to be properly registered, it has to repeat itself in the image of Gloria, a woman who also "looks like someone else" (she is another woman who replaced Anna for Sandro) but who is like Claudia in relation to patriarchal enjoyment (she is happy that she has just had another adventure). The realization of this truth is the primary reason for Claudia's horror, a much more important one than Sandro's unfaithfulness.

When, having encountered Sandro with Gloria, Claudia runs out of the hotel and into a car-park nearby, Sandro follows her there ashamed, collapses on a bench, and starts to cry. After Claudia approaches him from behind and hesitatingly puts her hand on the back of his head in order to stroke it in a gesture of forgiveness/reconciliation, the film cuts to a long shot from behind them, which is almost symmetrically divided between the view of Mount Etna on the left and the blank wall of a building on the right. This final shot of the film has usually been interpreted as representing an opposition: Claudia stands behind the bench to the left and is therefore supposedly related to Mount Etna;

---

[70] This appearance of a *doppelgänger* in the "mirroring" confrontation between Claudia and Gloria is prepared by yet another mirror scene which we have not mentioned so far. Waiting for Sandro in their hotel room in Taormina, Claudia encounters her reflection and "disfigures" her face by putting on clownish expressions—but it will be Gloria (a comic figure so far) whose face will disfigure Claudia's completely.

Sandro sits on the bench to the right and is supposedly associated with the blank wall. Thus easy oppositions come to mind: nature-culture, female-male, hope-despair. Moreover, these oppositions are often credited with the endorsement of Antonioni who seems to describe this shot in similar terms:

> On one side of the frame is Mount Etna in all its snowy whiteness, and on the other is a concrete wall. The wall corresponds to the man and Mount Etna corresponds somewhat to the situation of the woman. Thus the frame is divided exactly in half; one half containing the concrete wall which represents the pessimistic side, while the other half showing Mount Etna represents the optimistic.[71]

But, as we have tried to show, within the symbolic framework established earlier by the film these oppositions simply do not work. Images of "sublime" nature and especially the image of an active volcano, like Mount Etna or Stromboli, are continuous with what the images of architecture stand for in L'avventura, that is, patriarchal enjoyment. And in fact Antonioni himself undermines the above-mentioned oppositions supposedly present in the background by noting the continuity of what we encounter in the foreground:

> For she [Claudia] realizes that she too, in a certain sense, is somewhat like him. Because—if for no other reason—from the moment she suspects Anna may have returned, she becomes so apprehensive, so afraid she may be back and still alive, that she begins to lose the feeling of friendship that she once had for Anna, just as he had lost his affection for Anna and perhaps is also beginning to lose it for her.[72]

In other words, for Claudia's final gesture of caressing Sandro's hair to happen, her initial pain and horror at the sight of Sandro's unfaithfulness must have been turned into a realization that "she too, in a certain sense, is somewhat like him." But what is much more important than being "literally" like him (which Antonioni suggests: like Sandro, Claudia has also been "unfaithful" to Anna) is her perfect adaptation (like Sandro's too) to the obscene patriarchal scenario we have been describing, which grips Italy in its clutches and which Anna had rejected.[73] Although there are some critics who interpret Claudia's final gesture as heroic self-denial or metaphysical pity, it is in fact the gesture of resignation with

---

[71] Antonioni, "A Talk," 223.
[72] Ibid., 223–4.
[73] And whose rejection hovers over the characters throughout the film in the form of Anna's "absent presence."

which the moment of recognition of her complicity with patriarchal enjoyment is obliterated. Rather than act on the moment of insight and unmoor herself from the patriarchal plot, which would make for a true identification with Anna, Claudia thoroughly reinscribes herself into the patriarchal order by taking the position of the Madonna, the ultimate good female subject as it is imagined by the patriarchal gaze, and performs the supreme gesture that belongs to that figure: she forgives the man who has wronged her.[74]

That this is the moment of Claudia's *submission* is emphasized by the literalization of the patriarchal gaze in the final sequence. When Claudia, shown in a long shot, runs into the empty car-park, where the silent final scene between her and Sandro will take place, she crosses it and leans against the guardrail on the other side. Standing there, she is noticed by a man walking up a street, which runs uphill to finally reach the level of the car-park, who slows down and then stops to look up at her. Although the man does not reappear in the remaining three minutes of the film, one should not take his presence in the final scene as inconsequential. Because what happens in this concluding part of the film is shown more or less in real time, three minutes is about the amount of time it would take the man to reach the place from which the last shot featuring the wall and Mount Etna is taken (the end of the street he is walking up), so we may take the last image of the film as being from his point of view. Thus the presence of the volcano in the final shot seems very far from optimistic, because—like the cone of Stromboli and the dome of St. Peter's at the beginning of the film—it indicates the framing presence of the patriarchal gaze that objectifies Claudia and decides her "fate." In other words, the last shot takes us back to the Roman Charity painting we have encountered in the hotel. Like Pero, Claudia is framed by the "sublime" narrative of the Good Woman (mother/spouse/daughter), which is the fantasy that founds patriarchal enjoyment and allows for patriarchal domination. So, although in fact the blank wall takes up the whole screen (enjoyment has no image and is meaningless), on Claudia's side it is dissimulated by the "optimistic" image of a volcano, whose meaning, however, the film has previously established.

---

[74] It is not accidental that the emotional tenor of the final scene is not that of a confrontation of lovers—in the car-park Claudia plays the Mother to the infantilized Sandro. Claudia's "maternal vocation" is noted by Dominique Fernandez, "The Poet of Matriarchy," in *L'Avventura*, ed. Amberg and Hughes, 254.

2

La notte (1961)

Unlike other films by Antonioni in which temporal coordinates remain rather vague, *La notte* takes place in and around Milan in a period of less than twenty-four hours—between an early afternoon and the morning of the following day. The plot follows the peregrinations of a married couple: Giovanni Pontano (Marcello Mastroianni) and his wife Lidia (Jeanne Moreau), whose day consists of appointments they do not feel like keeping, but which they keep nevertheless ("One must do something," says Lidia[1]). Though the film will revolve around the couple's marriage crisis, the predicament they initially face is somebody else's. The first visit they pay is to their friend Tommaso (Bernhard Wicki) who is dying at a hospital, surrounded by an efficient staff and modern equipment which is nevertheless useless in saving this self-effacing, middle-aged yet old-fashioned man,[2] who, even on his death-bed, is aware of the contradictions his situation poses: he detests his circumstances[3] and tries to assuage his guilt by immersing himself in the piles of critical books that lie on both sides of his bed (a doctor picks up one of them with Brecht's photograph on it, and there is talk about Tommaso's article on Adorno).

An encounter with death (even if it is somebody else's death) which leads one to a reassessment of one's life, especially if this encounter happens during a midlife crisis, has of course for a long time been a conventional literary device, so a beginning like this sets the tone for the rest of the film, whose protagonists are, moreover, a novelist, and his wife, who "hangs out with intellectuals" (as Lidia's former acquaintance, Berenice (Roberta Speroni), reveals later in the

---

[1] Unless otherwise noted, all translations come from the 2008 DVD release of *La notte* by Eureka Entertainment.
[2] We learn of Tommaso's humble origins through the visit of his mother, and he addresses a nurse with old-fashioned courtesy.
[3] Tommaso comments: "It's everything I dislike in terms of style. I never thought I'd end my days like this ['così di lusso'—in such luxury]. I feel like a fraud ['frodare qualcuno'—cheating on/stealing from somebody]."

film) and therefore is, in a sense, estranged from her class (Lidia comes from a rich family). In addition, the "literariness" of *La notte* is reinforced from the very beginning in yet another way—the scene taking place in Tommaso's hospital room relies mainly on his introspective monologue for its effect, which is very untypical of Antonioni's cinema, known for oblique statements juxtaposed against ambiguous images. This verbosity, in which people attempt to explain themselves to others, keeps recurring in *La notte*, which has led the film to be seen by critics as being too reliant on dialogue. The prominence of language in *La notte* (sometimes to the detriment of the visual side, otherwise so inventive in Antonioni's films) is undeniable, but one may ask: Is it just a weakness of the film or does it have a purpose?

In connection with this intermittent overuse of language, another feature of *La notte* comes immediately to mind: there are scenes or sequences in the film in which language is either totally absent, or serves just as background noise, or, though used, is completely meaningless. In fact, this kind of scene takes place in the hospital immediately after the protagonists' visit to Tommaso. Having just left his friend's room (Lidia, overwhelmed by Tommaso's misfortune, had left it earlier), Giovanni is accosted in the corridor by a beautiful young woman (Maria Pia Luzi) and asked for a light. This, however, is just a ploy that allows her to drag Giovanni into her room and "pounce" on the writer: she clings to him violently and covers him with kisses, all of which is accompanied by inarticulate moaning sounds. What is more, during the entire scene Giovanni behaves like an animal charmed by a snake, remaining stiff and completely passive in the woman's embrace (both while being dragged in, that is, overpowered by the female patient who must be weaker than he, and while being caressed) and only finally proceeds to kiss the woman (usually referred to as "the nymphomaniac" by critics who write about the film) after she undresses and sprawls herself for him on the bed. But even in this action Giovanni's agency is doubtful, as it seems to be the consequence of his being "charmed"—he "mechanically" proceeds according to the (external) logic that the situation dictates, that is, he submits to being "devoured."

Although this scene with the unidentified woman is usually ascribed to (or written off as?) the familiar *malattia dei sentimenti* scenario (the "Eros is sick" theme discussed in the previous chapter), there are all kinds of problems with this approach. For instance, although the diagnosis of the "malady of sentiments" may be applied to most of the characters featured in *La notte*, if such is an interpreter's wish, it definitely cannot be applied to the woman—she behaves as she does precisely because she does not have sentiments like other people, even "disfigured" ones. We cannot speak in her case about quantitative difference—that the woman is just more alienated from her feelings than Giovanni or the guests at Gherardini's party (of which the final part of the film consists). The difference is radical and definitely qualitative—the woman belongs to a different order of "sentimental" existence; her behavior cannot be explained by resorting to common sentiments because she and her behavior, as they are shown to us in the film, are completely impenetrable. Giovanni, later trying to excuse himself before Lidia, says that the unidentified woman "was like a wild animal," but this is a very lame explanation, which relies on the image of a natural instinct not controlled by reason. This is precisely what cannot be said of the woman: flailing on her bed with her teeth bared and a provocative smirk on her face, held down with visible difficulty by two nurses who burst on the scene of Giovanni's "seduction," she seems to be possessed by some self-contained and inexplicable force, not by a goal-oriented instinct.

And in fact, although the film is just beginning, we have already seen an image of such utterly impenetrable self-containment. In the famous opening credits sequence of *La notte* the camera tilts up the facade of an old townhouse, catching sight in the background of the 127-meter-high Pirelli skyscraper completed in Milan in 1958, and then, after two short intermediate shots presenting metal constructions on top of it, the camera, in a long take, travels down the skyscraper's sheer glazed facade. Although the windows are filmed up close (we see only a fragment of one pane of glass of each floor as the camera moves downward), the inside of the building is virtually invisible—the glass just indifferently reflects the dwarfed city around it to which the skyscraper, in a sense, does not belong, and which the following long take only emphasizes: while the camera is still descending, the left part of the screen presents the panorama around the Pirelli building and the right part shows the reflection of the panorama in the building's curtain glass exterior.[4] Thus the skyscraper is shown as a sealed, self-contained alien object, not communicating with its environment but "cutting through it like a sword," as one architecture historian has it.[5] Moreover, as the opening credits sequence explicitly demonstrates, the building is completely

---

[4] There is a technical distinction between a curtain wall and a window wall but it is irrelevant to my purposes here. The point is that the Pirelli building's exterior has the look of top-to-bottom glass surface.
[5] Terry Kirk, *The Architecture of Modern Italy, Volume II: Visions of Utopia, 1900–Present* (New York: Princeton Architectural Press, 2005), 173.

"faceless"—its rows of reflecting windows make its "visage" entirely blank. Unlike the townhouse's façade/face, which has definite features and is therefore expressive of something—stylistically, historically, and existentially—and hence possesses a certain aura, the skyscraper is totally impenetrable, even if, theoretically, a transparent material like glass should "open up" the building and problematize the relationship between the inside and the outside of it.[6]

Like the heavy-set townhouse, which visibly contains something and provokes imagination by withdrawing behind the façade, Tommaso is a rounded character, an expressive sentimental man, with all the right sentiments in all the right places, as we learn from his conversation with the Pontanos. He is humble, he is generous, and he has an intellectual "work ethic": "This is the first time I've been off work for three years. ... You realize that there's still so much to do." This solidity, however, is precisely something that hollows him out, making for the interior whose "bottom" recedes into infinity: "Maybe I was watching from the sidelines something I should have been a part of. I lacked the courage ['forza'—strength] to go all the way ['andare fino in fondo'—go to the bottom]. I often cheer myself up thinking I probably wasn't clever enough anyway." In other words, it is with Tommaso, a solid "townhouse" character, that we encounter a problematization of the relationship between the inside and the outside: going to the bottom of something one should have been a part of is tantamount here to going to the bottom of oneself.

Unlike Tommaso, the unidentified woman in the hospital is faceless. Her face may smirk, it may get contorted, but its contortions are aleatory phenomena of the surface and are essentially meaningless—they do not reflect or represent anything, they are just surface ripples of something blank and impenetrable, turned upon itself. Tommaso's words are expressive because they painfully echo the void he finds within himself; the woman can only utter moans, which are a kind of foaming at the mouth of the substance she is the incarnation of, the substance of enjoyment. There are no sentiments here, sentiments which are always other-directed, only dumb self-stimulation, even if it may make use of an external object like Giovanni.

Although the parallel between the "cool" (aloof) Pirelli building and the "hot" (aggressive) woman may at first sight appear strange, the image of the blank

---

[6] Colin Rowe, "James Stirling: A Highly Personal and Very Disjointed Memoir," in *James Stirling: Buildings and Projects*, ed. Peter Arnell and Ted Bickford (New York: Rizzoli Publications, 1984), 23: "When considering intercourse with a building, its *face*, however veiled, must always be a desirable and provocative item."

skyscraper is definitely not unrelated to matters of enjoyment. For instance, poor Giovanni is "hypnotized" by the woman into becoming an acquiescent "victim," and the Pirelli tower is built to hypnotize and astound, too. Moreover, although Terry Kirk writes about it as a brilliant advertising tool for Pirelli's merchandise ("The Pirelli tower was designed like the billboard for latex stockings it replaced on this site, an advertising image complete with its own nighttime illumination"[7]), more than to advertise any specific commodity or business ("more effective in corporate imagemaking than any advertising agency's work"[8]), it was built to become, in the words of its creator, Gio Ponti, the "monument [that] would do honor to the city [Milan, the industrial capital of Italy] and society,"[9] that is, translating it into less lofty language, to become an (or, perhaps, *the*) icon of the Italy of the economic boom, and thus ultimately to advertise the contemporary Italian state itself, that shady nexus of business interests and the ruling DC party on which the boom grew. And in fact the skyscraper admirably achieved its objective—by becoming a symbol of Italy's economic success (it became a very popular image in advertising, illustrated journals, fashion magazines, etc.), the Pirelli building, as an emblem of the new industrial and commercial power, stood there to offer imaginary gratification to the population of consumers and thus awed them into submission to the brave new world of the Italian boom. But what did all the elation related to the building, its hypnotic force, amount to? With its blank reflecting surface and its utter indifference to its surroundings, the Pirelli tower was a "spotless mirror of placid affluence,"[10] in other words, a sheer materialization of the self-contained enjoyment of capital, the self-excitation that has no purpose, no meaning, and no message other than its own infinite perpetuation.

This configuration brings us, of course, to the industrialist Gherardini (Vincenzo Corbella), a familiar "elderly rich businessman" type, perhaps not unrelated to Alberto Pirelli himself. In a conversation with Giovanni, he characteristically presents himself in a heroic light: "I've always looked upon my businesses as works of art. Their financial profit was almost immaterial. The important thing is to create something lasting. … Life is what you make of it with your own resources." This is hardly surprising, because we encounter here

---

[7] Kirk, *The Architecture of Modern Italy*, 170.
[8] Ibid., 170.
[9] Ibid., 167.
[10] Ibid., 171.

in capsule form one of the most signal narratives of bourgeois culture: a success story (no matter whether imaginary or factual: from *Robinson Crusoe* to *The Autobiography of Benjamin Franklin* and further) in which wealth and position are reached by dint of high-mindedness and perseverance (both forms of sacrifice).[11] This story also has a typical continuation—both nature and history (progress) are the product of "captains of industry" like Gherardini: "I'm building my own [future], although the present keeps me busy ... When I was young, I imagined a world like this and set out to create such a future." And if people have reservations about the brilliance of the future thus materialized, it can only be due to a misunderstanding of the laws of nature and of progress.[12] But in fact there are plenty of people who have problems with understanding the heroic moral stature of Gherardini, and this concerns most of all his own workers. That is why he has a job proposal for Giovanni: "I want a better relationship between workers and the management. Do you know why? They don't know the firm history and my role in it. ... I want our company's history written." Thus, a better relationship between workers and industrialists, one that would remedy "misunderstanding" (that is, class antagonism), requires an understanding of the logic of necessity ("a sense of necessity, not a need for profit" guides him as it does a writer, says Gherardini). In other words, it requires a narrative that would present "captains of industry" as producers of automatic historical progress, and thus would inculcate the semi-religious (providential) belief in industry and technology as "mythic powers predestined to produce out of themselves a future world of peace, class harmony and abundance for everybody."[13] (This discourse, of course, has a very long pedigree going at least as far back as 1851 and the Great Exhibition of the Work of Industry of All Nations in London, with its free tickets to the workers to let them see the wonders of technology and hence to awe them into semi-religious submission.[14])

---

[11] There is even a success story mentioned in the film which pertains straightforwardly to Giovanni's profession—during Gherardini's party Ernest Hemingway is admired as "a real artist. ... [A] man who knows his business. Earns what he likes. Millions of dollars."

[12] Susan Buck-Morss, "The Flaneur, the Sandwichman and the Whore: The Politics of Loitering," *New German Critique*, no. 39, Second Special Issue on Walter Benjamin (Autumn, 1986): 135–6.

[13] Susan Buck-Morss, *The Dialectics of Seeing: Walter Benjamin and the Arcades Project* (Cambridge, MA: The MIT Press, 1991), 86–7.

[14] The awe-inspiring Pirelli building comes to mind again: not only did a worker visit the Great Exhibition to be stunned by the miracles of industry he saw, and thus was the fantastic image supposed to erase from his mind the drudgery of everyday exploitation; he was also meant to remain unaware of the autonomous logic of industrial-capitalist excess (enjoyment of machines fueled by exploitation of humans).

The heroic narrative of uprightness and perseverance ("the firm history and my role in it") is of course the story which Gherardini would like to present to the world, because he wants to recognize himself in such an idealized image. It is a story that proves his moral valour and thus justifies his elevated position not only as a millionaire but also as a man of bourgeois principles. ("Not everyone can create something lasting," says Mrs. Gerardini (Gitt Magrini).) But behind this figure of the symbolic Father, fittingly presented as a still agile elderly man (not surprisingly, also an actual father and a loving husband), whose main preoccupation seems to be instructing others in moral conduct ("Don't let money obsess you," etc.), we encounter his shady double, Roberto (Giorgio Negro), a slick young man with no moralizing story to him. Roberto's background is a blank—we can only be sure that he is rich. Moreover, he does not seem to be doing anything (when he tells Berenice, who knows him well, that he has just returned from a business trip, she laughs incredulously: "I'll bet!" ["Ma va'!"]). It is Roberto, not Gherardini, who is omnipresent during the latter's party and in a very oppressive way—he stalks Lidia and, like a vulture, swoops down on her when he realizes that her defenses have weakened (she has just seen Giovanni kissing Valentina (Monica Vitti), Gherardini's daughter). During all this he remains almost completely mute—he never says anything to Lidia (apart from "Don't play around" and "Get in the car"), until he gets her in his Lancia and drives off, only repeatedly emerging from the shadows like a specter to impose his silent oppressive presence on her when he notices that she is alone. And of course he does not have to say anything, because all the stories belong to Gherardini, and Roberto is just a mute solipsist, an equivalent of the unidentified woman appropriate for the party setting (though not less pathological), and a character in which the truth of Gherardini the high-minded industrialist is revealed—a figure incarnating predatory enjoyment with no rhyme or reason, craving only self-perpetuation, in whom economic (and symbolic) exploitation is transposed into the sexual realm.

Thus the memorable scene of Roberto's car with him and Lidia, moving slowly forward through the night and pouring rain, while on the soundtrack we only hear the car engine, the rain, and the windshield wipers, is far from presenting a happy encounter of two kindred individuals in a poetic way (which is how it is usually taken)—it is, rather, an equivalent of the hospital scene in which Giovanni is "hypnotized," dragged into the unidentified woman's room, and "devoured."[15] That the woman's hospital room is a capsule of mute enjoyment belonging to a different dimension than "ordinary" existence—in which people relate to themselves symbolically (in which people recognize each other)—is indicated by a famous shot: after the door of her room is slammed shut by the woman, the film cuts to a long shot of her with her back against a large, white, completely blank wall—there is not even a single object around.[16] The couple is isolated from "the world," the symbolic/social dimension (the woman speaks only outside the room, though even there she does not use speech for the purposes of communication/recognition); they are two figures drowning in the blank substance of enjoyment filling the entire frame, a substance which can be represented only as nothing (total whiteness) or the woman's meaningless moans, which escalate and transform into the sound of a helicopter (no self, no will—just an enjoying machine).[17] Roberto's car (another machine, a Lancia Flaminia Sport, which is as slick as its owner) is exactly the same kind of sealed capsule, even more explicitly removed from society and floating in darkness (an empty road at night), which is additionally emphasized by the absence of language[18] and the "liquefied" (blurred) image of the couple in the car, seen through the pouring rain.[19]

Roberto's relation to language is made even clearer later in the film: while he is virtually mute in his predatory incarnation, when he (for the only time in the film) says something among others (men, this time), his utterance is completely meaningless coming from him (which Giovanni recognizes in his reply to Roberto's words). In the context of a (lightweight) conversation between Giovanni and a few male party guests about writers and money ("My boy, never despise money," says one of them to Giovanni), Roberto in his characteristic

---

[15] Though there is one crucial difference: Giovanni is "saved" by the intervention of the nurses, while Lidia's final refusal to submit to Roberto is her own decision. I will have more to say below about the difference between Giovanni's passivity and Lidia's agency.
[16] The shot is too empty for the image to be a "realistic" one of a relatively small room in a modern clinic (we have just seen a full 360-degree panorama—split into several shots—of a room like that when the Pontanos visited Tommaso).
[17] To sound less arbitrary, this transformation is given a realistic pretext—a helicopter was previously seen by Giovanni through the window of Tommaso's room.
[18] Of course we see the couple's lips moving, so they seem to be conversing, but what we hear is the rain and monotonous, repetitive mechanical sounds: the purring of the motor, the swish of the wipers.
[19] Another important difference is a different "emotional tenor" of each "enjoyment capsule" scene. It is very instructive—especially if one takes into consideration the prevalent critical opinion that the female point of view reigns in Antonioni's films from *L'avventura* to *Red Desert*—that female predatory enjoyment is represented as pathological and aggressive (abstract whiteness, etc.), while its male counterpart is depicted as natural and poetic (rain, trees, night).

fashion suddenly appears out of the shadows and, apparently as a comment on Giovanni's remark, "It's hard to say what an intellectual might scorn," quotes from Robert Musil's *The Man without Qualities*: "Our time, sir, is vile and antiphilosophical, afraid to take a stand on values. As for democracy, in a nutshell, it means: take things as they come." Though it sounds "Adornian,"[20] coming from a man who is the best incarnation of what the quotation describes, the words can only be understood as a meaningless paroxysm of self-exciting enjoyment.[21]

Although Gherardini is an elderly man with a story to tell, he is also a man conscious of his times and therefore he knows that an individual historical account of a bourgeois heroism, no matter how edifying, is not enough for his purposes, and that, in fact, this moralizing story is quickly becoming antiquated. He is aware that a narrative like this has to be "sexed up" to become symbolically/publically effective, and that in present times the achievement of the objective demands constant effort requiring a full-time PR job. Such a job is therefore offered to Giovanni by the industrialist: "I want a press, advertising and public relations department with a special section devoted to internal relations." In other words, Gherardini knows that in order to have a future (his kind of future) in a society in which everything desirable is quickly being transformed into commodities whose value is mainly representational/symbolic,[22] he has to be able to manipulate the economic and legal signifiers and significations in order to continue being successful. This is the new power the command of which Giovanni is given.

Having established himself as a "critical intellectual" (in an early scene which takes place in Tommaso's hospital room Adorno's name is referred to, as has been mentioned already), Giovanni claims to be a writer in crisis. But what is the nature of his predicament? To Valentina, Gherardini's daughter, he says: "The way I feel, I don't know if I'll ever write again. I know what to write, but not how to write it." As far as the "what" is concerned, we learn about the things that fascinate Giovanni during his first conversation with Gherardini: "You have

---

[20] In fact, Arrowsmith ascribes this quotation to Adorno (*Antonioni*, 59).
[21] The above quotation is an English translation (the DVD subtitles) of the Italian translation of *Der Mann ohne Eigenschaften*. The English translation by Sophie Wilkins reads: "We are living in an unphilosophical, dispirited age; it doesn't have the courage to decide what is valuable and what isn't, and democracy means, expressed most succinctly: Do whatever is happening!" Robert Musil, *The Man without Qualities* (New York: Vintage, 1996), 904–5.
[22] Buck-Morrs, *The Dialectics of Seeing*, 81–2.

the advantage of real people, you create real houses, real cities. The pace of life is in your hands. Maybe even the future is." The problem is how to render this modern pace of life in writing, how to hang onto the force that is creating the future (capital)—it is too daunting a task for an individual of yore, sitting in his room on his own, while outside the forces of creation and destruction are raging: "Isn't writing an irrepressible but antiquated instinct? A lonely craftsman putting one word after another. The job can't be mechanised," Giovanni complains. But of course in a sense it can be mechanized, and this is exactly what Gherardini offers to Pontano: the job of executive coordinating the press/advertising/PR department. With his fascination with the powers that set the pace of life, his knowledge of newspapers ("Faccio molto pubblicazioni su giornali," says Giovanni to Gherardini[23]), and his position as an insider of the publishing world (as a known writer), he is ideally suited to coordinate the production of the new standardized (mechanized) form, which will be an amalgamation of news-literature-advertisement created for the similarly amalgamated purpose of information-entertainment-persuasion,[24] and which will conquer the future to such an extent that it will never arrive—by camouflaging class antagonisms and fixing people's desires to commodities, so that, hypnotized by them, they will become the collaborators of their own submission forever.[25] This is precisely what Gherardini intimates to Giovanni ("Probably the future will never come"), and he says it jollily, because from his point of view there is no menace in such a claim.[26] It just means that his dominion is secure: although on the manifest level capitalist industry seems to offer limitless progress and continuous change (imaginary capture),[27] it is only on the condition that nothing changes on the level of domination and exploitation.

In fact, the spectrality and repetitiveness of the futureless future are nicely illustrated for the viewer during Gherardini's party itself by Giovanni's pursuit of Valentina, who is yet another rich girl, like Lidia, only much younger (the cult of novelty and youth is of course the cornerstone of such a future, in which a change of a woman/commodity stands for a change of life), whom he tries to

---

[23] Translated on the DVD as "I contribute to many publications."
[24] Buck-Morss, "The Flaneur," 113.
[25] Ibid., 121.
[26] Of course in 1961 a statement like this would first of all be understood as a grim reference to the threat of nuclear war, especially in light of the presence of American missiles on Italian soil. But the Cold War context is completely external to the texture of significations produced by the film itself.
[27] Buck-Morss, *The Dialectics of Seeing*, 283.

get hooked on his internal crisis.²⁸ In relation to Giovanni, Valentina, unlike the partygoers, is from the very start represented as a materialization of a fantasy: young, beautiful, and a reader of Hermann Broch's *The Sleepwalkers* (as Lidia with an ironic smile describes Valentina to her husband even before Giovanni sees her)—in other words, the ideal of his dreams.²⁹ And Antonioni shows their first encounter by emphasizing this phantasmagoric get-up. In contrast to an almost classic shot/reverse shot exchange of looks between Lidia and Valentina when they first see each other (two subjects confronting one another: Lidia at the top of the stairs looking down on Valentina reading a book/Valentina at the bottom of the stairs looking up at Lidia looking down on her), the second time we encounter Valentina, we seem to see her through a large pane of glass playing with something (her compact) on a chessboard-like floor, but after a while we realize that, moving about the room we see, she is moving through some pieces of furniture, which seem to be in the room, like a ghost. Then, in the glass through which we seem to see Valentina, we see what seems to be Giovanni's reflection (his image is semi-transparent, hence we take it as his reflection), so we may imagine that he is looking at Valentina through the same glass as we are, and sharing our point of view. But then, while the camera is panning to the right, Valentina's and Giovanni's images dissolve into each other and we realize that we were looking through a glass at Giovanni (not his reflection) and then at another glass in which Valentina was reflected.³⁰ For Giovanni (and for us) this phantasmagoric presentation immediately establishes Valentina as somebody desirable, because she is dematerialized and mysterious, far removed from the fleshly ordinariness of female party guests like Resy (Rosy Mazzacurati) and

---

[28] That Valentina is just Lidia's phantasmagoric double is indicated by repetition or prefiguration of motifs. When Valentina says "Last year I thought I was in love with a boy ... " and that "Once, I lost everything," this of course prefigures the final confrontation between Giovanni and Lidia, in which the latter says, "I feel like dying, because I no longer love you." When (on a tape-recording) Valentina relates her "tree theory" ("A garden's silence is made of sounds, press your ear to a tree and listen. The sounds may be within us, I'd rather think it's the tree"), it takes us back to a scene in which Giovanni comes to pick up Lidia in Sesto San Giovanni (Milan's periphery) and finds her leaning against a tree, listening to an abandoned garden's silence.

[29] Similarly to Musil's *The Man without Qualities*, which shows the decay of Austria-Hungary on the brink of the First World War and tries to analyze the mechanisms which have led to the disintegration of the society and the individual, Broch's *The Sleepwalkers* attempts to portray and analyze the disintegration of values and its consequences to Germany between 1888 and 1918. In fact, the last part of this trilogy, *The Realist (Huguenau oder Sachlichkeit)*, includes an essay entitled "The Decline of Values" ("Zerfall der Werte") interposed among its chapters. These themes are of course strongly present in *La notte*, although the scope of the film is much more modest.

[30] Later in the film Valentina is repeatedly shown next to her reflection.

other commonplace giggling revelers.³¹ Moreover, the moment they encounter each other, Valentina drags Giovanni into a game, and of course does it by claiming that she does not want to play with him. The game we see onscreen is one of sliding Valentina's compact on the chessboard-like floor, but with this game another one starts: a game whose aim is yet again "hypnosis," the fixing of Giovanni's desire to the image of the mistress of the house. This is another reason why Valentina's image is initially mediated by her representations—from the very beginning (in relation to Giovanni and to us) she is self-consciously viewing herself as being viewed, in order to be able to construct and control her image as an object of fascination.

Moreover, Valentina's sex-appeal is not unrelated to the phantasmagoric setting (a modernist house of mirrors where glass predominates) that she languorously inhabits. On the one hand, the stylish and fashionable commodities she moves between and around (not to mention the ones she wears) add to her glamor and therefore enhance her appeal as a sexual object; in other words, her attractiveness as a fantasy image is at least partly mediated by commodities.³² On the other hand, these commodities, which exude the awareness of being hip, of being up-to-date with the pace of (commodity-oriented) life, give Valentina's sententious pronouncements³³—which against a different setting (even in the Gherardinis' garden, in fact) would sound hopelessly "old and grey"³⁴ (that is, rather vacuous and antiquated)—an air of being a current expression (an intellectual fashion may also be counted as a commodity) of "modern anxiety"

---

[31] "How prosaic. Sandwiches at this hour," jokes Pontano on seeing Resy, who is an admirer of his writing, eating.

[32] One may note that the solid and down-to-earth Mr. and Mrs. Gherardini (nothing phantasmagoric about them) do not go well with the modernist house and hence they are mostly shown walking or sitting in their garden. It is only the "de-solidized" and commodified Valentina who seamlessly fits into the abstracted and somewhat derealized setting, and therefore we hardly see her in the garden.

[33] Like: "I think love restricts a person. It creates misunderstanding ['vuoto'—emptiness] all around," or "Whenever I try to communicate … love disappears."

[34] This is how Mrs. Gherardini describes Giovanni's writing: "From your books, I expected you to be old and grey ['più vecchio'—much older]." Valentina offers her sententious discourse as a mirror to Giovanni's narcissism. Another example of this is Valentina's tape-recording, which she plays to Giovanni, a scene which links back to an earlier one in the film with another mechanical "speaking" device in it. When Giovanni comes home alone after his book promotion party, in his flat he finds a switched-on gramophone playing a record with an English lesson, which is obviously an "objective correlative" of what is going on in his head: a monotonously repetitive drone of words adding up to nothing (Giovanni is supposedly going through a crisis as a writer, but not only as a writer: "But in my case it's affecting my whole life," he says). Valentina's recording is an obvious reaction to such a state of confusion, an imaginary writer's wishes: "I don't want useless sounds, I want to select them. ['Così'—also] Voices and words … there are so many words I'd rather not hear … but you must resign yourself, like floating on the waves of the sea."

(*malattia dei sentimenti* again) and hence mystify Valentina's image to bring it to an even higher degree of desirability. But of course a sexual fantasy image cannot be kept too distant if it is to be effective, so Valentina keeps reminding Giovanni that, like every commodity, apart from her phantasmagoric side she also has a more down-to-earth aspect ("After all I like golf, tennis, cars and parties ..."), and even, when Giovanni, impressed by her "anxious" persona, gets carried out and insists that "It's a sin to waste such intelligence," she reminds him that intelligence is rather unfeminine (as if possessing it would spoil the image of her as an ideal male fantasy object),[35] and instead describes herself as alert ("I'm not intelligent, I'm alert ['sveglia']"). This once again sounds "deep" (and also "cool") in its anxious patrician self-deprecation, until one realizes that being alert (to male wishes predominantly) is precisely what a patriarchal discourse demands from women,[36] and is just what we have witnessed on Valentina's part in the course of the party (she is continuously alert to Giovanni's fantasy world). Though Valentina's subjective ("unspectral") aspect appears briefly outside her relation to Giovanni, when she confronts Lidia on her own (the two women are balanced as subjects both confronting and recognizing each other, as they did during their first encounter, as mentioned above), the specter-like status of Valentina during the night of revels is clinched by Antonioni in an almost humorous way—in the morning, after the Pontanos have left her room, Valentina "disappears" with the flick of a switch (only her black outline remains).[37]

Thus *La notte* presents us with the trio of figures who are necessary for the patriarchal discourse to function properly. We begin with a female monster, the witch—in other words, the all-powerful uncastrated woman, the incarnation of all threatening Weiningerian male fantasies.[38] She paralyzes Giovanni with her basilisk eyes and drags him into the abyss from which he must be saved (by women, incidentally). Then we encounter her caricature, Resy, who also

---

[35] An intelligent woman is, or at least may be, an intelligent man's partner and therefore a subject.

[36] Of course the list may be extended. For instance: "They are expected to be 'feminine,' that is to say, smiling, friendly, attentive [alert], submissive, demure, restrained, self-effacing. And what is called 'femininity' is often nothing other than a form of indulgence towards real or supposed male expectations, particularly as regards the aggrandizement of the ego." Pierre Bourdieu, *Masculine Domination*, trans. Richard Nice (Oxford: Polity Press, 2001), 66.

[37] There are other (not very serious) indications of the party as representing a descent into hell/a nightmare. For instance, on their arrival Giovanni, not hearing the noise of the guests, asks, "Are they all dead?"; we might also recall the title, echoing Rimbaud, of Pontano's novel *The Season* (*La stagione*).

[38] Because the uncastrated woman is an inconsistent male fantasy, we have such inconsistency in the image itself: the all-powerful woman is all-powerful precisely because she cannot control herself; she is at the mercy of her irrational female "substance."

throws herself on the writer and inundates him with her silly prattle ("Giovanni Pontano? The author of that great book? One of the best books ever written")—a figure who is not dangerous but nevertheless difficult to get rid of. She is a lower kind of a monster, a figure one can treat with disdain for the same reasons that one is afraid of the witch: she cannot control herself because she is an excessive incarnation of brute materiality. Because encounters with flesh-and-blood women within the bounds of patriarchal discourse necessarily result in the creation of this double-headed monster, a kind of defense formation is necessary to prevent constant oscillation between fear and disgust. Thus a dematerialized, spectral woman appears, a figure who has no substance, precisely because her role is to reflect to the man an image of his superiority/desirability (the monsters do not desire; they use men for their own evil or animal purposes). But it is easy to see which figure in this eternal-feminine trio represents its truth. Though Giovanni is made mute by the witch and keeps stumbling in his conversations with Valentina (the writer's crisis), when it comes to Resy, he has no qualms about telling her the story of his life (which is perhaps the explanation of the crisis in question): "I'll tell you about a hermit, an intellectual of course. He drank only dew, until he came to the city where he tasted wine and became an alcoholic."[39]

But let us return to another "anxious" woman in the film, Lidia, whose aura does not seem to rely on the commodities that surround her. In fact, what in *La notte* can be taken for her characterization takes place entirely outside in the street. When she leaves on her own and unnoticed the party celebrating the publishing of Giovanni's book, we may at first take her anxious state to result from the earlier visit to Tommaso at the hospital (where we saw her cry), but soon it turns out that the reason for her escape is not that she wants to be on her own in order to keep internally mourning her dying friend. After leaving the book party Lidia turns her attention outward and at first enjoys walking about—she pays heed to what is going around her, smiling at people, etc. In other words,

---

[39] The three modalities of the eternal-feminine are also shown against appropriate "symbolic" backdrops. We have already mentioned the "unrealistic" emptiness and whiteness of the hospital room (the fantasy of the witch). A counterpart to this shot is one of Valentina against a whitish wall of her room (she throws a big shadow on it, like the woman in the hospital) while Giovanni is being teased by her ("After all I like golf, tennis, cars, and parties"). There is nothing unrealistic about this shot, and, moreover, it includes a mirror—we are witnessing an "imaginarized" version of an enjoyment capsule, in which Giovanni is being hypnotized by his fantasies, which are being reflected to him by the spectral woman. In contrast, Giovanni always meets Resy among other party guests, and he tells her his story in a dark room full of people (interpersonal contextualization).

she has become *alert*, but the meaning of this adverb differs radically from what it will come to mean in the seduction context that connects Valentina and Giovanni at Gherardini's party,[40] where Lidia will behave differently—she will keep to herself, pay attention to nobody (apart from Valentina and Giovanni, for obvious reasons), and will even be accused by her husband of being a spoilsport ("Why is it that you never seem to enjoy yourself?" he asks her, while we still remember that she did enjoy herself, at least during the initial part of her walk).

What is she doing in the street and what is she looking for in this celebrated sequence? Why is she so restless? What finally makes her take a taxi and ride to Sesto San Giovanni (which lay on Milan's periphery at that time) where the city turns into the countryside? We have to wait for the answer to these questions almost to the end of the film, to the only moment in *La notte* when we find ourselves outside the bounds of the patriarchal-commodity discourse, which in advance has determined the female roles of a spectral mistress and a jealous wife (the discourse of melodrama is even more representative of bourgeois values than the providential success story already mentioned). When Lidia returns drenched from her ride with Roberto, Valentina invites her to her room and offers her a towel and a hair-dryer. Initially they continue with their female melodramatic act (animosity because of their relation to a man), but soon they decide to forget about it (Valentina: "Shall I tell you what happened?" Lidia: "Skip it") and proceed to speak about themselves outside the roles enforced on them by the patriarchal discourse. This is especially interesting in Lidia's case:[41] "You don't know what it is to feel the weight of years, in vain ['e non capirli più'—and not understand them anymore]. ['Stasera'—Tonight] I just feel like dying. An end to this agony, something new."[42]

But what is the agony she is speaking about? Before we turn to the finale of the film, in which the reason for the agony borrows its description from the

---

[40] Of course, there are men in the streets of Milan who give Lidia lascivious looks and therefore attempt to inscribe her into the seduction context. Strangely enough, there are commentators who, in a sense, identify with this look and suggest that Lidia is cruising. I think that this suggestion (which boils down to a ridiculous prejudice: an unaccompanied woman in the street must be up to something) is not supported by anything in the film. On the contrary, as my analysis tries to show, during Lidia's walk Antonioni creates (among other things) a counter-context to the phantasmagoric (and claustrophobic) seduction setup of the Gherardinis' villa.

[41] Valentina is less interesting, because we have seen her only in her spectral mistress incarnation, so we know nothing about her life outside of this role. The phrases in brackets do not appear in the English subtitles of the DVD.

[42] As if conscious of the role she plays in *La notte* (a lure toward a future which is a continuation of the same), Valentina answers: "It may be nothing."

conventional melodramatic vocabulary ("I feel like dying because I no longer love you"), we may note that the above complaint may be taken to be self-explanatory: the agony is the lack of "something new," the eternal repetition of the same (melodramatic) role whose sense one no longer understands. And something new is precisely what Lidia is looking for in the streets of Milan after having left yet another book party, a supposedly glamorous event (allowing one to be up-to-date with intellectual fashions) at which she once again has appeared in her usual, agonizing role: a writer's rich wife.[43] Out in the street, Lidia becomes a *flâneuse*,[44] projecting herself on what she sees (buildings, people, objects), trying to lose herself in the crowd, to dissolve her solid bourgeois identity-property,[45] to find release from her role. In the street everything is in a state of movement-becoming; every moment promises new openings, new possibilities, new identities; and this is especially so for a relatively new presence on Italian streets: an independent, unaccompanied woman. Lidia is excited by new possibilities immanent to the new world (which materializes in Italy with the economic boom)—movement, fragmentation, corporeality, even violence[46]—which promise also to realize female dreams of freedom and release.

This opening out is set in contrast to Giovanni's confinement. He returns to their flat, a cage of an apartment in a modern tower block, in which he is trapped with his thoughts and his role as a writer, a flat filled with the voice of a gramophone which mechanically produces random words that do not add up to any sense. When Giovanni, uncomfortable in his flat, finally lies down in his study, we see him casting a glance through the window which is over the sofa. Then the film cuts to a view of the dirty white/light gray blank wall of a tall building, seen from above, which fills almost the entire screen, and after a while the miniscule figure of Lidia appears at the extreme left of the frame. Because it

---

[43] Such discontent may perhaps explain a curious remark Lidia, a woman who has always consorted with intellectuals, makes during the final confrontation with Giovanni: "I used to spend afternoons reading in bed. ... All those purposeless books ... " Intellectual fashions keep changing, but they have never addressed the "something new" Lidia has been interested in—a role for the woman beyond the melodramatic clichés of the patriarchal discourse (like plain wife or spectral lover).

[44] For obvious reasons Lidia's walk has often been analyzed with recourse to Baudelaire/Benjamin's use of the figure of the *flâneur*—e.g., Torunn Haaland, "*Flânerie*: Spatial Practices and Nomadic Thought in Antonioni's *La notte*," *Italica* 90, no. 4 (Winter 2013): 596–619.

[45] In "Crowds" ("Les foules") Baudelaire writes: "The man who loves to lose himself in a crowd enjoys feverish delights that the egoist locked up in himself as in a box, and the slothful man like a mollusk in his shell, will be eternally deprived of. He adopts as his own all the occupations, all the joys and all the sorrows that chance offers." Charles Baudelaire, *Paris Spleen*, trans. Louise Varèse (New York: New Directions, 1970), 20.

[46] Marit Grøtta, *Baudelaire's Media Aesthetics: The Gaze of the Flâneur and 19th-Century Media* (London: Bloomsbury, 2015), 112.

frustrates the viewer's conventional expectation that the shot following one of a character gazing at something should be a point-of-view shot of that gaze (and Lidia is in a different part of Milan than her husband), the disorienting splicing of these two shots serves as an emphasis, because several different strands of meaning in the film, which we have analyzed so far, come together here. The second shot refers us back both to the scene in the unidentified woman's hospital room (the blank wall as a representation of solipsistic enjoyment) and to the blankness of the Pirelli building, that stalagmite of the self-perpetuating logic of capital (Lidia's tiny figure, hardly visible down on the pavement, is presented as if seen from the top of the Pirelli skyscraper). Thus these two variations on meaningless enjoyment turned on itself, which we have earlier associated on the basis of structural similarities in the film, are here explicitly brought together in one image. Giovanni's dissatisfaction with himself as an artisan (a producer of antiquated non-mechanized writing) has been presented as the feeling of entrapment and being haunted by meaningless phrases (the gramophone) he experiences in his flat, while his yearning for identification with the modern pace of life set by Gherardini-like capitalists finds its cinematic equivalent in the "panoptic" point of view (from the top of the Pirelli building) which gets attached to Giovanni's perspective. And no wonder that his supposed POV shot turns out to be "false"—by identification with Gherardini's aims (a peddler of news-entertainment-advertising), Giovanni abdicates all critical perspective and becomes, like Roberto, a man without qualities—a spectral omnipresent de-individualized incarnation of self-perpetuating enjoyment.

In fact, Giovanni's passivity and two-dimensionality—in contrast to Lidia and Tommaso, who are hollowed out by their desire for something new—are featured throughout the film. Although his first lapse happens in a hospital (a location that might suggest a liminal, extraordinary space), Giovanni's return to his and Lidia's flat is a continuation of this theme and clearly presents him not as a victim of some inexplicable external force but as helpless prey to something that wells up within him even when he is alone. The gramophone is a mechanical contraption, like a helicopter, the sound of which we heard in the woman's hospital room, where it was an aural representation of stifling and meaningless enjoyment. That the drone of the gramophone, which recites unconnected words of an English-language vocabulary lesson, is another aural incarnation of the invasion of stupefying and thus passivizing enjoyment is indicated by what we see next to the gramophone: in the central place of the living room there hangs a huge painting of a naked woman splayed frontally on a bed in the state of sexual arousal.⁴⁷ Also, Giovanni's behavior during the night of revelry in the Gherardinis' villa bears only superficial signs of his agency; he talks a lot about his crisis as a writer and a man ("But in my case it's affecting my whole life"), but he is entirely in the grip of a force he cannot resist, and hence he is the least interesting of the protagonists of the film.⁴⁸

Therefore it is not surprising that after such a splice we return to Lidia in a very different mood. Giovanni's false POV shot is followed by Lidia's medium close-up against a (different) blank wall filling almost the entire screen again. But this time there is no "continuity" between the wall and the female figure, as there was in the case of the unidentified woman in her hospital room (the wall representing the dumb enjoyment whose "emanation" she was). Now the wall clearly serves as an alienating background, which is only emphasized by the jarring sound of jet engines that we hear on the soundtrack.⁴⁹ During this later part of her walk, Lidia's initial excitement and high spirits dissipate. She finds out that the promise of the modern fluidity, of opening, of real transformation is illusory⁵⁰—what she has seen in the streets has not been possibilities opened to individuals, possibilities of a new life, but invitations to enjoy the world of commodities, the enjoyment in which people are stuck like insects in amber, like a man Lidia sees through the large window pane of a modern building sitting at his desk as if he were trapped in a cage of glass.⁵¹

But then a kind of flaw appears on the surface of the modern panoptic deterrence machine—while Lidia walks on, she encounters a figure that seems to be completely out of place: a poor old woman avidly eating what looks like an ice-cream cone, almost a fairy-tale figure (a fairy godmother) among the landscape of skyscrapers. But this is not the first time that something

---

⁴⁷ Although in the hospital sequence the camera showed the naked woman on the bed laterally, Giovanni's position in that shot exactly matched the point of view from which the woman in the picture is painted.

⁴⁸ If we were to return to the matter of cruising, we could say that it is Giovanni who constantly cruises, even when he is alone in his flat.

⁴⁹ Another connection with the unidentified woman's claustrophobic room where we heard a helicopter. In the hospital room, however, the source of claustrophobia was the woman herself "oozing" enjoyment which stifled everything around her. In the street scene described above Lidia is trapped by modern Milan, by the enjoyment known as the boom.

⁵⁰ Thus "being alert" (Valentina's claim) to the spectacle of commodified life necessarily ends in frustration.

⁵¹ This is the fourth shot after the one on whose soundtrack the jet engines are heard. We hear them in the following two, of which the second is the first shot of the building in which, after a cut and the silencing of the engines, we see the man. Thus the sequence which starts with the false POV of Giovanni is organized in such a way that the tension/anxiety rises and culminates in the "trapped man" shot, which might have come from an expressionist film or even from a horror movie.

like that happens—already in the "happy" part of her peregrinations, Lidia had encountered a gap in the consolidated time-space of panoptic urban modernity. In the center of Milan she came across a virtual ruin in whose yard she found a crying child and a broken clock, and from whose gate she peeled a piece of rust.

This sequence of the film is often criticized by commentators as a lapse, because they take it to be too facilely symbolic,[52] but I think they are missing something crucial here. They find this episode wrong because they think there is no place for "allegory" like that in an otherwise "realistic" or "factual" (though "modernist") film. In my view, however, the point being made by Antonioni is that upon entering the ruin (the child and the clothes drying on a line indicate that somebody lives there), Lidia, in a sense, finds herself in another dimension, which haunts the modern urban space without having a place in it, a surplus disavowed reality and hence an "oneiric" one (therefore the somewhat "unrealistic" dream atmosphere of the episode). In other words, the ruin represents a breach in the consolidated system of thoroughly organized urban hyperspace that aims at the absolute management of people and commodities.

Initially, because Lidia is looking for a different kind of opening, for something *new*, a transformation, by immersing herself in the flux of the *modern* street, that is, within the possibilities offered by the boom, she remains oblivious to what she has experienced in the ruin. Yet soon her hopes to find some release turn out to be completely groundless—she realizes that what modern life offers (especially to a woman) is only the role of different kinds of shop window mannequins, an infinite repetition of the same, a future that is futureless. So when the surplus "oneiric" dimension materializes once again in the form of the fairy godmother (like the ruin she is a real presence, but also a ghost from the impoverished Italian past), Lidia decides to pursue *this* opening, even though it does not seem to lead into the future but into some kind of reckoning with the past. Thus by taking a taxi to Sesto San Giovanni she is not setting out on a melancholy trip to revisit her younger and happier self in order to somehow consolidate her identity as a married woman (as this trip is usually interpreted)[53]; on the contrary, she goes there to find a solution to her present predicament, to find something new for herself, not to reinforce the failing old identity.

---

[52] For example, Lidia is childless (the crying child), getting old (the broken clock), her marriage is in crisis (when she is peeling the rust we can see the wedding band on her finger).
[53] Giovanni and Lidia used to live in Sesto San Giovanni when they were younger.

But what Lidia encounters in the dream-like world of the periphery, a liminal space-time where the rationalized modern city (a machine to control people and commodities) gives way to the myth-invoking rural grain fields, is ambiguous and, for her, disappointing. On the one hand, she does find there instantiations of the "renegade" surplus energies that, although pushed to the margins, haunt the consolidated urban-capital space. One example of them is an "irrational" fight of marginalized youth, which to Lidia appears to be pure and meaningless violence. Though some commentators find the fascination with which Lidia initially observes the fight to be of sexual origin, it seems more to the point to treat her attention in the context of her former *flânerie*, that is, precisely as fascination with a spectacle of energies that are beyond the control of and potentially subversive of the totalizing rational practices of unification, centralization, and uniformization (a statist form of violence) that have frustrated her hopes for something new. Another group she encounters is even more clearly related to the dream of the "outside"—this is the amateur rocketeers who, having set their launching contraptions in the grain fields, send missiles up into the sky. Although the rockets are small, therefore the altitude they reach is not great (though somebody in the small crowd gathered to watch says they attain three thousand meters), the utopian orientation of what these people are doing is quite obvious, and is emphasized by a question asked by one of the group observing the rocketeers: "Would you like to go to the moon?"

Although both "discourses" Lidia finds on the periphery (including violence) are potentially subversive of the panoptic capitalist machine, she finds out that they seem to be exclusively male—there are no women among the fighters as there are no women among the rocketeers.[54] Additionally, although neither group includes any women, both seem to presuppose a specific role for them. In the fighters' case, this is the role of prey—the winner of the fight pursues Lidia with clearly sexual intent, until she runs away frightened. In the case of the rocketeers, it is the role of spectator—Lidia can only join the crowd of observers whose mixed feelings about the rockets are expressed by the already-mentioned question about going to the moon and the answer to it: "Not really" ["Mi no"].[55] Moreover, looking for something new in the periphery, Lidia quickly finds

---

[54] The sex of the child crying in the yard of the ruined building (a girl) and of the "fairy godmother" was not accidental.

[55] The answer also emphasizes that the discourses that Lidia finds on the periphery are only *potentially* subversive.

out what meaning is given to this kind of desire in a region in which the grip of "modernity" (objectified not only in skyscrapers but also for instance by attitudes propagated in glossy women's magazines[56]) is not yet too tight—by the local women she is taken to be an "adventuress," that is, a more classy version of a "street-walker," and offered "a little hotel" ("una pensione") to meet with her man (no other purpose for Lidia's search is taken into consideration).

But this is not yet the end of Lidia's peregrinations. What she finally reaches in Sesto San Giovanni is quite enigmatic—she enters yet another yard with ruined buildings (a periphery within a periphery, a liminal region within a liminal region—this time "symbolically" including a church), but she does not find there an oneiric surplus-place that modernity finds difficult to contain and which therefore constitutes a potential opening. In fact we see what seems to be the same yard twice. The first time, when Lidia is entering the yard, there is a kind of over-the-shoulder shot in which Lidia is looking at a ruined building, then she turns and looks frame right, after which we see an abandoned church as her POV shot. Then, when Giovanni comes by car to Sesto San Giovanni to take Lidia home, we see him pass through the same gate to the yard we earlier saw Lidia enter through, but we no longer see the ruined buildings. In fact, the only thing we can see in this sequence (after Giovanni's arrival) is lush vegetation (grass, some trees, and some bushes) as if the gate were just the entrance to an imaginary (and lost) garden of their idealized past (they had formerly lived in Sesto San Giovanni, as mentioned already). Moreover, when Giovanni finds Lidia standing under a tree in the garden and turns back to look at the rest of the space enclosed by the wall, the camera only shows him looking and not what he sees. Standing next to the tree, Giovanni seems to be looking across the yard in the direction of the buildings Lidia saw earlier, but what he says while looking is surprising: "How strange, it hasn't changed at all." Does he mean that the landscape of ruins that once constituted the environment in which they lived has not changed? That the ruins were already ruins when they lived there? But this seems implausible, because as they leave the yard and cross the railway tracks he remembers that things used to be in better shape. ("This [railway] line was in use when we lived here.") And anyway, why would Lidia feel an urge to show Giovanni (or to see for herself) that what had been ruined was still a ruin? Moreover, why is the look, which sees that nothing has changed at all, situated

---

[56] That the periphery has already been infiltrated by such modernity to a significant extent is indicated by two young women who are discussing the latest fashion, while Lidia is walking about the place.

within the space of a garden, so unlike anything we have seen both in the center of Milan and on its periphery? What has Lidia found under the tree where she and Giovanni find themselves, looking like a latter-day Adam and Eve?

Before we answer that, we should note that the disappointment or confusion that Lidia experiences in Sesto San Giovanni has consequences over the rest of the day that culminates in Gherardini's party. While Giovanni tries to keep up with the pace of modern life by pursuing Valentina, Lidia, although present at the party in her old role as the writer's wife, attempts to test what she has learned that day in order to break away from what is expected of her. Although she is surprised by the presence of her old schoolmate, Berenice, who reminds her of her former traumas ("You used to be so plain"[57]), she quickly disengages from her and turns to practicing the role of *observer*, wandering among the party guests but keeping to herself without engaging in the fun. This, however, does not seem to lead in the direction of freeing her from playing the expected role. On the contrary, in the context of Giovanni's pursuit of Valentina, her behavior seems to fit very well the stereotypical carriage of a wronged wife in a melodrama— one who sulks and keeps to herself because she quietly suffers her husband's unfaithfulness. On the other hand, an attempt to abandon this role by partaking in the young party-guests' idea of fun (including diving into the swimming-pool after it starts to rain) finally lands her, as a *prey*, in the bubble of Roberto's sports car and, what is more, it looks as if she is here taking revenge for her husband's philandering (another typically melodramatic role).

None of these strategies to arrive at something new works, but then comes the already-mentioned moment when Lidia and Valentina finally find themselves together and attempt to speak about themselves outside the bounds of the patriarchal commodity discourse, which in advance has determined their roles as spectral mistress and jealous wife. This allows Lidia not only to explicitly formulate her desire for something new, while she is aware that Giovanni standing at the door is listening to her, but also to realize that for her, as a woman fully submerged in the patriarchal discourse, it is crucial that her message be delivered in an indirect way.

When the Pontanos are leaving the party in the small hours of the morning, Lidia suggests that they take a roundabout route to their car and walk across the golf course. On their way they pass Resy who is crying ("Take no notice. I'm

---

[57] Not a good prospect for a rich girl destined for marriage and the role of a society hostess.

just crying because I'm silly," she says to a female friend who is trying to console her), a woman who earlier during the party claimed to be the biggest admirer of Giovanni's talent as a writer. Although we do not know why she is crying at this moment,[58] we do know what makes her cry while reading novels:

> Resy: I'd like a novel about a woman who loves a man but the man doesn't love her. But he does admire her intelligence, her character. They live together ... She'd have to be a strong woman, who can sacrifice herself. She sacrifices herself for another woman's happiness.
> Giovanni: Why does she sacrifice herself?
> Resy: I don't know. It makes me want to cry.

Though Lidia might not be silly, she has well learned (and we with her) that a silly discourse is all she has. But perhaps there is a way to use such a discourse in a not-so-silly way. Thus, after reminding Giovanni of his enthusiasm for the captains of industry and their vision of the future by reviewing in brief Gherardini's argument for accepting his offer ("Why not? It's a good opportunity. Your life would be your own at last"), using the facts at hand (Tommaso had died while they were partying that night), she rolls out a melodramatic story that would no doubt make Resy cry, if she heard or read it. Since a stereotypical melodrama is a story about love with its sentimental side grossly exaggerated, Lidia claims that she wants to die: "I feel like dying, because I no longer love you. That's why I'm desperate" (it is no longer a desperate desire for something new that is agonizing). Because the female's role in a melodrama is to love and to sacrifice herself for love, her complaint is, "I wish I was old, and that my life's dedication to you was over." And of course the competition between a selfish man and an angelic one is also a staple of the melodramatic landscape, especially if the angelic man has just died, which allows for a further turn of the melodramatic screw to be able to rise to the higher level of verbal excess, also characteristic of melodrama:

> He [Tommaso] convinced me, despite myself, that I was cleverer that I am. He spent days trying to make me study even though I was not interested, I was concerned with my problems. ... He never talked about himself. Only me ... me ... And I never understood. I thought so little of myself. ... You [Giovanni] talked only about yourself. That was something new for me, I was so happy with it that nothing in the world was more beautiful. Because I loved you. You, not him.

---

[58] Or perhaps we do—during the party a man tells Resy to leave him alone.

Not surprisingly, Giovanni finds it easy to enter into the role prescribed to him by this Resy-like scenario: in a similarly verbose manner he confirms his selfishness as a husband and his worthlessness as the object of love, and promises to change himself and his life so that he can live up to the melodramatic ideal:

> I never gave you anything. I was completely unaware. I go on wasting my life, like a fool taking without giving, or giving too little. If you mean I haven't much to give, you may be right. … I have been selfish. Now I realise that what we give to others comes back to us. … Lidia, let's settle this. Let's try to hang on to something we're sure of. I love you. I'm sure I'm still in love with you. What more can I say?[59]

But instead of the curtain happily falling on the male villain's change of heart, the film continues as Lidia takes a letter out of her handbag and reads it out to her husband. Because it is a love letter to her from the young Giovanni, who does not recognize it until Lidia tells him that he wrote it, this scene is most often interpreted as Lidia's proof to her husband that his declaration of love is just "words" and that he does not really love her anymore. But we should note that although such an interpretation of the ending makes the story more "hopeless" (and therefore supposedly more "modern"—everybody knows that in the modern world a change of heart is an unacceptable fairy-tale or "Dickensian" resolution of the plot), it does not make it any less melodramatic, which seems out of place in a film which openly criticizes the discourse of melodrama in general ("Why does she sacrifice herself?"—"It makes me want to cry") and perhaps Giovanni's melodramatic leanings as a writer in particular (Resy is his biggest admirer).[60] One may also note that the final melodramatic confrontation takes place in specific surroundings which are unusual for this film, which so far has featured almost exclusively modern architectural and industrial landscapes as backgrounds. Giovanni and Lidia's conversation takes place against a background of nature, which is only fitting for a melodrama, which is supposed to emphasize the sentimental, that is, less rational and more "natural" (whether emotional or instinctual) human side.[61] But the landscape visible as a setting is not natural at all; it is a golf course, that is, a completely artificial creation,

---

[59] In the discourse of melodrama the sentimental bond constitutes the only true value in the corrupt world of wealth and power (the world of Pirellis and Gherardinis).
[60] One wonders whether in the ironic treatment of melodrama Antonioni is not also self-critical. All the plots of Antonioni's Italian films rely to a bigger or lesser extent on melodramatic devices.
[61] Also contrasted with the commodified background to Giovanni and Valentina's relationship.

a pseudo-natural landscape which has been created to serve a purely artificial purpose—it is the setting for a game. And in the context of Lidia's attempts to find something new, a new footing for the woman that would not rely on the hoary roles she is tormented by playing, her final melodramatic flight, which relies on invoking the most formulaic female roles of all, can only be taken for a game. But what is the game that she is playing?

Although the letter Lidia reads is a letter concerning their love, it is more than a confession of feelings. Surprisingly, it takes us back to a crucial matter we have discussed above, that is, the future, or in fact to the possibility of its arrival. While writing about his love, Giovanni is writing about an "eternal" moment which takes the couple out of time and from the perspective of which the future is seen as timeless:

> I was afraid of you being awake in my arms again. Instead, I wanted something no one could take from me, mine alone, this eternal image of you. Beyond your face I saw a pure beautiful vision showing us in the perspective of my whole life all the years to come, even all the years past. That was the most miraculous thing—to feel, for the first time, that you had always been mine. That this night would go on forever united with your warmth, your thoughts, your will. At that moment, I realised how much I loved you, Lidia. I wept with the intensity of the emotion. For I felt that this must never end, we would remain like this all our lives, not only close, but belonging to each other in a way that nothing could ever destroy except the apathy of habit, the only threat. Then you awoke and, smiling, put your arms around me, kissed me and I felt there was nothing to fear. We would always be as we were at that moment bound by stronger ties than time and habit.

The eternal moment is timeless because every moment of the future and of the past is transfigured by the vision of perfection in whose grip Giovanni is writing. In other words, the ordinary relationship of a flesh-and-blood man and a flesh-and-blood woman with all their ordinary callousness produced by habit and forgetfulness makes sense (has a future) only if it is simultaneously seen in (transfigured by) a utopian light that allows the relationship to carry within itself the dream of perfection, a transcendence (an outside) which is timeless, but which was visited on the couple in a particular moment of the past. This kind of vision is called love in Giovanni's letter and it is explicitly distinguished from the melodramatic emotional manipulation that had been described by Resy ("sacrifice") and was used by Lidia to get to Giovanni. Moreover, because this vision is presented in a letter, that is, as a specimen of Giovanni's writing, it is also a reminder to him of what writing might be about in its highest vocation. It is neither an antiquated artisan work nor is it keeping with the pace of life, as love is not changing a woman every few years to "rejuvenate" one's image according to the standards of the moment. The only way literature can be faithful to the future is to remain faithful to love, to a utopian light which transfigured the world in the moment of vision but which was then obscured by what Giovanni calls "the forces of habit," which obey the rules of the dumb self-perpetuation of enjoyment.

This reminder to Giovanni of his potential as a writer is of course not unrelated to Lidia's earlier peregrinations in search of something new, which she was unable to find. Lidia's challenge to Giovanni in the final sequence is precisely a challenge to him as a writer, a challenge he does not meet with his feeble "I still love you." This challenge is, in fact, emphasized by the setting. We have already said that it begins by invoking the discourse of melodrama (and with a vengeance), but one may add that these words, uttered by Lidia who is standing under a tree on a golf course, take us back to the already-mentioned "tree scene" in Sesto San Giovanni in which her husband saw something invisible (and therefore impossible to be seen on the screen) while he was perusing a landscape of ruins—he saw that nothing had changed, that is, that the future, the "something new" Lidia desires, is not a question of facts but of vision, that it is up to a writer to serve a better future by being faithful to utopian dreams of the past. It is up to the writer (or the critical intellectual) to open a future to Lidia, to come up with something new that would open a path forward and allow her to reformulate what it means to be a woman and a wife, leaving behind the roles enforced on her by the world of commodities, in which the verbosity of the melodramatic discourse and the silence of solipsistic enjoyment are two sides of the same coin.

Moreover, the utopian dimension that is "theorized" by Giovanni in his letter does not really come out of the blue at the conclusion of the film; its appearance has been carefully prepared by Antonioni. While Lidia is looking for something new in the streets of Milan, she finds surplus figures and locations that suggest an "outside" of the consolidated space of capital; yet when she takes the hint and visits the *actual* outside (the periphery), she finds it even more constricting. Therefore the redeeming dimension that appears to Lidia can only be construed as *virtual*—it is an immaterial surplus, which splits reality from within and insists that things do not—and should not—have to be the way they are. Thus it is hardly surprising that figures who represent this virtual dimension are three women who add up to a kind of historical "narrative": the old woman eating an ice-cream cone (a painful past in need of redemption), Lidia (the agonizing presence) and the girl in the yard of the ruined building (crying for the arrival of a real future). In contrast to what I called the eternal-feminine trio, which incarnates the ahistorical phantasmagoria that serves to consolidate the grip of totality (both patriarchal and capitalist), the historical trio undermines the dominion of the urban deterrence machine by showing its contingency and inconsistency.[62] Thus we may say that, at least within the bounds of the significations produced by *La notte*, the virtual dimension, which sabotages every whole, is female by definition, even if its instance is found in Giovanni's writing (but it is his "unofficial" writing; in his official persona Giovanni is "the author of that great book ... One of the best books ever written," as Resy enthuses).

Lidia herself uses the constricting melodramatic discourse to release its dormant utopian potential in order to remind Giovanni of who he might be. That this strategy does not work with him is indicated by his desperate attempt to stick to the letter of the discourse by forcing his kisses on Lidia, rather than understand what is demanded of him, that is, grasp the utopian potential of their situation. But this is not surprising, because we have already seen him failing to apprehend this distinction, and, moreover, during their final confrontation Lidia reminds Giovanni of the scene in which that happened—she claims that the thought that she wanted to die because Giovanni did not love her occurred to her in a nightclub which they visited before going to Gherardini's party. Bearing in mind that this claim is a part of Lidia's melodramatic strategy, we may see in it more than a make-shift fabrication[63] invented to serve its melodramatic purpose.

In the nightclub the couple watches an acrobatic act performed by a Black female dancer with a glass of wine which Giovanni is ironically enjoying ("Look at her, she's not bad at all"). When it is finished, while Lidia is applauding the performer, Giovanni utters a self-satisfied pseudo-intellectual witticism about what he has seen: "Life would be tolerably agreeable if it were not for its amusements." But in the context of Lidia's previous search for something new, and taking into

---

[62] Looking at the relationship between Lidia and Giovanni from a slightly different angle than before, we may say that the main problem Giovanni has with Lidia is precisely that she does not fit (or no longer fits) into a constellation he is comfortable with (the witch–Valentina–Resy), and thus undermines it.

[63] This would not be the first time Lidia has lied: in Sesto San Giovanni she says to Giovanni that she ended up there accidentally, which is obviously untrue as we saw her arriving by taxi.

consideration that the main performer is a woman,[64] Giovanni's comment seems especially obtuse—while he thinks he is criticizing the tawdry shallowness of modern Italy, he is really only showing his own shallow understanding of the performance. Although this is a spectacle of both patriarchal and colonial exploitation (an "exotic" woman performing almost naked for the mostly male patrons of the club), there is something in it that goes beyond its entertainment aspect and the patrons' blasé appropriation of it. During her performance the dancer goes beyond being just a commodity for sale—she is not just a beautiful object to be admired (like a model on a catwalk) but a woman who exhibits the perfect control of her body, something which her self-satisfied audience can only long for.[65] Thus her act carries in itself an emancipatory utopian potential—for instance, of "the harmonious reconciliation of subject and object through the humanization of nature and the naturalization of humanity,"[66] proposed by Marx as the communist goal in *Economic and Philosophic Manuscripts* of 1844. And of course it is not unimportant that it is a woman who shows this potentially emancipatory power ("something new") by overcoming the resistance of her own body in the very process of its commodification (display for money). How different does the transcendence that the dancer incarnates appear from Valentina's spectrality, which is thoroughly defined by the commodity! No wonder that Lidia, learning from the performance, counters Giovanni's ironic enthusiasm about it with "Please, don't belittle me. I have my own thoughts, too" (one has difficulty in believing that these thoughts are about her desire to die). Moreover, these thoughts first take form in Lidia's changed mind. No doubt prodded by Giovanni's smug comment on the performance, she proposes that they do what she had been reluctant to do earlier, and spend the rest of the night by *amusing* themselves at the Gherardinis' party (the amusement her husband would engage in so avidly) to demonstrate to Giovanni why their life together in its present form is far from being tolerably agreeable and to attempt to use things at hand (the materials the party will provide) to dissolve her subjection-attachment to him and carve an opening for herself, which would make her—or perhaps even their—future possible.

---

[64] There is a Black man performing with her but his role is mainly to assist the female dancer.
[65] Brunette notes something similar: "The female performer's gyrations are so gymnastic … that something beyond mere vibrant sexuality is suggested, a perfect at-easeness with her entire body" (*Antonioni*, 63).
[66] Buck-Morss, *The Dialectics of Seeing*, 146.

Finally, Lidia does not find what she has been looking for and her melodramatic strategy with Giovanni fails. But although Antonioni is generally held to be a poet of anxiety and desperation, this film is not entirely grim. Although so far we have been looking at modern architecture shown in *La notte* as an incarnation of the solipsistic enjoyment of capital, we can take inspiration from Lidia and try to find a glimpse of utopian potential in the very midst of urbanist domination and panopticism. And this is not difficult if we consider that the architecture featured in the film is mostly modernist constructions of glass and steel, which in Europe, at least initially, were associated with radical ideas about building a new society.

Urgently demanding "something new" after the slaughter of the First World War, Walter Gropius wrote in 1919 that "[n]ot until the political revolution is perfected in the spiritual revolution can we become free," and that only then "will the people again join together in building the great art work of their time ... the freedom cathedral of the future."[67] Being an architect, he did not use the word "cathedral" in a metaphorical sense. In later Bauhaus publications this building of the future (also called "the cathedral of socialism" or "the cathedral of freedom") was described as crystalline and connected with glass and light.[68] Although Bruno Taut at first imagined such "glass architecture" (which according to him would banish hatred, war, and aggression) as made of colored glass, which for him was related to joy (after the pain of the war),[69] for other Bauhaus architects, and for Ludwig Mies van der Rohe, the use of large glass areas seemed to be more effective for the transformation needed, because it allowed for the interiors of buildings to be flooded with sunlight—a necessary condition, they thought, for establishing "new, more honest, human relationships," conducive to creating a better society.[70] In other words, the idea of the high-rise modernist European building made of glass and steel, which gives people better access to light, sun, and fresh air, which are necessary for both bodily and spiritual health, originated in a utopian vision of transcendence—the dream of a non-commodified society of equal and honest men and women. Thus, although in *La notte* the modernist buildings of Milan (and especially the Pirelli tower) are

---

[67] "Baukunst im freien Volksstaat," in *Deutscher Revolutions-Almanach*, Hamburg, 1919, 135–6. Quoted in Barbara Miller Lane, "Modern Architecture and Politics in Germany, 1918–1945," in *Housing and Dwelling: Perspectives on Modern Domestic Architecture*, ed. Barbara Miller Lane (Oxon: Routledge, 2007), 260.
[68] Lane, "Modern Architecture," 262.
[69] Ibid., 262.
[70] Ibid., 265.

presented as the materialization of suffocating capitalist enjoyment, there is also something in them (something invisible) that makes them more (or less) than they seem to be, and thus destabilizes their aggressive imaginary dominance. Therefore, Antonioni's "fixation" with modernist architecture (in *La notte* but in his other films as well) should not be taken (or at least not only) as a personal interest, nor as a predilection for abstract shapes that are suited to his abstract cinema, but as a persistent search for strong images through which something invisible can break through, offering a glimpse of redemption, if only for a flash.

3

L'eclisse (1962)

Of all Antonioni's films, *L'eclisse* has perhaps the most rudimentary and stereotypical plot: a young woman breaks off a relationship with a man only to embark on another one with a stockbroker met by chance, which continues uneasily for a number of weeks (June–September 1961), and expires one day when the couple arranges a meeting at 8:00 p.m. at "the usual place" for which neither of them turns up. Although the protagonists we encounter—a typical aggressive male narcissist and a typical submissive woman looking for a missing element in her fantasy of life—are far from gripping, and nothing extraordinary takes place in the plot between the dissolution of the first relationship and the second one, the film is often considered to be the most interesting of the so-called trilogy, beginning with *L'avventura*, which catapulted Antonioni to international fame.

L'eclisse opens with the disintegration of the relationship between Vittoria (Monica Vitti) and Riccardo (Francisco Rabal): after what we may assume to have been a night of fruitless bickering, which has taken place in the latter's apartment, the couple decides to separate. This ordinary narrative event is significantly made strange by Antonioni's "eccentric" stylistic choices, which, rather than help the viewer to orient him- or herself as to the ground-plan of the apartment and the spatial relationships between the two protagonists, present the objects and the characters from strange angles and employ misleading shots, for instance, ones that suggest a point of view but then withdraw the suggestion. The resulting fragmentation and confusion is augmented by the omnipresence of rectangular shapes in Riccardo's apartment—apart from multiple doors and windows, the walls are full of paintings and other kinds of framed objects. These paintings are mostly abstractions of the Jackson Pollock type, that is, ones in which the very notion of the centered composition is questioned. But even this kind of decentering is not enough—the interior in which the protagonists find themselves is additionally reflected by mirrors (and other polished surfaces like the floor), which constitute yet another type of framing and multiplying device. The overall effect of such a mise-en-scène (and the lenses that are used) is flattening, fragmenting, and decentering of the space due to the overabundance of objects in the rather cramped interior and a kind of wicked game that the director plays with the rules of continuity editing.[1]

These forces of disintegration that Antonioni incorporates into the dynamics of the image seem to meet with resistance. Although the first shot of the film cues us for the "confusion" that will follow (we see a switched-on table lamp, some books, and what looks like a white shapeless object, which, when the camera starts to pan right, turns out to be Riccardo's white-shirted forearm; we see him look at something off-screen and then cast his gaze toward the floor in frustration), in the next two shots we see Vittoria trying to center an abstract object within an empty picture-frame that she is holding. Then, seemingly dissatisfied with what she sees in the picture-frame, she looks at a large painting of a little town hanging on the wall. Because it is a specimen of "naive art," the painting's representation of space is two-dimensional ("flat"), and its composition is rather decentered, but the effect the painting creates is the opposite of the disintegration-disorientation of the sequence in which it is featured as filmed by Antonioni, because, as is often the case with paintings of this sort, it is a vision of a fantasy of the good life, a vision in which an ordinary reality that is possibly drab is transfigured by a utopian impulse (though the film is black-and-white one can "feel" that the painting must be very colorful). It is a very untypical painting for Riccardo's apartment, in which the other large paintings are abstractions and the rest of the space is cluttered by all kinds of art objects, which, even when they are "representational," are so congested that they give the impression of being patterned in an abstract and mechanical manner in a modernist space whose soundscape is determined by an electric fan, which remains on throughout the initial sequence, and an electric razor, which Riccardo uses before Vittoria leaves. Within the stifling atmosphere of Riccardo's place the "naive" painting (which includes lots of greenery and a waterfront) offers a draught of fresh breath and seems to suggest how to puncture the suffocating cocoon that Vittoria finds herself in—a look at the painting makes her go to one of the windows to part

---

[1] This decentering of space and the flattening of the image are of course noted by most commentators on the film.

the curtains and look outside.² But what she finds there does not really help her: through the window she sees (or at least the viewers do) the motionless branches of trees, creating yet another decentered abstract pattern in a part of the window that she has uncurtained (later in the film Vittoria's gaze will often be associated with tree branches moving in the wind). Thus we have witnessed two failed attempts by Vitoria to escape disintegration by centering her space and therefore herself: firstly, by creating her own perfect (referential) frame (a fantasy) within the chaos of other frames around her, using available objects typical for the apartment (centering an abstract object within a picture-frame), and secondly, by finding among the patterns of internally referential objects (objects which point only to other objects in the apartment, like frames/rectangles referring only to other frames), an exception that arrests the centripetal movement and points to an outside which may function as an external support point (outside of the window) in reference to which the internal chaos can be given some meaning or/and reorganized into some semblance of order.

But why do both these attempts turn out to be failures? Why do both centripetal and centrifugal ways of escape not work? The answer is provided in the most "uncanny" part of the opening sequence. Although there are obvious narrative reasons for the initial sequence to be spatially and editorially perplexing (the emotional turmoil of the protagonists, perceptual exhaustion after a sleepless night of struggle), the confusion is also due to a structural discrepancy between two kinds of centering "devices": apart from Vittoria's aforementioned attempts at centering, there is another centering force present on the scene: Riccardo keeps following Vittoria with his eyes throughout the sequence and thus she remains the virtual center of this formally decentered fragment of the film. Yet Riccardo's look cannot really be treated here as external to Vittoria—the symbolic point from which Vittoria is looked at (and of course it is not an accident that the point is inserted here in a male figure) has been partly internalized by her, that is, it has become a part of who she is.

This is demonstrated precisely when, for the only time in the sequence, Riccardo's look "disappears." When Vittoria returns from the kitchen, where

---

² In order to "congest" the atmosphere even more, the film juxtaposes two POV shots. After showing Vittoria in medium close-up looking off-frame right, the film cuts to the full view of the naive painting, then to Riccardo's following something with his eyes, and after that to the head-on shot of Vittoria's legs among all kinds of furniture legs, all of them doubled by their reflection on the polished floor. The last is, typically for the initial sequence, a fake (disorienting) POV shot—in order to see Vittoria's legs from such perspective Riccardo would have had to lie down, or at least sit, on the floor.

she has taken some empty coffee cups, she sees Riccardo sitting in an armchair staring intently into space with unseeing eyes. When she tries to confront that look by standing right in front of him and looking directly at him, there is no reaction. Frightened by this, Vittoria very slowly takes a few steps back, still staring intently at Riccardo (as if "taking over" his empty look with her own eyes), retreating with the camera, until we see her reflected frontally in a nearby mirror. After a moment, she takes her eyes off Riccardo and looks straight into the mirror, where she confronts this strange object (the look) she has taken over from him (and which we as viewers are, of course, unable to see), which causes an attack of panic that makes her run to another window and draw back the curtains. What she then sees through the window is one of Antonioni's more memorable images (also because it is so often reproduced): a strange modernist mushroom-shaped construction, a water tower in the EUR district of Rome, called *Il Fungo* by Romans. The construction looms threateningly, overwhelming the landscape, so that its windows seem to look back at Vittoria and down on her, as it were. In other words, apart from Riccardo's wistful "personal" look, which constantly follows her, the situation also includes the impersonal gaze of the Other (the gaze that questions her and for which she performs), which "belongs" to her (it is a part of her subjective universe) though she is usually not conscious of it.[3] When, due to an "unrailing" situation, she becomes aware of its presence, it gets separated from its material bearer (Riccardo) and appears on the horizon externalized in a threatening, looming form that has a phallic shape.

Although at first sight the Fungo seems to be an "eccentric" choice to relate Vittoria to, in fact it is perfectly fitting because its uncanniness is of a Freudian kind: it is both threatening and familiar. Its form might be "unnatural" (modernist-abstract) and thus unsettling, but it is a water tower, which is necessary for the proper functioning of the EUR—the residential and business district of Rome where both Vittoria and Riccardo live, and which is the main setting (together with the Borsa—the Roman stock exchange) of *L'eclisse*. In the film this district is shown as being under construction—like the contemporary Italy of the economic boom—and we can see that it has been envisioned as a modern low-rise suburb with lots of large green spaces needing plenty of water for irrigation, not to mention more water for potential fire-fighting, always a

---

[3] Restivo postulates the presence of the gaze of the Other in this sequence but what he means is quite different from my point. Angelo Restivo, *The Cinema of Economic Miracles: Visuality and Modernisation in the Italian Art Film* (Durham: Duke University Press, 2002), 117.

threat in a densely populated area. In other words, what the Fungo embodies in the film is a point of view with which Vittoria, more or less consciously, identifies a point of view which represents the values of the Romans whom the EUR is being built for: a fashionable, well-to-do group of people who are rising with the tide of the economic miracle, people who are not necessarily only business-related, but also include "mainstream" intellectuals like Riccardo (otherwise how would he be able to afford such a "trendy" location?[4]). In fact, Riccardo's affiliation with the establishment is cleverly indicated later in the film. If we take his apartment as representative of who he is, he turns out to be only a "moderned-up" version of Piero's parents, whose large upper-middle-class apartment in the center of Rome Vittoria visits. The parents' place is overstuffed with "aesthetic objects" (full of "representational" paintings and sculptures, as well as mirrors, photographs, knick-knacks, and designer utility products), their style going back to the "solid" fashions of the late nineteenth century and gesturing toward the "classical," while Riccardo's apartment is just as overcrowded with a plethora of objects illustrating the aesthetic and intellectual fashions of his day: mostly abstract or abstraction-oriented, and gesturing toward the primitive or exotic (not forgetting the socialist journals lying on his desk).[5]

Thus, rather than being a symbol of modern alienation or even a premonition of nuclear catastrophe (for which it has often been taken), the appearance of the Fungo indicates something much more prosaic, a certain desublimation in Vittoria's life resulting in an indefinable discontent that materializes on her horizon, which, when asked about, always produces the same answer on her part: "Non lo so" (I don't know).[6] But the uncanniness Vittoria experiences at the sight of the Fungo seems to be something relatively new.[7] From the conversation

---

[4] A figure going back to Giovanni Pontano in *La notte*.

[5] Moreover, there is a ghost which literally haunts the landscape of the EUR in the film—the district was a Fascist project begun in the middle 1930s for the 1942 World Fair (hence its name, which is an acronym for Esposizione Universale Roma) to celebrate the twentieth anniversary of Fascism. But the most famous examples of Italian Fascist architecture, like the Palazzo della Civiltà Italiana, are absent from *L'eclisse* (as "repressed from memory" of the brave new Italy) and in their place the buildings and places constructed for the 1960 Olympic Games appear. This is a typical example of (collective memory) displacement: in the 1940s the EUR was supposed to show the greatness of Fascism; in 1960 it was to show the greatness of the Italy of the economic boom (not to mention the Fascist obsession with sporting activities). The telling absence of Fascist architecture in *L'eclisse* is mentioned in Sitney, *Vital Crises*, 151.

[6] "The lack at the core of Vittoria's self-examination resonates throughout the film." Sitney, *Vital Crises*, 156.

[7] It is a nice coincidence that what we see with Vittoria through Riccardo's window is just a photograph of the Fungo, because it was not in the vicinity of the apartment in which the opening sequence of *L'eclisse* was shot.

between her and Riccardo in the initial sequence we learn that things used to be otherwise. "When we first met, I was 20 years old. I was happy then," says Vittoria, and this of course does not mean that meeting Riccardo made her former happiness disappear.[8] We can surmise that it was precisely the other way round, that is, that meeting him had a lot to do with the happiness at twenty she is now so nostalgic about. Although we do not learn anything specific about the nature of that past happiness, there are two sequences in *L'eclisse* in which Vittoria seems to be very happy, one of which bears a kind of "negative" resemblance to the spectacle of tension and "alienation" taking place in Riccardo's apartment.

We have already mentioned two overstuffed living spaces which make Vittoria squirm: Riccardo's apartment in the EUR and an upper-middle-class apartment in the center of Rome. But there is yet another, in many ways similar, apartment which she visits, but which has the opposite effect on her. One night she and her friend Anita (Rossana Rory) are unexpectedly invited to pay a visit to their neighbor's apartment. The neighbor, Marta (Mirella Ricciardi), is the daughter and wife of white landowners in Kenya, where she was brought up, and her apartment is as overstuffed with frames and "aesthetic" objects as the two mentioned above. Only in this case instead of paintings we have photographs of the landscapes, animals, and natives of Kenya, and instead of designer utensils and bric-a-brac, we see indigenous arts and crafts products or other exotic objects.[9] Unlike the aesthetic trophies that hang on the walls of Riccardo's apartment, which seem to weigh down on Vittoria, Marta's collection of picturesque objects, which project (a fantasy of) the unknown and exotic world of Africa, reinvigorates melancholy Vittoria and puts her into high spirits, which are on display in the mock-African-tribal dance she performs among the exotic objects. This reaction to the fantasy of an exciting and colorful life may indicate to us the way we should understand Vittoria's youthful happiness with Riccardo. The aesthetic trophies hanging on the walls of Riccardo's apartment once also represented for her an unknown and exotic world of excitement—in that case of high modernist aesthetics and intellectual debate—and offered a glimpse of something else, a fantasy of a better, more fulfilling life, an opening up of horizons, but which turned out to be a glossy covering over of the material

---

[8] Unless otherwise stated, all translations come from the subtitles on the DVD *L'eclisse* (The Criterion Collection, 2005).

[9] Each of the mentioned apartments is of course a relatively pure representation of a certain type of aesthetic taste, but the values they incarnate are not necessarily incompatible.

interests of the beneficiaries of the Italian boom, which are manifested in the ominous outline of the Fungo. Thus Vittoria breaks up with Riccardo because she finally finds the fantasy of his world empty ("I know you know about these things, but I don't know," she says), that is, finds him constricted or even paralyzed by the discourses whose representations hang on his walls. But what may seem surprising at first glance is an antidote Vittoria finds for the desublimation of her relationship with an intellectual—the substance of the plot of *L'eclisse* is her love affair with Piero, a Roman stockbroker.

We visit the Borsa with Vittoria—where she goes to meet her mother (Lilla Brigone) and where she also encounters her mother's broker, Piero—just after her break-up with Riccardo. But before their relationship starts to develop, we are able to look quite closely at the substance of the "I don't know" Vittoria keeps offering to her male admirers and which infuriates them so much—we get introduced into her fantasy world. This world has two aspects, which are exemplified by two "scenes of happiness" that we witness in the film. The first of these scenes has already been mentioned: in Marta's apartment, among the photographs of Africa and indigenous objects, Vittoria puts on blackface, dresses up in Kenyan garb, and performs a mock-ritual dance, fantasizing about "going native." What we encounter here is of course an old modernist fantasy of "instinctual happiness," of going back to the biological roots of existence, which should lead to the fulfillment of the appetites of the body and with it to ecstatic being in the world, in which petty concerns of an individualized (that is, civilized) self are left behind. This is a "dark," or even "black," naturalist fantasy, because the eclipsing of the individual by the instinctual means also the eclipsing of moral precepts by biological laws.

The second aspect of Vittoria's fantasy life is also "naturalistic," but in it all the "base" elements emphasized in the black fantasy disappear. The night of the "primitive" dance in Marta's apartment is followed by a day when Vittoria, Anita, and her husband fly to Verona in a small airplane. The flight introduces us to nature in its "ethereal" aspect, that is, completely unrelated to the instincts. In fact, in the film this aspect of the fantasy turns out to be literally white because of Vittoria's fascination with the view of the clouds from the air (she even asks the pilot to fly into a cloud for her). On the ground, this initial elation is transformed into a more palpable form of the pastoral:[10] they land at the grassy aerodrome of

---

[10] Gilberto Perez, *The Material Ghost: Films and Their Medium* (Baltimore: The Johns Hopkins University Press, 1998), 381.

Verona Aeroclub, the sun is shining, it is peaceful and quiet, a nostalgic melody is playing in the background on a juke-box. In other words, what we witness here is not the nature of the body (chaotic instincts), but nature as something to feast one's soul upon: a perfect order, which is both beautiful and good—the Verona Aeroclub sequence starts with Anita's comment "Che bello" (How beautiful) and ends with Vittoria's "Ma sita così bene qui" (But it's so good here).[11]

These two fantasies of nature (black and white), although at first sight unrelated or even mutually exclusive, actually implicate each other. The black fantasy of instinctual release, although interrupted by Marta, has an ironic coda, in which Marta's black poodle Zeus escapes from the confines of civilization (her apartment) to band up with other dogs and run about the EUR in the night. Marta and Vittoria go out to catch the dog and when Vittoria finally approaches him, Zeus gets up on his hind paws and does a circus routine to crown his escape with. So much for the fantasy of the releasing primeval instincts.[12] Moreover, what may seem to be a naïve and relatively innocuous fantasy of the overcultured about going primitive is not so harmless after all because it has a violent foundation, which is explicitly stated by Marta. Although she refers to the natives as "my people" and presents herself as a child of wild nature to whom elephants are more or less what cars are to Europeans ("Weren't you afraid?" "No, I was born there. Are you afraid of cars?"), she reveals the hidden underside of such a primitivist fantasy, which is ultimately racist: she claims that black Kenyans are simply monkeys who recently lost their tails and now irrationally want to become like their "masters," that is, they do not participate in the fantasy of nature, because they know the life of the "monkey" is a life of human deprivation and penury (or service), and thus very far from releasing. Marta also claims that, in order to keep the "natural" fantasy going, all whites have to carry guns in Kenya—no doubt to make sure that the monkeys are kept separate from their masters, so that the masters can fantasize about the ecstatic life of a monkey who does not suffer from the alienating shackles of civilization. In other words, although the primitivist fantasy sports blackface, it is in fact a white fantasy of death, which is nicely indicated when Vittoria, submerged in the world of the Kenyan memorabilia in Marta's apartment, looks at a large photograph of Kilimanjaro and speaks aloud the title of Hemingway's short story "The Snows

---

[11] Translated on the DVD as "That was lovely" and "It's so nice here," respectively.
[12] In order to emphasize that the core of the black fantasy is white, Zeus, a black poodle, is accompanied by a *white* dog.

of Kilimanjaro," in which a flight in a small aircraft into the eponymous snows is used as a dream-like image signifying the descent into death.¹³

Thus it is not surprising that we encounter precisely such an aircraft in the introduction to the second incarnation of the fantasy. The white pastoral fantasy of the Verona Aeroclub is a fantasy of the perfect balance between nature and culture: an airport and in a sense the sky too are turned into a grassy field on which the planes (and clouds) seem to be at home, almost turning into sheep. But, surprisingly, what Vittoria finds at the center of the white pastoral is the disturbing mute presence of two Black men sitting in front of the airport bar (a remainder to us, and to Vittoria, that we are not finished with fantasy yet—a few minutes earlier in the film we have seen Vittoria "going native" in blackface), and when the dreamy atmosphere is re-established inside the bar by the wistful glances of men at Vittoria and the sentimental melody that a juke-box is playing, we realize that we are in a foreign country—this is not really Verona, Italy, but a fantasy of what the EUR is ideally supposed to be,¹⁴ peopled not by Italians but by American soldiers (both Black and white).¹⁵ In other words, the white fantasy of "wholesome" nature is not only a foreign import (the American suburb of 1950s Hollywood movies: white prefab houses and green lawns), but the very possibility of its existence is founded on American military dominance (violence) both in Italy (where after the Second World War the Americans bolstered Christian Democrat rule to prevent the communists from overturning the Fascist state structures) and throughout the world. A very "black" core indeed is active within this fantasy and is hardly dissimulated by all the surface beauty and serenity.

Thus it is ultimately not very surprising that Piero so easily finds his way into Vittoria's fantasy world. He is the antithesis of Riccardo, who is associated

---

13 Although Kenya was a British colony and thus unrelated to Italy politically, the conjunction of the EUR (originally a Fascist project) with Africa necessarily brings to mind Mussolini's colonial dreams and exploits. David Saul Rosenfeld in his internet site devoted to L'eclisse claims that a photograph of Vittoria's father that she and Piero peruse in Vittoria's mother's apartment shows him in the uniform of Mussolini's African expeditionary force. "Michelangelo Antonioni's L'eclisse: a broken piece of wood, a matchbook, a woman, a man," accessed June 8, 2019, http://www.davidsaulrosenfeld.com/.
14 Although the EUR that we are shown in the film seems to be based on the fantasy of happy reconciliation between the city and the country, Antonioni undermines this fantasy constantly by inserting ominous views into it (the Fungo, the building under construction at the usual place of Vittoria and Piero's meeting, Piero's car with the body of a drunk, who has stolen it, being pulled out of an artificial lake).
15 We hear some (white) men speaking American English, and although there are no explicit signs that they are soldiers, we may conclude that an exclusively male American group in a country with American military bases are soldiers, which would also explain the presence of Blacks within the group. In the published script of L'eclisse the men are explicitly identified as American soldiers.

with rigidity, patterns, and aesthetic objects (that is, rules or values)—as is emphasized a number of times in the film, Piero is spontaneous and constantly on the move ("You never stand still," says Vittoria), he has a passionate attachment to the stock exchange, and his job there seems to be a perpetual improvisation in which intuition plays a major role. In this way, he fits very well into the framework of the dark "African" fantasy—he seems to be an incarnation of pure "dark vitality" (life-energy itself): oblivious of limits and spontaneous, but also primitive and ruthless (exemplified, for instance, by his treatment of the clients when they come to plead with him after losing money in the stock-market crash). And at the same time, he is the white fantasy's "foreign import": a narcissistic Italian incarnation of American individualism and materialism, driving fancy (white) cars and fascinated by money ("I had dinner with seven billions," he brags to Vittoria), supposedly in denial of his solid upper-middle-class Roman roots (exemplified by Piero's parents' apartment).[16] And of course Piero is also related to both aspects of Vittoria's fantasy because in the final analysis her fantasy of nature is a fantasy of love: in the natural order of things spontaneity is the defining characteristics of love, understood as the privileged case of the state of happiness, both sensual (black) and spiritual (white). This is explicitly voiced by Vittoria in the context of her African fancy: "Maybe you think less of happiness down there [in Kenya]," she says to Marta, "Things just unfold on their own. But here everything's so difficult. Even love." But this appealing (white) belief in love has also a less appealing underside: what from a certain distance looks like spontaneity (the impulsive mutual attraction between Piero and Vittoria), when examined closely seems to be nothing but blind obedience to natural repetitive cycles (in case of Vittoria: first ..., then Riccardo, then Piero, then ..., etc.; in case of Piero: first ..., then *la bestiola*,[17] then Vittoria, then ..., etc.).

Because the fantasy of nature as happiness is central to Vittoria's world, throughout the film her image is related to green branches, often swaying in the wind (indicating the vivacity of her inner life). Although this trite juxtaposition (woman—nature) may be automatically related to its conventional meaning

---

[16] Piero's American aspect is emphasized by the soundtrack. When Vittoria visits his childhood room in his parents' apartment, we hear non-diegetic music: a twist with which *L'eclisse*'s opening credits began.

[17] An unnamed young woman whom Piero breaks up with to start his affair with Vittoria. He refers to her as "la bestiola" among his co-workers (translated as "a hot number" but meaning a little creature or beast), which emphasizes the artificiality (and aggressivity) of the supposedly natural impulse.

(nature as something motherly and therefore positive) by the viewer, *L'eclisse* undermines such an easy association with other images in which the natural is featured. The EUR, which is supposed to be a district in which nature and the city are reconciled, is strangely lifeless and depopulated. Moreover, in its center death awaits those who act on "natural" impulse in search of happiness: a sympathetic drunk, having stolen Piero's car in order to go for a joyride, drives into an artificial lake and drowns.[18] We have already mentioned Marta's dog and its circus routine, which is a comment on Vittoria's African fantasy of "natural" release from the difficulties of emotional life enforced by modern civilization. And, most humorously and pointedly, in the film nature is associated with artificial tranquilization: an elderly man who has lost 30 million lire in the stock-market crash goes to a pharmacy and then to a cafe where he swallows a tranquilizer and draws flowers on a piece of paper to calm himself.

There are, however, two scenes in *L'eclisse* in which happiness is not related to a fantasy and its connection with the natural is actually undermined. Both of them can be found in the longer fantasy sequences we have already discussed, where they are included in order to undermine the main fantasy configuration. The first of these scenes takes place after Marta's dog has been found by Vittoria. While he performs on his hind paws, she hears a strange sound, which turns out to be made by the lanyards of a row of flagpoles, shaken by the wind. Although the propelling force (the wind) that creates this effect is natural, the instruments that are being played are products of human technology and rather ordinary ones to boot (they are "ugly" and therefore not very suitable for fantasy). But most importantly, the image and the soundscape produced by such interaction suspend the fantasy projections (related to spontaneity and vivacity) and create a kind of standstill—an ecstatic and visionary moment for Vittoria, in which the ordinary, stifling world, where everything is difficult and nothing makes sense, suddenly becomes transfigured, infused with a mysterious meaning, which suggests a new dimension to existence, and thus produces a virtual opening, an epiphany, which explodes the constraining horizon of what comes naturally. In other words, what takes place here is the opposite to what happened when Vittoria encountered the Fungo outside Riccardo's window, the image that weighed down on her, making her feel that her narrow horizon—defined by

---

[18] Another deathly core to a fantasy of nature along with the snows of Kilimanjaro and the American military.

the happiness understood according to the values of the EUR—had trapped her for good. A similarly ecstatic moment occurs when Vittoria is flying to Verona. Before we encounter the false pastoral of the Aeroclub, Vittoria is "beside herself," overwhelmed by the spectacle of the clouds, which is "natural" but which she could not participate in without modern technology.

That Vittoria does not learn from these experiences and remains stuck in her fantasy world is made explicit in the penultimate sequence of the film, which takes place first in Piero's office and then outside it. The scene in the office is yet another example of Vittoria engaging in her fantasy of natural happiness, and the only one in which Piero features. Thus far in the film the relationship between the lovers has been shown as uneasy, and this has just been emphasized for the viewer by the previous scene, in which Vittoria has claimed that when she is with Piero she feels estranged ("I feel like I'm in a foreign country," says Piero in the EUR; "Funny. That's how I feel around you," responds Vittoria[19]). This uneasiness, or even anxiety, is absent in the scene in Piero's office and the couple seems to frolic in perfect understanding and amiability, making fun of other couples and of past events in their own relationship. But their spontaneity is stilted, it is just an act—precisely because this is their last meeting, they are able to play out the fantasy of the perfect ("natural") relationship, which in fact they have never had. This interaction excites them and gives them thrills, which may be wrongly perceived as spontaneity by the viewer.[20] In other words, what happens in Piero's office is precisely what had happened in Marta's apartment where Vittoria and Anita (but not Marta, who was brought up in Africa) played out their fantasies of what it is to be an African, and this reference is even explicitly invoked when Vittoria pretends to be a lioness (a photo of lionesses on the savannah features prominently in Marta's place and we see it in close-up) and attempts to scratch Piero's face in jest. Moreover, just as the "primitive ritual," when it had been going on for too long, was interrupted by an irritated Marta (who, as we have indicated, was at least half-aware of the lethal forces that lie at the origin of such a fancy), the office fantasy of the natural relationship is interrupted too, although this time the identity of the "spoilsport" remains unknown. The couple's frolics are interrupted by a buzzer, which in L'eclisse we

---

[19] Though this is ambiguous in the film—being in a foreign country (his "Americanness") is also Piero's drawing power.

[20] The play reinvigorates each of them separately—it boosts their own self-images, not the image of the couple.

hear only once apart from the office scene and in very telling circumstances—it rings in the Borsa as an introduction to the announcement of the death of one of the brokers, which is the ominous context of Vittoria and Piero's first meeting.[21] Marta could not bear Vittoria's supposedly happy acting out of the fantasy of primitive release because she was aware of the lethal forces it dissimulates and the acting out of the fantasy of natural relationship has to be stopped for the same reason.

So what is the origin of this fantasy of natural relationship? It is not difficult to find it if we remember that with Vittoria the black fantasy ("Africa") is always only one side of the constellation and that the white fantasy also belongs to the scene. In fact, on the stage of her fantasy the very incompatibility of certain elements emphasizes their crucial importance and indicates their deeper mutual implication.

In the case of the office scene, the important incompatibility is that it starts with the couple making fun of "serious" amorous gestures, but ends with the kind of act that they have earlier ridiculed. When Vittoria is about to leave, the couple wistfully recites: "We'll see each other tomorrow, and the day after tomorrow. And the day after that, and the next. And the day after that. And tonight. 8:00 ... the usual place." Apart from the fact that such behavior is gratingly at odds with their earlier "spontaneity," we note immediately that this prolonged and smooth parting dialogue seems out of place not only in this particular scene, but in the entire film, in which meaningful words are rare and, even when they appear, are usually contained within fragmentary, broken-up utterances, which peter out inconclusively. And no wonder these words feel out of place, because they belong to the white side of the natural fantasy that is being acted out in Piero's office: they sound as if they were the lyrics of some dreadful pop song about ideal (that is, natural and spontaneous) love[22]—in fact they would easily fit as the lyrics of the sentimental juke-box song that was heard playing as the musical background of the false pastoral at the Verona Aeroclub. While the almost wordless ("African") acting out of the fantasy of spontaneity might at first seem natural, its prolongation by use of melodramatic pop lyrics instantly qualifies it as fake. So when the play is over, everything can

---

[21] That this association is emphasized can be shown by pointing out that when Anita visits Vittoria's apartment, her ringing of the door-bell is edited out.

[22] Noted by Rosenfeld.

go back into the old ruts, back to the repetitive "natural" course. When Vittoria leaves the office, Piero returns the telephone receivers to their proper places and they start to ring.[23] Thus, he is back to what he is really passionate about and what comes to him naturally—in order to ironically emphasize this a soft breeze wafts through his office. Vittoria goes downstairs and into the street, where she stops at the barred window of a shop—although she does not know it, this is exactly where Piero had ruthlessly broken up with *la bestiola*. When, dejected, Vittoria turns her head up to look at the upper branches of the trees in the park across the road, the camera tilts to follow her look. Although after a while the noisy street disappears from the screen and we see just an expanse of greenery above the wall of the park, the camera films it from behind the bars of the shop, suggesting entrapment in the "natural" fantasy. But after a cut the bars are gone and Vittoria reappears under the canopy of the same trees with a smile, in order to stroll away (screen left) from our view, to find a successor to Piero, one may suppose, that is, to repeat the natural pattern with the renewed reliance on her fantasy of nature.

But then comes the famous ending, the so-called final montage, a seven-minute sequence in which nothing happens and in which none of protagonists appear. It just shows the passing of time at a crossroads in the EUR where Piero and Vittoria used to meet and which they assigned as a meeting place in their final conversation at Piero's office. We watch daylight turn into dusk; we see people and objects we have seen earlier in the film at the same place when the protagonists were present (a nurse with a child, a man driving a horse buggy, a lawn sprinkler, etc.); people come and go, buses arrive and leave. We are presumably waiting for Piero or/and Vittoria to arrive but they never come. The corner sports as usual a notice board and a metal drum filled with water, which is now (in the final montage) leaking. Both belong to a building site containing an unfinished construction covered with scaffolding and reed or straw mats. Finally night falls, street lamps come on, and the final image of the film is a close-up on a bright street light, accompanied by what many commentators take for ominous music.

---

[23] We are back in the context of death, back to the Borsa, where, after the buzzer, came a minute of silence for the dead broker, in which the unanswered telephones rang in exactly the same way. When the superficial human element is silenced in the Borsa (normally the soundscape of the place is men shouting at the top of their voices), the essence of it is expressed in this insistent mechanical-impersonal ringing.

What is the purpose of such a strange ending? The most frequent interpretation again relies on Antonioni's famous comments on the *malattia dei sentimenti*. The final montage is supposed to show the alienation and reification of modern life:

> The two subjects, failing to understand each other by affecting a mutual transfer of sense …, are gradually swallowed by things, and can no longer act upon the latter. … At the end … the gestures of that human being who was Vittoria are no longer present: only the things remain. Again we see the whole neighbourhood appear to us in a rigorous sequence in which the posthumous testimony of the missed appointment negates itself even as testimony. … It seems to me that the film indirectly compels us to become aware of objectification so that we might change, become human, and avoid disintegrating into things and objects.[24]

Moreover, this objectification is supposed to be given an even more ominous twist by the appearance in the final montage of a man who gets off a bus reading a newspaper (*L'Espresso*, September 10, 1961), which the viewer can peruse in two close-ups and whose most legible headlines announce: "La gara atomica" (nuclear arms race) and "La pace è debole" (a fragile peace). Thus, the reification is given the context of the Cold War arms race and the final shot of the bright streetlight is taken to be a premonition of the hydrogen bomb holocaust.[25]

But is the final montage really so grim and desperate? Is it just the continuation by other, more abstract and non-narrative, means of the rendering of the "difficult" and fragmented reality we have already witnessed in the body of the narration? And if so, why do the protagonists have to disappear, if it has been precisely Vittoria's "anxiety," through which the representation of the broken-up world has been filtered throughout the film so far? Because there is no denying that the world presented by the narration is grim, broken-up, and desperate, and what makes it even more so are the fantasies that Vittoria relies on to introduce a modicum of happiness into her existence. As we have seen, both of these fantasies are founded on death (self-justifying naked violence: of colonialism, of the struggle for world domination) and there is no doubt how this propelling force of the modern world is represented in the film: whether its drawing power is straightforward (Vittoria's mother, Piero) or rather convoluted (Vittoria), it is the Borsa, which constitutes the center of *L'eclisse*.

---

[24] Enzo Paci, "Uomini, scimmie e cose," ed. Roberto Leydi, *L'Europeo* (Milan), April 22, 1962; quoted in Sitney, *Vital Crises*, 157–8, 148 (Joan Esposito's translation).
[25] This suggestion is repeated in virtually all critical works devoted to *L'eclisse*.

But what *is* the stock exchange in the film? On the surface it is represented as chaos: a crowd of unappealing men running about screaming (these men represent other men and women who, as we can see, seem to behave just as irrationally) and rows of ever-changing digits. Yet, even though such an image seems "crazy," it is in fact a domestication of what is going on at the stock exchange, because it can be taken for a humorous or ironic representation of *personal* foibles (like Vittoria's mother's unhealthy obsession with money), which might be interpreted (as is possible in Piero's case) as resulting from an excess of life energy. And after all the screaming men are not just madmen but are supposed to be professionals doing their job. The really lethal side of the stock exchange is presented to us casually, when, after the stock-market crash, Vittoria asks Piero: "All those billions lost—where do they end up?" "Nowhere," Piero answers; and when Vittoria uncomprehendingly insists that they must go somewhere, he just shrugs his shoulders.[26] To substantiate this shrug, we can say that what constitutes the center of the world in *L'eclisse* is impersonal and unrepresentable; it is the sublime black vortex not only into which money disappears, but which sucks reality dry and gray (it is the ultimate source of the reification and fragmentation). Much has been said about reification in *L'eclisse*, but the modern world the film represents consists of things only secondarily—at its heart there is a virtual dimension, an uncontrollable mechanism which transforms and governs everything according to its own aleatory-inhuman (il)logic and which is death itself—unrepresentable self-justifying violence, whose immediate incarnations are colonialism or the struggle for world domination.[27]

But this is not the only virtuality that we encounter in *L'eclisse*. Although the characters (including Vittoria) are totally shot through by fantasies, which are ultimately fantasies of death, and thus they participate in the deathly enjoyment the Borsa stands for, we have already mentioned certain experiences which are visited on them that briefly break the spell of the black vortex. In the film this is most clearly exemplified by the epiphanic moment when in the middle of

---

[26] The whole exchange is as follows: V: "All those billions lost—where do they end up?" P: "Nowhere." V: "The guy who wins takes the money, right?" P: "Right." P: "From the guy who loses it." P: "It's not that simple." V: "But if someone loses, where does the money go?" Piero shrugs.

[27] Piero, for whom the Borsa constitutes a passion, is throughout the film associated with death and violence. Piero and Vittoria's first conversation takes place in the Borsa against a minute of silence for the dead broker. Their second meeting is occasioned by the death of the drunk who stole Piero's car. The only time we encounter Piero in his own apartment, we see him reading a newspaper in which the murder of a prostitute is reported.

the night Vittoria encounters the music of the flagpoles and is transported—a virtual dimension opens the night for her, the night that was originally the night of fake "primitive happiness." As we have noted, Vittoria does not learn much from such moments, but she does not necessarily have to be our representative, because the film includes experiences of this sort as being addressed not to the protagonist but immediately to the viewer—images which suggest the possibility of another virtuality, which may break the dominion of the black vortex. In fact, what may be called an epiphanic moment comes right after our first experience of the Borsa in the film. After the first sequence in the stock exchange (in which Vitoria meets Piero for the first time), the film cuts to an extreme long shot of Vittoria's apartment building. In the lower part of the shot we see the lighted entrance lobby through the huge panes of glass that separate the lobby from the outside world. It is night, and the upper part of the frame is almost completely black. Suddenly an opening appears in this blackness—this is Vittoria, who has just returned home and opened the door of her apartment. Then she switches on the light and two openings appear: a balcony door and a window. We see Vittoria moving further into her apartment, and then the film cuts to darkness. When we are disoriented this way, the light is switched on again and through the window (the camera is a few meters outside the window or a telephoto lens is being used) we can see the back of a woman in an old-fashioned dress looking out of the window into the light of day. This image is what we see for about five seconds, until the figure of Vittoria appears between the woman and the window, and we realize that what we have seen is a poster of an impressionist painting hanging on Vittoria's wall.[28] It is a magic moment in *L'eclisse*, because the poster has been placed so cleverly that for a moment we take the painted woman to be "real,"[29] and with her also the daylight she is looking into. Although we do not see what she sees, or rather precisely because of that, a new dimension appears to the viewer for a moment (when the woman is taken to be a character in the film), puncturing the darkness and opening a virtual daylight space beyond the dark dominion which later that night will become the stage of "going native." And it is only the viewer who has access to this vision, not Vittoria, so even before the epiphany of the flagpoles, the

---

[28] It appears to be a preparatory sketch or painting for Paul Signac's well-known "Sunday."
[29] In order to emphasize this effect, the figure of the woman is not only a flat shape on the wall but is additionally reflected in the "real" (diegetic) pane of the open window of the room in which the poster hangs, which gives the figure a fake three-dimensionality.

audience is offered an experience which suggests the possibility of breaking out of the confines of the world represented in the film.[30]

This "lyrical" little scene, which briefly suggests an opening into the "bright" virtual dimension, must be taken as a preliminary device to prepare us for the final "epic" solution attempted at the end of *L'eclisse*. No wonder, therefore, that the final montage is centered around a building site—by including certain indifferent (meaningless) sights, people, and objects in the background of the love affair between Vittoria and Piero, the film has been building up to the finale, in which the lovers are absent but in which these sights, people, and objects take on a new life. Of course, some of these objects may have a meaning within the protagonists' story if we chose to interpret them symbolically. For instance, the meeting point of the lovers depicted as a building site can be interpreted as suggesting an endeavor by Vittoria to build a new center for her life by means of the love affair (suggested in the initial sequence by an attempt to center an abstract object within a frame), and also suggesting that her endeavor is doomed from the start, because we know that for Piero their "usual place" will always remain peripheral—his true center is the Borsa. The creation of the new relationship around a plain water drum might be taken as representing an attempt by Vittoria to engage with a different source of life than the one represented by the Fungo (associated with Riccardo as a representative of a certain social group), and so on and so forth. But in the final montage *the drum is leaking*, that is, all symbolic meanings we have poured into it are disappearing quickly. During the last seven minutes we gradually become oblivious to the main protagonists (who were never too engaging anyway) and instead concentrate on what we actually see. These objects and people lose their connection to the story and become what they are, what they seem to be. And for those who hang on to the love story too persistently, Antonioni in the fourth minute of the montage introduces into the cityscape the back of a blond head looking very much like Vittoria's—but which, when it looks in another

---

[30] The importance of this scene is emphasized throughout the film by a certain mannerism (or shall we call it a stylistic device?)—the characters (especially Vittoria) are often presented looking at something, while the camera shows the back of their head included in the frame. It is not done in the manner of the standard over-the-shoulder-shot, in which the head is usually "peripheral," but precisely to emphasize the back of the head. This strategy is introduced with a special "estranging" emphasis right at the beginning of the film, in Riccardo's apartment sequence, when the shot of Vittoria looking at Riccardo with the back of her head visible almost exactly in the middle of the screen is spliced together with exactly the opposite shot—Riccardo looking at Vittoria with the back of his head visible also in the middle of the screen.

direction, turns out to be someone else's—to force us to abandon the story of the couple and look on this world with new eyes. I am in complete agreement with Mirella Joan Affron when she writes, "the composition of the edited sequence and its placement in the emphatic position are such that it takes on a form and meaning of its own, tending to replace the film at the conclusion of the viewing experience as well as in its recollection,"[31] but my interpretation of the sequence is exactly opposite to hers.[32] She claims that Antonioni's aim in the final montage is to extinguish all (symbolic) meaning so that "[a]bstraction breaks away from narrative altogether";[33] in other words, so that he has a field day with juxtaposing abstract shapes for purely aesthetic reasons.[34] But although abstract shapes and technological materials are featured in the final montage, so are clouds, ants, majestic acacias, and freshly sprinkled leaves; and of course people, who are not very amenable to being abstracted. Some of these people seem to be anxious (a young brunette waiting for something or somebody), some don't (the man reading the newspaper); there are even children playing and laughing. In fact, when dusk descends we even have a "homely" scene of people descending from a bus and returning home. Affron claims:

> Antonioni misleads the audience when, in the earlier sequences shot at the intersection, he has the camera insist upon particular shapes and objects (house, curb, wood, and so on), and invest them thereby with apparently inescapable significance. Following the direction of the camera, the viewer is bound to attempt to construe the sense of the repeated images. Only towards the end of the montage does she or he become sufficiently discouraged by change and novelty to abandon all attempts at allegory.[35]

But Antonioni misleads nobody. The camera "insists" on certain shapes and objects to include them into the meaning of the love story,[36] precisely in order

---

[31] Mirella Joan Affron, "Text and Memory in *Eclipse*," *Literatue/Film Quarterly* 9, no. 3 (1981): 146.
[32] Affron is in a minority here. The majority of the commentators on *L'eclisse* seem to think that the final montage is "meaningful" only because the absence of the lovers haunts the places presented in it; otherwise, it would not make sense. For instance: "The final sequence, I believe, creates nostalgia for the subject, so that by film's end the audience senses the full weight of Piero and Vittoria's absence" (Joseph Luzzi, *A Cinema of Poetry: Aesthetics of the Italian Art Film* (Baltimore: The Johns Hopkins University Press, 2014), 104).
[33] Affron, "Text and Memory," 150.
[34] Affron does not treat it as a liability, but of course a lot of commentators on Antonioni do. It is enough to quote Pasolini: "I don't like Antonioni, abstract art, or electronic music" (quoted in Sam Rohdie, *Antonioni* (London: BFI, 1990), unpaginated page).
[35] Affron, "Text and Memory," 150.
[36] Sometimes to give them the possibility of meaning, sometimes to give them much more—e.g., Piero is distracted from Vittoria by a nurse pulling up a stocking—suggesting that he is *this* kind of man.

that this *conventional* meaning (or its possibility) be erased in the final montage and so that these objects patterns, situations, and people stand on their own as *interesting in themselves*. To abandon all attempts at allegory is here the opposite of finding everything in the montage meaningless (as Affron suggests). The non-narrative final sequence brings to the fore what had been the background to the main narrative, and presents it in such a way that what we have taken for the reified world becomes suddenly transfigured by a mysterious light, radiating an aura which we cannot fathom, but which is indisputably there.[37] In other words, we are put in the position of Vittoria when she was confronted with the spectacle of the "singing" flagpoles in which the ordinary world (an unreconciled world of nature, technology and humanity, the world of both anxiety and joy) opens up to an imageless utopian dimension (a bright virtuality), which can only be represented by white light puncturing the black screen and which is the only antidote to the stifling dispensation of the black vortex. This, however, can happen only when the water drum (the conventional narrative) is completely empty of water (allegory). Thus, in the penultimate shot the empty water drum (it must be empty—it was leaking for hours), shown in the long shot, is lit up (like Vittoria's window in the night scene we have discussed earlier). Then the camera pans right to show us a nighttime street in the EUR focusing on a row of lampposts (Vittoria had her epiphany in front of flagpoles). And finally the film

---

[37] The indisputability of a strange "aura" is confirmed by the prevalent reification/nuclear holocaust interpretation—evidently the commentators who push it find the final montage "pregnant" with something. The problem is that they attempt to explain it with the most conventional (in fact, sentimental) meaning possible, which makes the ending *continuous* with the main story (reification of human relations/*malattia dei sentimenti*), while it seems quite obvious that such an "abstract" ending is there to "sabotage" the preceding narrative. Moreover, while so much ado has been made about the above-mentioned headlines in *L'Espresso*, in order to end the conventional interpretation on the ominous note, hardly anybody (apart from Rosenfeld) mentions another sinister newspaper, the one Piero reads in his apartment, in which the murder of a prostitute is reported. Does its presence mean that the murder has some bearing on the meaning of the film? Was Piero involved? These are ridiculous questions (although one has to ask them sometimes)—all of these references (and others we have mentioned) simply portray modern Italy (or the Western world in general) as the realm of imminent violence and death serving the black virtuality and have no bearing on the meaning of the final montage, which has to be contrasted with the main (but in a strange way secondary, as Affron notes) body of the film. Another way a case has been made for the "grim" interpretation of the final sequence is by maintaining that "anxious" music accompanies some parts of the final montage. Though Fusco's composition does not necessarily sound menacing, and can just be taken as additionally "estranging" the visual content, I find it a mistake that Antonioni in the final montage sometimes abandons his usual strategy to rely on diegetic or semi-diegetic sound. However, Fusco's music is more ambiguous than it seems, especially if one takes into consideration the soundtrack to the opening credits of *L'eclisse*. The credits are at first accompanied by a twist, which after a while turns into the "anxious" music. Aren't they closely associated this way? Isn't Fusco's "modernist" composition just a conventional musical illustration of the devouring darkness (the black vortex), which the white light aims to defeat?

cuts to a close-up of one of the streetlights, as it did previously to show us the strange woman looking at night into the light of day.

But this is not the final reflection to be made here, because this virtual light is perhaps not entirely virtual—perhaps it has an "earthly" incarnation. In the old days, when *L'eclisse* was released, it was enough to turn back to spot it, when the word "*Fine*" appeared on the screen: a projector radiated a light into the dark auditorium. Thus, what we have in the last shot is also a kind of meta-cinematic gesture: the bright virtual dimension must appear in the material world to be able to transform it, and the cinematic apparatus, usually so efficient in subverting the utopian impulse (both aspects—black and white—of Vittoria's fantasy are ultimately also the fantasies of mainstream cinema), may be used in order to help it appear. And such is the case in *L'eclisse*, so often accused of being depressing and pointless.

4

Red Desert (1964)

Red Desert, Antonioni's first production in color, begins like a weird futuristic movie: after the oneiric opening credit sequence, we see a close-up of fire bursting out of a stack, accompanied by a loud naturalistic series of explosions, and we find ourselves in an industrial landscape, including cranes, cooling towers, etc. We also see a crowd of people, some of them dressed in transparent plastic raincoats, who, in the rain, are watching a person who is being escorted by two uniformed men to the gates of the industrial works part of which we have just seen. Their overcoats and the landscape around them are the color of gray mud, so they look like the dispossessed underclass dominated by a police state that we have seen in so many cinematic dystopias. And in fact this is what they seem to be—it turns out that they are workers on strike and the man under escort is a strike-breaker. In this desperate landscape appear two creatures who do not fit the depressing image, Giuliana (Monica Vitti) and her son Valerio (Valerio Bartoleschi), dressed in what seem to be designer clothes in the colors of nature (green and brown). Yet their "aristocratic" appearance is immediately undermined by what Giuliana does: she buys a half-eaten sandwich from one of the strikers, runs for cover, and devours the food ravenously. We will have to return to this strange behavior, but for the moment what interests us is not what she does but what she perceives while she is eating. Hidden from the workers by a mound overgrown with blackened bushes, she looks at the landscape around the works and sees only filth: smoking ashes, mud, scraps of plastic and cardboard, rusted metal, and burning nondescript rubbish (to which she adds by dropping the paper in which the sandwich is wrapped). This is a landscape worthy of any post-apocalyptic dystopia.

But this is the end of the futuristic movie. Although the next sequence takes place inside a modern industrial plant (with a few intercuts to other establishments of the same sort, one of which is owned by Philips), complete with dials and levers straight out of Fritz Lang's *Metropolis* (1927), it turns out that we are in the Italy of the early 1960s in the modern petrochemical complex built outside Ravenna, among managing engineers with their technocratic and personal problems. Ugo (Carlo Chionetti), Giuliana's husband, is visited by his friend Corrado Zeller (Richard Harris), who is looking for workers willing to go with him to Patagonia, where he wants to start some industrial enterprise (unspecified in the film). But although they are in a workplace and the troubles they discuss are ordinary (problems with finding workers, a wife recovering from the shock caused by a car accident), their conversation takes place against the interior of the plant, which is radically different from the gloomy world outside, where we have seen the striking workers and Giuliana: it is clean, well-lighted, and full of colorful installations, in bright, mainly primary colors (red, green, blue, yellow, orange, lilac).

However, in the following scene the strangeness of the images we have seen so far seems to become qualified by a psychologization—in Ugo and Giuliana's home we watch as she goes through an anxiety attack and thereby a suggestion is offered that we witness the world as it is felt by a "neurotic" wife, who from now on becomes the main protagonist of the film. Giuliana suffers from repeated panic attacks and chronic state of depression (though this term was hardly ever used at the time the film was made), which causes her to have dreams about sinking into shifting sands, but when it comes to expressing what she feels in more abstract terms, Giuliana says, "She had to ask herself 'Who am I'?"[1] So what has happened that she no longer knows who she is?

There is a long critical tradition, going back to Antonioni's own comments about the film, which sees the cause of Giuliana's "neurosis" in her failure to adapt to the world around her, a world that has been transformed materially and symbolically by the modernization of Italy (especially in the north) in the 1950s during the so-called "economic miracle."[2] Antonioni obviously gestures in this direction, setting the action of his film in and around Ravenna, and prominently featuring in it the imposing petrochemical works built there, because one of the most important events that allowed the "miracle" to happen was the discovery of methane gas in the Po valley in the late 1940s. To exploit methane, ENI (Ente Nazionale Idrocarburi), a state holding company, was created in 1953, managed

---

[1] Giuliana is speaking about herself pretending she is speaking about a girl she met at a (possibly psychiatric) clinic, in which she spent some time after her car accident, which, as we learn later, had in fact been a suicide attempt. Unless otherwise stated, all translations come from the subtitles on the DVD/Blu-ray release of *Red Desert* by British Film Institute (2011).

[2] "Giuliana cannot adapt to the new 'way' of life and she goes through a crisis, while her husband, on the other hand, is content with his lot in life." Antonioni, *The Architecture of Vision*, 284.

by Enrico Mattei, who quickly turned it into an industrial empire. Using the profits from the methane gas he "soon diversified through five major operating companies into a bewildering number of activities, including petrochemicals, motels and *autostrade*, synthetic rubber, steel piping, contract engineering and construction, textiles, and nuclear power and research."[3] What is interesting, however, is the fact that, although the ensuing rapid modernization changed the image of Italy forever, unlike in his previous three films, in *Red Desert* Antonioni avoids showing the most visible urbanizing and architectural effects of the "miracle." Its only material traces are modern petrochemical and scientific installations (the works outside Ravenna and the radiotelescope in Medicina) and industrial pollution.[4]

Giuliana's fantasy, recounted by her to her sick son (and shown visually against her voiceover), of an island where a sun-tanned adolescent girl spends her time alone but happy among "the cormorants and sea gulls and wild rabbits" on a beach of pink sand is usually taken as representing Giuliana's ideal world and hence constituting a comment on the source of her "neurosis": the island is a natural paradise in which peaceful enjoyment of one's life is finally possible. However, there are a number of problems with such a facile opposition (industrial Italy vs. the paradisial island) and they register in the film even on the most superficial level of vision. For instance, the sand is said to be pink in Giuliana's voiceover but we cannot actually see this; or (which we do see) a "happy" rabbit appears on the beach but suddenly goes crazy and jumps blindly into the sea, not a perfect environment for a rabbit, to say the least.[5] It is also interesting that although, according to Antonioni,[6] the island fantasy was the only part of the movie in which the cinematographer did not alter natural colors—while *Red Desert* production is famous for altering "crude" reality for the purposes of Antonioni's artistic vision (by painting the grass green, etc.[7])—the fantasy looks much more artificial than the "gothic" industrial images. So perhaps the status

---

[3] Ginsborg, *A History of Contemporary Italy*, 163.
[4] There is one exception, however: the unfinished, and therefore somewhat desolate, workers' housing estate in Ferrara, where Corrado goes to recruit a worker, accompanied by Giuliana.
[5] In his critical commentary in the British Film Institute DVD/Blu-ray edition, David Forgacs claims that the beach sand on Budelli island, north of Sardinia, where the sequence was shot, really was pink but it did not register in Technicolor. As to the rabbit, when released from its cage, it was probably so scared that it did not know what it was doing, but Antonioni left it at that.
[6] Antonioni, *Architecture of Vision*, 285.
[7] Antonioni did not trust the laboratory to create the desired effects while developing the film, so the alterations of color had to be done by hand-painting the objects (Antonioni, *Architecture of Vision*, 204).

of the fantasy in the film is not so obviously "happy" and its natural imagery is more ambiguous than it seems.[8] But how could the fantasy be related to the rest of the film if its status as an image of the ideal of the good life seems suspicious?

Red Desert is a film in which naturalistic images of degraded nature abound. Although they seem to be contrasted with the island fantasy created by Giuliana, her fantasy of nature is not the only one in the film. Interestingly, while her fantasy is explicitly "anti-social" (as the voiceover explains, the girl is bored and frightened by grown-ups, and does not like children her own age, so she is always alone), another fantasy of nature pops up in the only "festive" sequence of the film, the party that takes place in a cabin on the seashore which belongs to Ugo's associate, Max (Aldo Grotti).

After a meal consisting, among other things, of wine and quail eggs, the party—Max, his wife Linda (Xenia Valderi), their friend Mili (Rita Renoir), Ugo, Giuliana, and Corrado (all representatives of the new managerial class and their wives)—enter a small compartment, painted flaming red and containing nothing but a huge bed, to engage in mild sexual games, which revolve around the efficacy of quail eggs as an aphrodisiac. Their antics are interrupted by the arrival of a couple who turn out to be one of Max's workers, Orlando, and his girlfriend. Orlando joins in the discussion about aphrodisiacs and raises the stakes by describing the ultimate "real thing," "the stuff that the Negros use" in Africa "made from crocodile fat and some spicy herbs" to prolong erection "for several hours"; after which other examples follow: crushed rhinoceros horn, dried sharks' fins, queen bee food. Thus we are presented with another fantasy of nature that allows true enjoyment of life (this time an excessive one), which, moreover, is also a social fantasy. While for the managerial party the only aphrodisiac effect of quail eggs is produced by talking about the aphrodisiac effect of quail eggs (it is the signifier that arouses, but disappointingly[9]), the secret of true satisfaction seems to belong to the worker, who is supposed to be less alienated from his body,[10] or even more to the phantasmatic Negro who has his secret "natural" ways to make the best of life. Moreover, it is also important to note how, in Max's fantasy, the worker's enjoyment operates: "He has a different girl every day; he's fantastic," he says. And similarly, as we can see, in Max's cabin

---

[8] At least one critic finds the fantasy poisonous: Arrowsmith, *Antonioni*, 97–9.
[9] Having eaten the eggs, Giuliana announces to everybody that she wants to make love, but she has obviously joined in the "talking" erotic game, that is, she is emulating the behavior of the others.
[10] This fantasy is clinched for the managerial party by the worker's girlfriend when she emphasizes the separation between words and deeds: "I'd rather do certain things than talk about them."

(or at least for Max) all the female members of the party are interchangeable—they are just anonymous sexual objects (of course, Max invites Orlando's girlfriend to join them the moment he notices her). This is emphasized, on the one hand, by the disappearance of intimacy—that is, separation between the bodies—when they all cavort on one big mattress,[11] and, on the other hand, by shooting the bed scene in such a way that the bodies of the participants, and especially the female bodies, become fragmented by the mirror hanging above the bed: in the same shot we see a fragment of a human figure in one place filmed by the camera "straightforwardly" (e.g., Mili's legs) and another fragment of the same figure reflected in the mirror (Mili from the waist up); or we don't see a given person in a shot, only a part of her or him reflected in the mirror and mixed up with the other characters. Therefore we can be quite sure that the worker joins in the discussion about aphrodisiacs so eagerly because, on the one hand, he feels at home in this fantasy of nature, and, on the other hand, because from his position a mirror social fantasy is superimposed on it—from his perspective those who possess the secret of enjoyment are the knowledgeable managers: they surely must get much more of what they are doing together in one bed than he can get out of his single girlfriend. In this solidarity between the worker and the "ruthless capitalist"[12] over the phantasmatic object of enjoyment, class differences seem to disappear when political/social antagonism is dissimulated by the common ideology of individual satisfaction. Max's (and Orlando's) African fantasy, therefore, is not really a natural fantasy at all; it only has an exotic African envelope, painted flaming red to mark its imaginary intensity, while behind the artificial coloring it is the fantasy of the consumer's paradise—the social cement of the new Italy.

Moreover, although at first sight Giuliana's fantasy seems radically different from Max's, they have a number of things in common. The island is also an exotic place for the full satisfaction of the girl's private needs (she is always alone), and this imaginary fullness is emphasized by the saturated colors: the azure sky, the emerald water, the (supposedly) pink sand. In other words, what we see as the island fantasy is the "hyperreal" nature known from tourist brochures—an idealized holiday destination in which nature is exclusively "nice" (its dangerous or unpleasant aspects, like annoying insects, have disappeared)

---

[11] Noted by Forgacs in the DVD commentary.
[12] Max has all the characteristics of such a stock figure: "He's always ready to pounce—on a bankrupt factory or a woman in difficulties," says Mili.

and where one does not have to go to school or work. In other words, this happy image of balanced enjoyment is simply a consumer product of an industry—the Italian (or, in fact, international) tourist industry. Therefore Giuliana's and Max's fantasies of nature have to be taken as complementary,[13] because consumerism can function only by offering *both* of these fantasies of enjoyment at the same time: to experience life as ecstatically as possible and, as an antidote to that, to fulfill ourselves by establishing a balanced satisfaction. Moreover, despite appearances, the "antidotal" attitude is not secondary, that is, "reactive" in this pair, but, in fact, constitutes a matrix for it: the excessive fantasy that in spite of its "wildness" does not destabilize anything and the balanced life that in spite of its repetitiveness is constantly exciting and/or fulfilling.[14] Therefore, contrary to what most of the critics claim, there is no discontinuity between the colors of the island sequence (natural) and the colors encountered in the factory or Max's cabin (primary)—the difference is quantitative, not qualitative, like the difference in "arousal effect" between quail eggs and crocodile fat with herbs.

The "artificial," non-naturalistic use of colors in *Red Desert* has often been noted, but usually this has been ascribed to Antonioni's "delirious" aestheticism[15] and/or to his interest in modern art.[16] His statements on this matter, however, point in a more interesting direction:

> In *Red Desert*, we are in an industrial world which every day produces millions of objects of all types, all in color. Just one of these objects is sufficient—and who can do without them?—to introduce into the house an echo of industrial living. Thus, our houses are full of color, and our streets and public places are full of colorful posters. With the invasion of colors we have become addicted to them.[17]

Colors have invaded all aspects of modern life and have irreversibly transformed the world we live in. But how was this invasion possible?

Because the factory presented by Antonioni in *Red Desert* is a petrochemical plant, one cannot avoid associating it with plastic, that most revolutionary and

---

[13] To be more precise, the complementarity concerns only the first part of Giuliana's fantasy, before the sailing ship appears. We will return to this.
[14] Alenka Zupančič, *The Shortest Shadow: Nietzsche's Philosophy of the Two* (Cambridge, MA: The MIT Press, 2003), 67.
[15] "[Antonioni] has finally succeeded in representing the world seen through *his* own eyes *because he substituted, wholly, the world-view of a sick woman for his own vision, which is delirious with estheticism.*" Pasolini, "The Cinema of Poetry," 553; Pasolini's italics.
[16] See, for instance, Angela Dalle Vacche, *Cinema and Painting: How Art Is Used in Film* (Austin: University of Texas Press, 1996), 43–80.
[17] Antonioni, *Architecture of Vision*, 283.

colorful product derived from oil, which has been transforming the face of the Western civilization, since the 1950s, that is, from the start of the Italian economic "miracle." Yet the excessive "painting over" of modernity with the colors of plastic does not come without a price. While industry creates plastic as the first universal substance (a substance which can imitate any other substance[18]), it also brings about the universal presence of filth as its by-product. On the one hand, this is the "real" filth of non-biodegradable industrial pollution, which destroys specific indigenous forms of life around Ravenna (and of course throughout Italy), turning the landscape into a kind of polluted marsh (a "universal" form of landscape that can be created almost anywhere), and, on the other, the metaphoric filthiness of the possibility, which quickly becomes a necessity, of gaining absolute control over matter and society by recreating it out of plastic: by mass production of affordable objects (including plastic copies of almost anything), and by creating a society in which bonds between lone individuals are to be mediated by these consumer products, that is, by reducing all difference to the universal plastic substance of consumer enjoyment. In other words, with the appearance of plastic and the universal invasion of artificial colors the reign of consumerism is instituted, which abolishes all particularisms and for the first time in history unifies Italy under one idol, the market.[19]

One can, however, object that this universal invasion is precisely what is *not* shown in *Red Desert*, because the film meticulously avoids showing "our houses, … our streets and public places" which Antonioni speaks about in the above quotation, and when they are shown they are presented as almost colorless—"antiseptic" (like Giuliana's home and Corrado's hotel room) or melancholy (like the Via Alighieri, where Giuliana wants to open her shop).[20] But this is precisely the point: despite appearances consumer Italy is a filthy place (even the fruit at a vendor's stall has the color of ashes in the Via Alighieri), and because of that the artificial plastic coloring of modern industrial civilization is reflected back at the place from where products offered for consumer enjoyment

---

[18] In a famous discussion of simulacra, Baudrillard marks out stucco as the first attempt to create such a substance, but of course plastic is the final fulfillment of this idea. Jean Baudrillard, *Symbolic Exchange and Death*, trans. Ian Hamilton Grant (London: Sage, 1993), 52.

[19] In a famous article, originally published as "Il vuoto del potere in Italia" ("The Power Void in Italy") in *Corriere della sera* on February 1, 1975, Pasolini discusses the consumerist unification of Italy in similar terms (but without the reference to plastic): the caesura between "fascist fascist" Italy and the "fascist consumerist" Italy is the disappearance of fireflies because of the industrial pollution. English translation by Christopher Mott, accessed September 24, 2019, http://www.diagonalthoughts.com/?p=2107.

[20] There is one exception, a street seen from the lobby of Corrado's hotel, to which we will return.

come, the factory itself, but in its spectral incarnation as yet another fantasy of nature. While "real" nature (trees and bushes) is dead outside, inside the plant the machinery seems to have taken on some mysterious life, producing not "plastic" (artificial substance of enjoyment) but a wind which ruffles Giuliana's hair (she comes to visit her husband at work and thus meets Corrado) and geysers of steam at her feet. But not only that, the plant as a whole seems to possess some kind of mysterious vivacity—the life of a potentially dangerous but controlled animal: at the beginning of the strike sequence we see it spitting fire into the air and creating desolation all around; at the end of Ugo's conversation with Corrado we see the breath of the dragon[21]: a massive release of steam which fills the whole screen and causes the filthy world to disappear. In other words, we are back in the (phantasmatic) jungles of Africa, and therefore the locus of excessive enjoyment, but now it is the factory which really "enjoys," while people who serve it, like Ugo, look thoroughly drained of life.[22]

Giuliana's question "Who am I?" is at the core of her depression. When in Ferrara—where they go to persuade a worker to work for Corrado in Patagonia—she tries to explain to Corrado her feeling of sinking, she speaks about the lack of support, "of being on the verge of drowning, with nothing … not even a husband." But, in the world in which traditional social bonds and supports have disintegrated and every relation is mediated by individual satisfaction (the support of the market), what is a husband (or a lover)? And what does it mean to lose him?

Although Giuliana's problems have a lot to do with her inability to answer these questions, she comes close to an answer in their later conversation on an offshore rig when she says to Corrado: "If Ugo had looked at me as you do, he'd have understood many things." In other words, her loss of herself is related to her loss of Ugo's look of love. But what does such a look consist of? Its structure too is in a sense phantasmatic: the lover sees in the beloved an enigmatic object which the lover lacks but, because it is not reducible to any of the beloved's positive features, it is as enigmatic to the beloved, since s/he is not able to grasp what it is and therefore locate it in him/herself. In other words, the beloved, rather

---

[21] Murray Pomerance, *Michelangelo Red Antonioni Blue: Eight Reflections on Cinema* (Berkeley: University of California Press, 2011), 71.

[22] One can say that Ugo serves the factory not only at work but also at home, indoctrinating Valerio about the beauty of instruments like a gyroscope or a microscope (he keeps saying about them: "Que bello!").

than being plagued by the question "Who am I?" (whose fuller version is "Who am I *for the Other*?," that is, ultimately, "What is my worth?"), finds that for the lover, s/he is not an anonymous and interchangeable object (e.g., of enjoyment, as in Max's and Orlando's fantasy), but that there is something special in the beloved, which binds the lover to him/her and which is inexplicable for both of them. To put it differently, a beyond is created by the lover in the beloved, which makes the latter lovable but which is inaccessible to both of them. This structure of love, however, does not allow for a "harmonious" relation—even if love is reciprocal, the lovers are not two halves of a Platonic whole. Precisely because the elusive object, which instigates love, is inaccessible, while at the same time it constitutes the enigmatic "essence" of the beloved, the love relation is always "unbalanced": "I love you, but, because inexplicably I love in you something more than you … I mutilate you."[23] Rather than being satisfied with the positive features of the beloved, the lover always reaches for the beyond, the beloved's inaccessible essence, and therefore must destroy whatever balance has been tenuously established in the relationship. Thus dangerous excess (in the form of a death drive, of repeated reaching for this "beyond") is endemic to any real love relationship, but it is also precisely what feeds the love, what makes it alive. Although one can say that this is the "African," dark and excessive, aspect of love, it is something entirely different from Max's consumer fantasy.

And in the film there seems to be an image which relates to such a state of affairs in the earlier stage of the relationship between Giuliana and Ugo. As well as Max's cabin, in which the "African" sexual fantasy stakes its claims, there is another cabin in *Red Desert*, belonging to Giuliana and Ugo, which they visit briefly in the company of Corrado. It is in a state of advanced disrepair. Before Ugo enters it, he says that he has not visited it for two years and he touches Giuliana's arm affectionately, as if remembering the old days or trying to fortify her before a painful memory. Inside the cabin we see a natural landscape featuring zebras, which has nothing "flaming red" about it, but knowing it depicts the *wild* nature of Africa, we are sure it is not the image of Giuliana's island paradise. Seeing this African landscape Corrado, who is becoming more and more fascinated by

---

[23] Jacques Lacan, *The Seminar of Jacques Lacan, Book XI: The Four Fundamental Concepts of Psychoanalysis*, ed. Jacques-Alain Miller, trans. Alan Sheridan (New York: W. W. Norton, 1981), 268. The above conception of love is, of course, the Lacanian one (see, for instance: Jacques Lacan, *The Seminar of Jacques Lacan, Book VIII: Transference*, ed. Jacques-Alain Miller, trans. Bruce Fink (Cambridge: Polity Press, 2015), 52–3.

Giuliana, senses something that makes him a stranger there and immediately claims: "Sometimes I feel I have no right to be where I am."

But Giuliana's loss of love is not just a melancholic ailing—its effect is a state in which she not only loses interest in the world around her (everything looks like filth) but also experiences repeated panic attacks. When, during one of them, Corrado asks her what she is afraid of, she answers: "The streets, factories, colours, people—everything!"[24] Moreover, this complaint is "negatively" mirrored earlier in the film, when, speaking about herself under the guise of a patient she met in a clinic, she claims that the girl ended up there because "she wanted everything." The same "diagnosis" is repeated when Giuliana complains about the doctors' advice that in order to get better she should "learn how to love," love one thing at a time, "Love your husband, your son, a job, even a dog." Resisting this, she comes up with another, potentially infinite, list: "But not husband-son-job-dog-trees-river ...."

Strangely enough, the mechanism of infinite listing related to melancholia was described by Walter Benjamin in *The Origin of German Tragic Drama* (1928). Benjamin claims that the horizontal movement of allegory is at the center of the discourse of mourning. While the symbol is vertical and aims to embody a transcendental (and thus redeeming) truth, allegory is immanent to the secularized world of "the insuperable despair": "[T]he allegorical physiognomy of the nature-history ... is present in reality in the form of the ruin."[25] In other words, whether they are verbal or pictorial, images used in the allegorical discourse of melancholy become "designified" in the sense that they no longer have any autonomous meaning (which would allow for a hierarchy of importance); they become completely interchangeable, because each of them is simply yet another allegory of something which is the cause of "the hopelessness of the earthly condition,"[26] the missing value of the world. And because everything in the world, looked at from the melancholic perspective, is always already a ruin (even a newborn baby is an image of mortality), the images are not only interchangeable—their enumeration is potentially infinite and any end of the list is arbitrary.

---

[24] There are other lists related to the same kind of anxiety, for instance: "My hair hurts, my eyes hurt, my throat, my mouth ...." The list does not continue only because Giuliana has no strength to go on.
[25] Walter Benjamin, *The Origin of German Tragic Drama*, trans. John Osborne (London: New Left Books, 1977), 78, 177.
[26] Ibid., 81.

Giuliana's lists function in a similar manner: wherever she looks she sees ruins and emptiness, which in the modernized world takes the form of industrial filth. But the filth and her infinite lists are clearly related to the aforementioned question she has asked herself: "Who am I?" If she knew who she were, that is, if there was some principle in her life that could bring a hierarchy back into her reality, the lists would not have to be extended to encompass everything.[27] This is precisely what she is seeking when she complains to Corrado: "But what do people expect me to do with my eyes? What should I look at?" The ordering principle was precisely what she lost with Ugo's love, because in order that reality not be a chaos of unrelated phenomena it has to be enframed by an element that incarnates the transcendence of the positive elements of reality. In the context of the baroque *Trauerspiel*, Benjamin calls this element a symbol, which, if it existed, would give meaning to the dead objects in the world and make the world alive once again. But in the context of *Red Desert*, it was Ugo's loving look that installed an enigmatic object in Giuliana and hence created a transcendence (her feeling of being worthy of love) by the mediation of which she could relate to both her symbolic roles as a wife and a mother and other aspects of reality. Without this mediation she is constantly at the mercy of opaque objects which can never be perceived as neutral (distanced through mediation) and therefore impose themselves as either exciting (why not love everything) or threatening (I'm afraid of everything). In other words, Giuliana's anxiety is produced by permanent excitation, the effect of which is melancholic paralysis, with intermittent bouts of anxiety when a meaningless object attacks.[28] In this way the omnipresent filth that covers everything takes on its full metaphoric meaning: it figures not only the emptiness (lack of value) that Giuliana sees all around her but also the *painful* substance of excitation. Giuliana would like to have everything, but it is only through the mediation of "one" (installed by the loving look) that she can have it, and, when this "one" is lacking, others to whom she feels attached (husband, son, friends) can only be imagined by her as a protective shield to separate her from the attacks of the exciting/frightening

---

[27] A similar point is made by Luzzi: "Part of her problem is hermeneutic, for she cannot distinguish between what is and is not important in her life." *A Cinema of Poetry*, 48.

[28] Thus Giuliana's seemingly innocent remark about her looking for colors to paint her shop that do not disturb the objects may bear relation to her anxiety. One of the examples of an attack by an object is a newspaper which unexpectedly floats down toward Giuliana and Corrado in front of her shop in the Via Alighieri. Giuliana approaches it with a sort of interest (not as a source of information but as an object) but when it wraps itself around hers legs, and she steps over it to let the wind blow it down the street, we immediately find that she feels "ill" and has to sit down.

objects of the world—"You know what I'd like? Everyone who's ever cared for me, I'd like them all around me like a wall," she tells Corrado.[29]

In light of the above, what happens in the second part of the island fantasy is crucial. In it, the static world of idealized enjoyment (perfect weather, pink sand, "nice" animals and plants, happy solitude as the absence of any intrusion) is disturbed by the appearance on the horizon (in the distance, not too close) of an element which destroys the peace of the girl. It is "a real sailing boat" with white sails, which "could brave the tempests and oceans of the world; maybe even beyond, who knows?" The girl notices the ship and swims out to meet it—"seen from afar, it looked splendid; but near to, it was mysterious." However, it turns out that there is nobody on board and before the girl reaches the ship it turns away and disappears in the distance. Disappointed, the girl returns to the beach, but there she comes across another mystery: she hears a disembodied voice (the same female voice we have heard in the opening credits sequence of the film) and while searching for its source she notices that the limestone rocks lining the shore look like human flesh. Although the source of the voice is never found by the girl, when, at the end of the story, Valerio asks Giuliana who was singing, she answers: "Everyone was singing" ("Tutti cantavano").

The fantasy is clearly one in which an enigmatic (and empty!) object appears on the horizon in order to disturb and reconfigure the elements of the girl's world by introducing mystery into it, a beyond of the world, which is rough (tempests-disturbance), that is, different from the peaceful world of the girl. But in fact this beyond does not exist "beyond the world"—it is immediately reinscribed into the girl's world as another enigmatic event, a singing voice, the pursuit of whose origin makes the girl realize things she has not noticed before about the objects she has known so well: the fleshy appearance of the rocks. Thus the appearance of an enigmatic object unbalances the stasis and introduces interpretation, that is, the movement of desire into the static desireless constellation (isn't the Technicolor "cuteness" of the island images, its tourist brochure quality, another kind of filth that stains the paradise?) and lets the girl breathe the fresh air of the beyond, which is, however, not external to the constellation, but divides it from within. What the girl notices about the rocks is, after all, something that she also notices about herself and her own flesh: the mystery of her awakening

---

[29] Another instance of the same complaint is when she says to Corrado that if she were to leave she would take everything with her, even the ashtrays. This time "everything" does not mean the whole world, but all the objects and people in it to which she feels attached, that are "hers" (including ashtrays).

sexuality.³⁰ When the chaos of static objects is put into order by the mediation of the beyond of desire, all of them begin to sing.³¹

Although the constellation present in the island fantasy, which is recounted by Giuliana about three-quarters of the way through the film, mirrors the situation she finds herself in in her life and therefore should be taken not as a passive escapist fantasy but as an attempt to break out of her depressed state, one still has to ask where the imagery that is employed in the fantasy comes from. Its sources are not difficult to find. When, after meeting Giuliana for the first time in Ugo's plant, Corrado finds her in the space she wants to turn into a shop in the Via Alighieri, he briefly speaks about his life, in which he has often moved from place to place, and tells her that because he likes it "neither here nor there" ("né qui né là"),³² he "decided to leave" Italy. But of course, he comes to the shop not to speak about his life but because he is attracted to Giuliana who, apart from being a beautiful woman, also intrigues him. They go together to Ferrara and Medicina, they talk a lot (Ugo throughout the film is presented as a rather reticent man), mostly about Giuliana, and in the words that are exchanged between them, in the words that Corrado uses to find his way into her world in order to seduce her, she feels that the look she has been missing, the look that constructs the enigmatic object in her, is being reconstituted again through the man. And we do not have to wait long for the special object which is a correlative of this look to appear in the film: when the members of the party which will end up in Max's cabin are meeting, Giuliana looks the other way and sees a strange, mysterious image on the horizon: a cargo ship (Corrado is about to go away) moving through a group of trees (it is moving along a canal hidden from our view), which nobody else sees. "What are you looking at?" Corrado asks her, surprised that she is staring into the distance, but he is not answered. In this case Giuliana knows perfectly what she should do with her eyes.

---

[30] Using a Lacanian context and particularly Michel Chion's work on acousmatic voice, Restivo interprets the singing voice in *Red Desert* as "a manifestation of the pure invocatory drive" and argues, using Joan Copjec's remarks on Roland Barthes's "The Grain of Voice," that "what erupts in *Red Desert* is always drive, never desire" (*The Cinema of Economic Miracles*, 139). Although my interpretation has a number of points in common with Restivo's and its context is also Lacanian, for the reasons explained above I do not believe the voice serves as a manifestation of drive in the island fantasy.

[31] The girl is alone on the beach but both the adolescent sexual context of the desire and Giuliana's "tutti cantavano" suggest an interpersonal (phantasmatic) or even social (utopian) potentiality which wakes the girl to the singing of the world.

[32] BFI DVD translation: "I don't like to stay in one place."

But this is not the first time we see a cargo ship moving away, one also appears in the opening credits sequence, which bears a curious resemblance to Giuliana's island fantasy. Here, to the accompaniment of electronically distorted sounds, we see out-of-focus images of strange towers and other constructions wrapped in smoke.[33] At first the objects, presented in extreme long shots, are pale and yellow-grayish, like the smoke, but gradually the camera moves closer and the installations become more and more colorful. As in Giuliana's island fantasy, in which there is nothing unpleasant about nature, there seem to be nothing unpleasant about the industrial installations; the smoke makes them simply more mysterious, like the fog which wraps about a castle in a Romantic painting, and the pastel colors of the plant make it look like a strange fairyland. This fairyland effect is, in fact, reinforced when, just as the saturation of colors begins to take place, another element is introduced into the constellation: the electronic noises are joined by a female singing voice and, if one pays attention to the moment the voice appears in the opening sequence, it is against a shot which shows an installation consisting of domes and spires which look almost like Hagia Sophia complete with its minarets. Hence the "muezzin" (even if female) voice, although strange, does not seem out of place and greatly contributes to the oneiric effect of the sequence which ends with a crane shot of a cargo ship slowly moving away down a canal.

Compared with Giuliana's island fantasy, the opening sequence reverses the order of the appearance of the voice and the ship: the voice appears "out of nowhere"[34] and accompanies the images to the final shot of a leaving ship. Therefore rather than an enigmatic beyond incorporating itself into the familiar rocks and making them mysterious flesh, like in Giuliana's island fantasy, we see here the opposite operation: the enigmatic "flesh" of the factory externalizing itself into a mysterious beyond. It is not difficult to guess whose fantasy rules the opening sequence: Corrado's. Yet unlike the beyond of Giuliana's vision, the beyond of the fairy factory offers only stasis in the form of infinite repetition of the same. Whereas in Giuliana's fantasy the beyond appeared as an empty object which exploded the configuration of the static world in which the girl lived, the beyond of the factory fantasy relies on infinite expansion, that is, reproduction of the mysteriousness and sweetness of the vision of the sublime factory. In

---

[33] To be exact, the first image we see in the first traveling shot, before we find ourselves among the industrial installations, is of leafless trees.
[34] Out of "Hagia Sophia," in fact—it is the chant of the new religion.

other words, the factory can only export the cleaned-up, colored, and hyped-up vision of itself "beyond." And this is precisely what Corrado wants to do: liking it "neither here nor there" in Italy (which is full of industrial filth), he is exporting Mattei's vision to Patagonia in a nice, clean, and colorful phantasmatic envelope (when asked by Giuliana what he believes in, he says he believes in progress and perhaps even socialism). In other words, although Corrado seems to be presented as a "romantic" capitalist, different from other managers (Ugo, Max), who are satisfied with themselves and the world around them, because he is restless and feels always out of place, it is he who incarnates most fully the fantasy which is the essence of "the miracle"—the infinite colonization of the beyond by the same.

The deceitfulness of the opening sequence fantasy is related to yet another of its strange features—it is shot out of focus. Initially, the blurred visuals add to the mysterious atmosphere of the sequence by bringing to mind the distortion of vision created by (e.g., desert) heat and therefore enhancing the "mirage" (miraculous) effect. But, as it turns out, the out-of-focus background or foreground is a technique on which Antonioni relies continuously in the film[35] to make the world represented in it more claustrophobic, or, one might say, to indicate the clandestine presence of the intrusive and formless substance on which the fantasy is founded, whose other incarnation in the film is filth.[36]

Moreover, Giuliana's island fantasy does not tell us everything about the nature of the figure of the ship: it does not have only a magnificent-mysterious incarnation. When everybody in Max's cabin is happy getting off on discussing quail eggs and Mili is trying to arouse Max by "massaging" his knee, Giuliana inadvertently leans against Corrado and immediately hears a cry. While Max valiantly blathers about his "sweet" excitement, so that it should materialize, the cry is a puzzling warning of the imminence of something opaque and terrifying. And when the pseudo-orgy—in which only words are the means of enjoyment—peters out in sexual frustration, released in the form of jubilant aggression when the participants demolish the wooden interior of the cabin to feed the fire in the stove, and Giuliana's closeness to Corrado becomes too overwhelming ("I can't

---

[35] Unlike in his earlier movies in which everything is usually perfectly in focus, no matter what distance from the lens.

[36] Another technique often used in the film is to shoot the scene (especially in long shots) with a telephoto lens. The effect is "flatness" (the three-dimensionality, that is, "openness" of space is reduced) and a slight blurring of the image. In other words, in the telephoto shots, a similar effect is achieved as in the blurred backgrounds or foregrounds which completely destroy three-dimensional space, creating a stifling lack of depth.

look at the sea [Corrado's element] for long, otherwise I lose interest in what happens on land," she says), we witness the arrival of an enormous dark hulk, whose crew is immediately pronounced infected (the yellow flag of contagion is hoisted on the mast), while Giuliana's sinking feeling returns. This time the ship is not a mysterious appearance on the horizon that opens a beyond and with it the space of desire; on the contrary, it appears at the very door of the cabin and its presence is opaque and completely overwhelming. Giuliana's too close proximity to the object of her fantasy (Corrado "in the flesh") materializes in the warning cry (rather than a singing voice) and then the opaque ship, and with it the invasion of excitation (panic, anxiety), which cannot be stopped by being surrounded by everyone who has ever cared for her. In fact, when the other members of the party are lined up before Giuliana on the pier next to the cabin, a wall of fog separates her from the world and the sinking feeling becomes unbearable—she gets into a car and almost drives into the sea (she stops the car at the very edge of the pier).[37]

After that, as if in order to make up for the horror of the encounter with the lethal hulk, the images of "good" ships start to proliferate in the film—they are lightly colored or white and on the move, so one might expect that their presence is stabilizing (in a kind of "scientific" joke on Antonioni's part, Ugo even explains to Valerio that every ship has a gyroscope to keep it steady in rough seas). So all seems to be going well, when, unexpectedly, Giuliana's other symbolic anchor ("husband" was the first) is removed. Now it is Valerio who becomes another tester of her "gyroscope." Moreover, this time it seems that it is nature itself which has knocked on Giuliana's door to show its ugly side: Valerio tells her that his body is failing him, that he cannot feel his legs.[38] Giuliana's first reaction is, helplessly, to offer him her own medicine: "Come and look at this beautiful boat. It's so big, and all white." When this remedy does not work, the feelings of guilt that she does not know how to be a mother (she wonders whether she

---

[37] Linda also claims to have heard the cry, which is an early indication of Corrado's mistaken assumptions concerning Giuliana. Among the members of the party it is Linda (not Corrado) who seems to have the strongest empathetic connection to Giuliana: concerning aphrodisiacs, Max tells her, "you keep quiet, you're well away as it is," and, when pressed by the men, she concedes that perhaps the cry she heard came from a novel (fantasy) she was reading in the "red room" before the others entered it. Moreover, when Giuliana almost kills herself, Linda bursts out crying—instead of Giuliana, as it were.

[38] When talking to Corrado in Ferrara about having "nothing, not even a husband," Corrado (understanding that she is speaking about herself under the guise of another) also questions her about her son: "Not even her son?" To which Giuliana answers, putting also this symbolic attachment in doubt: "Yes, him. But that girl had no children."

has forgotten about an installment of polio vaccine) are awakened in Giuliana, and her panic rises. Then, when she finally finds out that her son has only been pretending,[39] to the panic is added a feeling of alienation from him ("He doesn't need me," she says: in her estimation she has neither husband nor son now), which leads to another anxiety attack. Thus she runs to the only person who, she thinks, can offer remedy.

Giuliana's arrival at Corrado's hotel is rendered explicitly as a recourse to the stabilizing ("normalizing") force of the ship fantasy—when we cut to the hotel lobby, it is painted uniformly white—the walls, the furniture, including even plants (two ficuses on each side of the entrance)—and while Giuliana is entering, through the window and transparent doors of the lobby, we can see, for the only time in the film, the ordinary life of a city street in naturalistic colors: a yellow Agip van passing by, some people walking, a cyclist carrying a green plant on his bike, a parked Fiat 500. The "normality" of life is literally enframed here by the white-sail fantasy related to Corrado (even his car is white), but it is only from the film-viewer's perspective, not Giuliana's.

But what she encounters in Corrado's room is no longer the releasing fantasy of the beyond that he has so far represented, but the realization of what she sensed in Max's cabin, the very premonition of which made her lose her balance and want to drive off the pier. This is emphasized by the gesture by which the "normal" world we have just seen outside the hotel lobby is erased. After Giuliana claims that she would like to have everyone who's ever cared for her form a wall around her, Corrado does precisely that—he takes a seat on the bed (which will be the place of Giuliana's "undoing") right in front of Giuliana, and cuts her entirely off from the view of the camera.[40] And when the world is gone, the fantasy of the beyond must disintegrate, too. We recall that the first appearance of the mysterious ship of Giuliana's fantasy (moving through a group of trees) was accompanied by Corrado's question: "What are you looking at?" In his room Corrado repeats the same question when Giuliana begins staring intently at the white wall, which looks ordinary to him. But when we see it from her point of view, the "good" stabilizing object is nowhere to be seen; there are only suffocating free-floating colors, which dissolve the world. Thus begins the plunge into the void, opening in the shifting sands, which, however, is not the void of nothingness, but of excitation. Yet it is very different from the

[39] Whether Valerio pretended to be ill or his disability was a "hysterical" symptom remains unclear.
[40] As the fog separated Giulaina from the world on the pier next to Max's cabin.

imaginary "flaming red" enjoyment of genital pleasure that Max dreams about in his African fantasies—it is a convulsive experience unimaginable for the visitors to Max's cabin. In order to emphasize this contrast, Antonioni's way of rendering the sexual encounter between Corrado and Giuliana explicitly refers to the scene in the red compartment of Max's cabin: the bed-railings in Corrado's room are bright red and the bodies become fragmented by the framing of the camera (with special attention to Giuliana's convulsively twitching legs and hands).[41] The sexual act in the hotel room is made to look almost the same as an anxiety attack.

Moreover, the image of Corrado's room, painted uniformly pink (including the formerly red bed-railings), with which the hotel sequence ends, obviously takes us back to Giuliana's fantasy: we are back on the pink beach (which this time does look pink). The white ship has been visited and the source of the song among the fleshy rocks has been found[42] but it has turned out that both the ship and the voice were pure semblances not connected to any positive features of Corrado but only to the place he represented in Giuliana's fantasy. The "realization" of the fantasy has caused only what it was supposed to prevent: more sinking. So, after Corrado has driven her from his hotel to her shop, Giuliana tells him that she no longer feels attached to him because the enigmatic object is gone—to her he is now no more than her former partner in yet another symbolic role to which she cannot really relate: an unfaithful wife.

Yet because she knows (she has just experienced it) that, as she says to Corrado before he leaves, "there's something terrible in reality,"[43] it is time to confront the real Thing dissimulated by the mysterious-beautiful fantasy ship on the horizon, the real meaning of going away. This is done in the nightmarish penultimate sequence in which, at night, Giuliana confronts the "contagion" itself, the overwhelmingly huge and motionless hulk that had caused her to try to "go away" in front of Max's cabin, and in her earlier suicide attempt. The mysterious ship as a promise of "a place in the world when one goes to feel better" has exerted

---

[41] The fragmentation of Giuliana's body is reinforced by disorienting editing which disrupts continuity. For instance, Giuliana is lying on the bed being undressed by Corrado when she sees the "attacking" colors again, but after a cut we see her sitting in an armchair with Corrado standing next to her. This is not primarily an example of elliptic editing but displacement for the sake of disorientation.

[42] Arrowsmith, *Antonioni*, 102: "And in the writhing bodies of Corrado and Giuliana, Antonioni clearly *requires* his audience to see again those twisted torsos and buttocks discernible in the island's rocks ... and thus to recognize the actualization in the bedroom of the erotic suggestions so vivid in the Sardinian beach fantasy" (Arrowsmith's emphasis).

[43] "[A]nd I don't know what it is. Nobody tells me"—it is beyond words.

a strong pull on Giuliana, but the presence of this one is sheer oppressiveness: no whiff of mystery but incredible weight, no sweet song but an interminable scream stifled in the throat. When, in spite of her terror, she hesitatingly starts up the gangplank to enter it, she meets a sailor who speaks to her in a language (Turkish) which is the opposite of the sweet singing voice: although his voice is also incomprehensible, he is not an exotic stranger promising mysterious things, just a confusing and overwhelming presence, an obstacle blocking her entrance. So she hastily retreats ashore where she tries to gather her thoughts to explain herself. Although what she says is ambiguous and incoherent, it is interesting that, in spite of her former despairing attitude toward her social roles, her words articulate her resistance to the final plunge in the void of obliteration in terms of her position as a wife and a mother ("I'm not a single woman") and separation from enjoyment as a necessary condition of functioning in the symbolic ("the bodies are separated, ... if you prick me, you don't suffer"). Therefore it seems that, in spite of her problems with finding her place among the people around her, the vestiges of her symbolic attachments have been strengthened and not weakened by her repeated frustrations (with Ugo, Valerio, and Corrado) and her walking away from the shore, when her shadow disappears among the shadows of waterfront installations, is to be taken as at least a temporal overcoming of the fixation on "something terrible in reality."

Yet the confused language in which she "explains" herself indicates the tenuousness of her position, which the film reinforces in its last sequence. We find Giuliana, dressed in the same green overcoat we saw her wearing at the beginning of the film, with Valerio once again in front of the gates to the petrochemical works. When Valerio asks whether the birds flying through the poisonous yellow smoke belching from the works will die, Giuliana answers that "the birds have learnt that and they don't fly through it." This remark has often been taken to be an oblique reference to her own condition and therefore to indicate that the healing process is underway. There are also critics who see in this return to the beginning of the film that the cycle we have seen will repeat itself. But the ambiguity of Giuliana's position is indicated by the last two shots of the film, which come after her answer to Valerio's question. In the first, Giuliana's head is shown in the foreground in close-up against the background of colorful out-of-focus smears (reminding the viewer of the way objectless colors were shown "attacking" her in Corrado's room); in the last one we cut to a long shot showing Giuliana and Valerio in the foreground, the chemical works in the background, and in the middle distance stacks of colorful metal drums containing nitric acid (a sign next to the fence says, "Isola B: acido nitrico"). The pure colors of anxiety (the acid of excitation, which consumes objects) that we thought we have just seen (as out-of-focus smears) are for the moment contained, but are always ready to overwhelm Giuliana's world.

However, the last sequence not only returns us to Giuliana's "neurosis," it also goes back to the post-apocalyptic landscape in front of the petrochemical works where the strike was taking place, a collective effort against the colorful factory, growing out of the filthy ground, which caused the already-mentioned strange reaction of Giuliana: she bought a half-eaten sandwich from one of the strikers and devoured it ravenously. Why did she do this? Food is, in fact, mentioned in the strike sequence: the man who is probably a trade union representative addresses the scab and invites him to join the strikers because he is one of them: "You work to feed your children …." But of course, the managers (or at least some of them, like Ugo) also work (among other things) to feed their children, so the signifier "children" must stand here not primarily for the empirical children of the workers, but for something less definite—for that which distinguishes the strikers from what they oppose: "You are not one of the managers," the trade union man says. In the film we have seen three different types of manager: Max, the ruthless capitalist; Ugo, the devotee of applied science (that is, the factory); and Corrado, the romantic capitalist. All of them have one thing in common: whether they work to feed their children or not, their dominant fantasy is the infinite expansion of the same, the "miracle" they are devoted to.[44] So the workers' children must stand for the "beyond" of this fantasy, for a future which will put an end to it. This fantasy of the beyond is essentially negative, that is, empty: a society which is not like the existing one, one in which the fact that the scab is "one of us" counts more than his individual satisfaction (or a place to feel better). In other words, a new utopian society, the dream of the Italian left after the end of the Second World War, which was betrayed by the Christian Democrats and replaced by consumer filth into which the strikers seem to melt. Therefore Giuliana's already-noted reaction to the presence of the striking workers, although desperate, is perhaps not so strange—by buying a worker's sandwich and eating it agitatedly, she tries to incorporate into herself a beyond which is not

---

[44] Max's element is temporal expansion—his motto is: "Comprare, vendere subito, via, via" ("Buy, sell quickly, away, away"; untranslated on the DVD). Corrado's project concerns spatial expansion into the New World. Ugo's fantasy is "metaphysical" expansion: the continuous field of knowledge extending from the microworld (Valerio's microscope) through the macroworld (gyroscope) to outer space (radiotelescope in Medicina); thus, it is not surprising that he teaches Valerio that $1+1$ can equal 1.

just an individual fantasy (like the mysterious ship) which may help her to find or re-find meaning in the family constellation as a wife and a mother, but which would include a wider social bond that could tell her who she is beyond the domestic roles. And thus perhaps the surprising verbal conclusion of Giuliana's fantasy—when her voiceover says, "Everyone was singing," while we hear a solo female voice and see a lone girl among the rocks—does not simply testify to the personification of the natural phenomena around the girl by Giuliana (the rocks, the sun, the air, the plants, the living creatures are singing), but is evidence of her yearning for the "everybody" included in the strikers' utopian imagination.

But of course the strikers are not the only workers in the film. We have already mentioned the solidarity between Orlando and Max over the phantasmatic object of enjoyment, in which class differences seem to disappear, dissimulated by the ideology of individual satisfaction. There are also workers who are lectured to by Corrado about his enterprise in Patagonia. Unlike the strikers at the beginning of the film, who are presented as a group mainly in long shots and against the muddy landscape into which they melt, the prospective migrants are shut up in a nondescript storeroom and presented against empty demijohns wrapped in wicker. The workers are themselves wrapped in their overcoats (many of them the color of wicker) and the camera lingers on their individual faces. Moreover, the storeroom seems to be a former cinema—when we see Corrado talking to the workers in a long shot, we see what looks like a screen frame painted on one of the shorter walls of the rectangular storeroom. And, in fact, Corrado's speech is like a movie presenting the wondrous prospects of life and work, and perhaps even adventure ("Is it true that women are barebreasted?" asks one of the workers) in exotic Patagonia. In other words, what we see here is the verbal equivalent of the factory fantasy we have seen in the opening credits sequence, with the content of which the workers are filled like the empty demijohns to which they are compared, invited like Orlando to join the phantasmatic party. But we have already noted that the colorful substance (plastic) with which the exciting consumer dreams are filled has a dangerous tendency to transform itself into filth, when looked at from a certain perspective, and this exposes the dream as a nightmare from which one has to awake for the sake of one's "children." Thus, in the final sequence, rustic transparent demijohns are replaced by drums full of dangerous content. And they appear at the former site of the strike: the strike is over, so the corrosive substance (nitric acid) is for a while contained, but the colorful factory's control over it is always ever tenuous. After all, 1968 is just a shot away.

5

Blow-Up (1966)

Appearing on screen in late 1966, *Blow-Up* was Antonioni's first English-language film made for a big American studio (MGM) and released in the United States "to first-run theatres, thus becoming the first European import to compete openly with Hollywood fare on American screens."[1] Unexpectedly for some (but evidently not for MGM executives), it became a big commercial success and also a *cause célèbre* for cinematic and cultural criticism. Yet, although a wide range of critics, philosophers, and anthropologists felt compelled to say something about it, the interpretations one comes across are strangely similar, even if they may be contradictory. They usually follow two related routes and differ from each other mainly in the emphasis that the main (unnamed) protagonist (David Hemmings) is given: he is treated as an exemplary case of the youthful and professionally successful "mod" London or more individually as an artist (or what by the 1960s was left of such a figure) and thus the director's representative to a certain extent. Obviously, both approaches are not mutually exclusive which some critics demonstrate by superimposing the latter upon the former: the protagonist is at first presented as a typical narcissistic representative of his milieu (he is a successful fashion photographer who works with supermodels and drives a Rolls-Royce); yet, an unexpected encounter with death causes an identity crisis and his initiation into matters epistemological and existential, the result of which is his transformation into an individual and an artist.[2]

As already noted, interpretations pursuing this royal way may be and often are contradictory, but what they have in common is an emphasis on the same

---

[1] Pomerance, *Michelangelo Red*, 237. The sentence continues: "*Blow-Up* had netted more than twenty million dollars worldwide by the end of the decade and has taken in more than six million dollars in video rentals in addition."

[2] The most interesting example of this approach is the chapter devoted to *Blow-Up* in Arrowsmith's *Antonioni*.

motifs which are usually organized into a series of binary oppositions.³ The series begins at the very beginning of the film in the opening credits: we see a wide expanse of lawn in a long shot upon which letters are superimposed after a while. Within the body of the letters we can spot a female model posing on the roof of a building, who is being looked at and photographed from below by a group of people. The colors of the fashion show are radically different from the "natural" green of the lawn: they are highly "synthetic" and fluorescent. This opening is said to set the scene and develop throughout the film as the opposition between the life of fashionable, affluent, and youthful mod London, which is restless, flashy, and noisy; and the quiet of the park to which the lawn belongs and which the photographer enters on impulse later in the film (impulses are also supposed to be "natural"). The peace of the park is, of course, also an answer to a nebulous yearning of the photographer's world, which is a restless milieu in which everybody wants "to try something else," like the young owner of an antiques shop (Susan Broderick) the photographer wants to buy, who dreams of escaping to Nepal ("Nepal is full of antiques," counters the photographer) or Morocco, supposedly to live an imaginary "quiet," that is, more "natural" and therefore fulfilling, life. Moreover, within the symbolically loaded scenery of the park, we encounter another facet (or perhaps the core) of this fantasy: in the idyllic circumstances the photographer comes across what looks like an idyllically sentimental relationship, which he photographs on the sly in order to put it into an album he is about to publish.

This is, therefore, the first commonplace about *Blow-Up*: the fantasy of the natural ("peace and quiet" obviously stand for balance and contentment) is contrasted with the modern civilized as represented generally by mod London which gets high on "sex, drugs and rock'n'roll" (other pop culture developments like fashion photography included), and in particular by the photographer who is successful and narcissistic, who treats everybody as means to his ends and who is, therefore, free of all attachments, which allows him to exercise protean abilities to adapt himself to whatever the moment demands in order not to "lose his cool."

Another commonplace about the film is also related to the idyllic scene in the park. What was shot by the photographer as a representation of peace turns out

---

³ Most often the claim is that the oppositions are Antonioni's, but, for reasons enumerated later, I find it unconvincing. For instance: "the intercuts between the merrymakers and the homeless men emerging from the 'doss house' (shelter) with which the film opens are heavily, almost didactically, oppositional and seem meant to nudge us in the direction of seeing the film as a set of binary oppositions." Brunette, *Antonioni*, 110.

to be a scene of murder featuring the photographed couple and the photographic trace of a murderer hiding in the bushes. The photographer is taken by the natural beauty of the scene (both in its natural (light) and human (love) aspects[4]) but when he develops and inspects the photographs, in order to find out why the photographed woman is so desperate to retrieve the negative from him, he finds out—in a series of blow-ups of the pictures—that what he took for an amorous scene seems to have been a plot involving the woman and the man in the bushes to have her "lover" killed.[5] Hence we encounter a master of illusion (a fashion photographer) who, because he knows how it works, considers himself above it (in fact he thinks he contests it[6]), but who turns out to be a paragon of naïveté when it comes to the issues of reality. Therefore, the "deeper" level of the murder story (a surface lure to the audience) is supposed to present us with the problem of epistemological uncertainty, which finds its narrative incarnation in the disappearance of the evidence of the crime (the photographs get stolen and the body is no longer in the park the following morning) and creates the inconclusiveness of the film (the murder mystery is not solved).

In this approach, the basic level of meaning—the moral uncertainty of a world in which the difference between good and evil no longer seems to be clear (a theme relatively popular even in the Hollywood cinema of the 1960s and the main source of *Blow-Up*'s mass appeal: "lax" behavior on screen)—is interpreted as being reinforced by a more rarefied level which introduces doubt about the possibility of reaching the truthful image of reality located beyond self-serving pop cultural illusions. The theme of uncertainty seems to be clinched with the ambiguous ending. In the morning, a group of revelers, their faces painted white[7]—whom we saw at the beginning of the film (the previous

---

[4] "The light was very beautiful in the park this morning," he later says.
[5] What takes place in the park is often taken as another opposition: mod London vs. the establishment. As many critics have noted, there are only two characters in the film who are more than thirty: the assistant in the antiques shop (a stock grumpy old man out of "Dickensian" Hollywood movies complete with the routine of blowing dust off some old letters into the photographer's face) and the oldish boyfriend in the park ("Your boyfriend is a bit past it," the photographer cannot resist saying to the woman, who is more or less his age). But one does not have to think too hard to see that the opposition is a false one: the mod London youth *are* the new establishment.
[6] "But even with beautiful girls, you look at them, and that's that. That's why they always end up by … And I'm stuck with them all day long," he says to the woman from the park when she comes to visit. But more explicitly to Ron, his editor: "I hate those bloody bitches."
[7] Arrowsmith is ingenious in identifying the revelers: "Everywhere in Europe matriculating freshmen, usually at the end of March, celebrate Rag-week, *la festa delle matricole*. Dressed in costumes akin to those of comedia dell'arte, they run about the streets performing improvised games and tricks, cadging money for charity" (*Antonioni*, 108).

morning) noisily descending on the West End to scrounge money from passers-by—appears in the park, from which the dead body has disappeared, and mimes a game of tennis with an imaginary ball. The photographer observes them with amusement and when the players pretend the ball has just gone over the fence separating the court from the rest of the park and mutely ask him with their eyes and gestures to retrieve it, after a moment of hesitation he trots toward the imaginary ball and pretends to throw it back over the fence and into the court. While some critics take the scene to have a "positive" meaning (the photographer as an individual against the faceless society of make-believe) and others a "negative" one (the photographer joining the make-believe and disappearing as a subject),[8] both interpretations converge in emphasizing the social origin of values and epistemological standards, which, being constructs of the society, are mutable, that is, unstable.[9]

Matters, however, seem to be more complicated than what a series of binary notions can suggest, and we might start unraveling them by returning to the incipient opposition between nature and (mod) culture. There is something really strange in such a hoary coupling being applied to the period in which Western (post)modernity started to articulate its critical self-knowledge by, among other things, positing the natural reality as always already lost and claiming that it is only with the loss of nature that the very idea of nature itself (as the lost thing) is constructed. In this context, it is interesting to see that there are some critics who, although they are prepared to follow the nature vs. culture interpretive route, seem to feel somehow uneasy about it, which gets articulated in a peculiar way. They have a problem with the greenness of the grass in the park: while Arrowsmith claims that "[t]he trouble with English grass is that it is *too* green," Brunette sees it as "sickly looking."[10] Yet the point that the grass is either too green or not green enough just covers a more important one: this strange "denaturalization" has an obvious source—"nature" is in fact the battle cry of the culture these critics take to represent hyper-artificiality. The dominant injunction of the mod world of *Blow-Up* is "Be natural!" In other words: do not follow artificial (constraining) rules; remain true to yourself and act on impulse.

---

[8] While Arrowsmith, for instance, allows for the photographer's individuation from the crowd in the final sequence, Freccero, working generally with the same motifs in the film, interprets it as the artist's ultimate defeat and collapse into conformity. John Freccero, "*Blow-Up*: From the Word to the Image," in *Focus on* Blow-Up, ed. Roy Huss (Englewood Cliffs, NJ: Prentice-Hall, 1971), 127.

[9] For example, Brunette, *Antonioni*, 117.

[10] Arrowsmith, *Antonioni*, 107; Brunette, *Antonioni*, 115.

This is most obviously demonstrated by the plot line and the construction of the main character of the film: as is often noted, his life consists of isolated episodes (impulsive acts) which do not add up to any consistent character.[11] I have already mentioned the desire to be elsewhere (Nepal, Morocco, out of London) which is repeatedly expressed in the film and which stands for a fantasy of a different, more natural, "fulfilling" way of life.[12] Moreover, on a semi-humorous or ironic level the very image of the expanse of (suspicious-looking) grass brings to mind one of the crucial objects in the film, that is, "grass," "pot," or marijuana, whose purpose is also to make one "natural," that is, more "spontaneous" and less "inhibited." Finally, the uselessness of the nature/artifice opposition is additionally and conclusively confirmed when the natural image itself visits the photographer's studio (where he also lives[13]). When the girl seen in the park (Vanessa Redgrave) appears at his door to demand the negatives again, the photographer asks her in and, after observing her for a while, he marvels at her *natural* gift for *modeling*: "You've got it. ... Not many girls can stand as well as that." He imagines her acting spontaneously or instinctively, unlike the affected behavior of the nameless models the photographer had worked with in the morning. Thus the distinction between nature and culture (artifice) collapses: in order to reach the summit of artificiality (to be an ideal fashion model), you have to be artificial "naturally."

According to Brunette, the setting up of binary oppositions at the beginning of *Blow-Up* as the key for the viewer to the rest of the film does not end with the credits (nature/culture) but is continued by juxtaposing the revelers who are causing a bit of harmless confusion among the new skyscrapers—the prosperous London of finance and the media—with the homeless people leaving Camberwell Reception Centre (later called a "doss house" by the photographer).[14] At first sight the montage does look like an opposition or a provocative collision of images,

---

[11] The photographer is only the most obvious example of this general condition which afflicts even minor characters (the teenyboppers are scared of the photographer, but a moment later they cavort happily with him on the seamless mauve background paper). The most flagrant example of this is, of course, the pot party where Ron, the photographer's editor, is not even able to remember what has just been said to him.

[12] Characteristically there is one exception to this rule in the film, the exception which confirms the fantasy status of "going elsewhere." The supermodel Verushka, whom the photographer meets at the pot party and asks "Weren't you supposed to be in Paris?" answers "I am in Paris." Because her job is to be every day in a different place, she knows that whether in Paris, London, or Morocco a pot party is always the same.

[13] This is yet another example that the main strategy of the film is dissolving rather than reinforcing binary oppositions.

[14] Brunette, *Antonioni*, 110.

and that the revelers belong to the scintillating world of the photographer is confirmed by a shot in which, after they are given money by the photographer, whose Rolls-Royce they stop, they run away, and in the background, which so far has been hidden behind them, can be seen the figure of a homeless man walking down the street. Yet such a non-problematic contrast is undermined by the fact that, earlier on, one of the men emerging in the morning from the shelter looks around and, when everybody is gone, trots up the street and jumps into a Rolls-Royce parked there. This is of course our first encounter with the photographer in the film and supposedly the introduction of yet another binary opposition: between reality (the photographer is rich) and illusion (he pretends to be homeless in order to photograph the destitute in the doss house).

The status of the doss house in the film and in the photographer's world is rather ambiguous too. Although the opposition between the mod and the destitute London is essentially an example of political antagonism, it is not the source of any "insight" but photographic "material," that is, "art." That the doss house is peripheral in all meanings of the word is emphasized by its "topographical" lack of contiguity with the photographer's world which encompasses fashionable London (including the park as one of its fantasy spaces): it is an empty and depressing morning landscape of dirty brick and of desolate "nature" represented by one stunted tree. But as the doss house guests reappear in the film transformed into aesthetic photographic objects that fashionable London can accommodate or even enjoy, political antagonism, which is impossible to repress without some residue, reappears in a more "fashionable" form within the "beautiful districts." Returning home in his fancy car from lunch with his editor, the photographer comes across an anti-war or anti-nuclear demonstration bearing placards saying: "Go Away!" "Not this!" "Not our lads" "Stop the war" and most interestingly "No No No" as well as "On On On." While the episode adds another level of meaning to the title of the film (atomic bomb explosion), one may note that this potentially ominous narrative thread is treated rather lightly and that it transposes an internal antagonism (e.g., the fashionable vs. the destitute) into an external one (international conflict). Moreover, some of the placards strangely echo the social and existential problems mentioned earlier (everybody wants to go away, would rather have something else than this). And of course this is fitting because, if one were to imagine which world the demonstration belongs to, there is no doubt that it is an extension of the photographer's and the revelers' domain, which is emphasized by the photographer's treating the demonstrators (and the revelers too) in a friendly manner (while virtually everybody else in the film is treated rather badly by him). Hence this supposedly political theme is thoroughly depoliticized starting on the most basic level of self-contradictory and therefore neutralized signifier (no no no—on on on) and ending with contextualization of the demonstrators as yet another group of revelers.

This neutralization of the political is not accidental, because the world we are presented with has moved "beyond" political meanings. The fate of the photographs taken during the night at the doss house may serve as an example here. The photographer brings these newly developed prints to the lunch with his editor (Peter Bowles), where the two of them peruse the content of the photographer's planned photo-book. These are the photographs of the destitute and downtrodden. Some critics see this as another, more compassionate, and therefore "authentic" side of the photographer, a sign of "bad conscience" or thirst for truth as an antidote to the world of illusion that he exploits in his fashion career. But the fact that the photos are being arranged into a sequence during a tasty meal between sips of beer means not only that their content makes no impression on the arrangers, but also that the arrangement is being made for the prosperous to be looked at in similar circumstances: the book is being prepared for their coffee tables to add some spice or thrill to their comfortable lives.[15] Because the poor and the violence present in their lives are turned into aesthetic objects, there is hardly any difference between the fashion photography we have seen in the film and the destitute which are photographed here—both kinds of pictures aim at maximalization of surface effect at first glance, which is perhaps most evident in the photographs of butchers splattered all over with blood in front of a "Home killed" sign. That this is the most disposable kind of "social-realism," which does not have anything to do with internal conflict or the feeling of guilt, is emphasized by the photographer's decision to end the book with the photos of the couple in the park (they are "very peaceful, very still"). "Yeah, that's best. Rings truer," says Ron, the editor, about this sentimental ending, which aims at a fake humanitarianism, with his instinctive understanding of the truth of the market.

That the book is supposed to end with such "reconciling" image reminds one of what a number of commentators on photography have repeated: that the photographic perception of the world creates a false reality in which everything is reconcilable. The primary untruth of photography is not that it creates an artificial world of fantasy (like fashion), whose artificiality is obvious enough (nobody believes commercials), but that its technical veracity (the photographed object

---

[15] Arrowsmith, *Antonioni*, 111.

must have been present in front of the lens, it left its trace on the photographic film[16]) creates a fake image of reality by replacing it. Photography takes fragments of reality out of the contexts that give them meaning, and therefore makes them mute. When the meaning disappears, the image becomes neutralized and it can be easily manipulated by being inserted in a different narrative, a different framework. Moreover, while reality is contradictory (there are mutually exclusive things, there are conflicting meanings or narrations which cannot be reconciled), in a photographic representation of it everything can exist side by side with no conflict: the world becomes a collection of inert (decontextualized) fragments. And, finally, there is no end to it because a fragmentary collection like this can be infinitely expanded.[17] Taking into consideration that the 1960s was precisely the decade when (at least in the West) photography and other visual media began to make all other representations of reality subservient to their purposes (the leading motif of postmodernist theories), the universal repression of the reality by its image sanctioned the non-contradiction principle as the new foundation of the world.

In the world of *Blow-Up*, images, objects, even language get neutralized in this way. Whether it is a propeller in the antiques shop (a modern and streamlined thing which stands out against the more or less exotic colonial loot that seems to have come from various territories of the former British empire), which the photographer does not really know what to do with in his studio, or the piece of a broken guitar for which he dives eagerly into a crowd of fans but then, after escaping from the club, throws away, the objects have attracting power in one isolated context but lose that power completely in another one, which one finds by simply turning a corner. In language, too, the principle of contradiction no longer seems to operate: "This is a public place. Everyone has the right to be left in peace," says the girl in the park when she becomes infuriated by the intrusion

---

[16] This is, of course, true only of pre-digital photographic image of the world to which *Blow-Up* belongs.

[17] This paragraph paraphrases by now familiar statements in critical thinking about photography, the most eloquent examples of which are perhaps Susan Sontag's *On Photography* (London: Penguin, 1979) and John Berger's essay, inspired by Sontag's book, entitled "Uses of Photography," in *About Looking* (New York: Pantheon Books, 1980). Both Sontag's and Berger's favorite example of the lack of contradiction in the world represented by photography and its infinite inclusivity is the following: "In the most famous photographic exhibition ever organized, *The Family of Man* (put together by Edward Steichen in 1955), photographs from all over the world were presented as though they formed a universal family album. Steichen's intuition was absolutely correct: the private use of photographs can be exemplary for their public use. Unfortunately the shortcut he took in treating the existing class-divided world as if it were a family, inevitably made the whole exhibition, not necessarily each picture, sentimental and complacent" (Berger, "The Uses of Photograpy," 57).

of the photographer. And when she comes to retrieve the negatives, he treats her to a story about his "wife": "It's my wife. ... She isn't my wife, really. We just have some kids. No. No kids. ... She's easy to live with. No, she isn't. That's why I don't live with her." Critics often connect the final disappearance of the corpse from the park with the vanishing of the body of the photographer from the last shot of the film, and they try to make sense of this parallelism, but, in a sense, it is the wife's body which is the first to disappear[18] and the body is desubstantialized into nonsense: meaningless phrases, contradictory fragments of sentences, free-floating particles of language.

This substitution for and fragmentation of the world brings us back to the most critically celebrated narrative thread in the film: the photographic murder story. By blowing up the photographs of the couple in the park the photographer first notices that the woman, while being embraced by the man, looks attentively into the bushes, so he blows up the fragment of greenery she seems to be staring at and finds at first the face of a man, then his hand holding a gun. After a moment of elation (he thinks he had prevented a murder), which is interrupted or perhaps expanded by sexual shenanigans with unexpected teenage guests (yet another example of narrative discontinuity), he notices something suspicious in the final photographs taken in the park, and with more blow-ups he discovers the upper part of what seems to be the corpse of the earlier photographed "boyfriend."

We have already mentioned the usual critical take on this story which emphasizes epistemological uncertainty. Reality is elusive: one photographs what one takes to be a scene of two lovers; one blows it up, and it turns out to be the scene of a murder; one blows it up further and the scene disappears entirely, transforming itself in an abstract pattern of the silver halide grains with which a photographic film is covered. In this context, a fragment of an interview with Antonioni is often quoted:

> We know that under the revealed image there is another one which is more faithful to reality, and under this one there is yet another, and again another under this last one, down to the true image of that absolute, mysterious reality that nobody will ever see. Or perhaps, not until the decomposition of every image, of every reality.
>
> Therefore, abstract cinema would have its reason for existing.[19]

---

[18] Admittedly, we never see her and therefore there is no certainty that she exists, but the phone call which is supposed to be from her is an answer to an earlier call by the photographer from the phone booth outside his studio which we do hear.

[19] Antonioni, *The Architecture of Vision*, 63.

But this comment by Antonioni does not really seem to fit what happens in the film, because the photographer's pursuit of truth, as it develops in *Blow-Up*, does not have much to do with depth. Although, by blowing some photos up, he finds photographic traces which were too small to be noticed at first, the photographer very quickly gets to the level of disintegration of the image (abstract dots) beyond which one cannot go. The process shows as the characteristic feature of photography what we have already noted: a photograph represents a fact (the object was incontrovertibly there) but not a truth. In order to find the truth, that is, the meaning of the fact (what happened) the photographer moves not deeper *into* the frame but *beyond* the frame. In other words, he has to (re-)construct the story, create a narrative, introduce the element of time. This is precisely what he does in the most celebrated sequence of the film: he arranges his photographs into a sequence. In other words, he makes a "film" out of them, complete with some tricks of the cinematic trade, including eye-line match and close-up (a photograph of the woman who is staring at the bushes—cut—a photograph of what she sees there: a man—cut—a close-up on what the man is holding: a gun).

Yet there *is* perhaps some truth retrievable from the disintegration of photographic reality into the abstract pattern of dots, if we relate it to other cases in which this kind of abstraction appears in *Blow-Up*. An obvious clue here is a comment by Patricia (Sarah Miles; the wife or girlfriend of Bill, the painter) regarding the biggest blow-up of the corpse in the park, in which it is on the brink of decomposing into an abstraction. She says, "It looks like one of Bill's paintings." We have seen two pictures by Bill (John Castle) at the beginning of the film: one is not really an abstraction; it looks rather like a cubist-inspired work from which a human figure is slowly emerging. Bill says: "That must be five or six years old. They don't mean anything when I do them. Just a mess. Afterwards I find something to hold on to, like [he points] that leg. Then it sorts itself out and adds up. It's like finding a clue in a detective story." Another picture he shows to the photographer is still in the state of being "a mess": a chaos of monochromatic dots on a white canvas. As many critics have noted, the remark comparing a painting to a detective story constitutes an additional link between Bill's painting and the photographer's pictures (detective stories often involve death, too). It is usually interpreted as pointing to the common problematic that various arts (including of course cinema—the photographer is supposed to represent Antonioni in this interpretation) have to grapple with: primarily the elusive nature of reality and the search for its truth. Without going further in this direction, which, for reasons discussed above (photography replaces reality), I consider unfruitful, one can observe that Patricia's comment is not exactly correct: although the mess of dots she sees on the blown-up photograph reminds her of Bill's paintings, for the painter a mess is the initial state of his paintings, which he later develops into something recognizable (a human figure in the painting we saw), while the "abstract" photograph is the end-product of exactly the opposite process: from the love affair through the murder story to a mess.[20] This is actually a commonplace: painting synthesizes, while photography analyzes—both technically and intellectually they do not have too much in common. But perhaps they have something in common within the framework of the film, something different than both being a futile search for reality.

Do the abstract dots encountered in *Blow-Up* present to us the zero-level of meaning? Although I think that Bill's comment about painting as a detective story is largely a red herring serving to confuse the critics,[21] the painter is not a superfluous character in the film. On the contrary, his paintings give us an important clue. Not when he delivers his witticism about detective stories, however, but precisely at a moment when everybody's attention is diverted from them by what constitutes the commercial allure of the film. For the second and last time we see Bill's painting (or at least something that looks like Bill's painting) toward the end of the film, when the photographer visits the couple, having returned from the park in which he found the corpse of the man he had photographed in the morning.[22] The photographer enters their apartment through the open door and finds the couple making love. He observes them for a while and then, at the moment of sexual climax, the camera starts to pan down the red blanket with which they are covered until it reaches its end, and we see

---

[20] The opposition here works also on the aesthetic level. The initial state of a "mess" is aesthetically least appealing, while the final painting appeals the most. The photograph of the love scene contains appealing human characters, beautiful light, and scenery; the blow-ups which show the murder story are less satisfying: they are dark and blurry; and the final abstraction is just a mess.

[21] "Bill represents a curious doubling, on Antonioni's part, of the artist figure and suggests that one character was not sufficient to explore the ambivalences and nuances of this thematic area." Brunette, *Antonioni*, 118.

[22] The status of the corpse is a bit uncertain in the film, and not necessarily in the "epistemological uncertainty" sense some critics prefer. The photographer finds himself in the park at night and sees the corpse in the sinister light of a greenish neon; all of this looks really nightmarish. Bearing this in mind, it is perhaps important to recollect a number of facts: the photographer probably did not sleep the previous night, which he spent in the doss house making photos; almost the first thing he does when he returns home is open a bottle of wine; he continues to drink during the day; when he inspects the blow-ups we see him finish a bottle and we do not know if it is still the "morning bottle"; when the girl from the park comes to visit, they have a drink (which looks like whisky on the rocks) and then they smoke a joint. After all this, it is not hard to conclude that he has perceptual problems with reality.

some blue-gray background densely and irregularly covered with multicolored little flecks or dots. At first it looks as if it is a carpet, but with the passing of the sexual climax (heard on the soundtrack) the dots gradually become less and less dense.[23] Finally the camera stops and after a cut we see the couple "subsiding." Thus, "almost didactically," the abstract pattern of dots is connected with something quite difficult to represent, which at the same time is a crucial component of the world that is shown in the film: intensity (sex, drugs, and rock'n'roll are only some ways of pursuing it).

The connection between art and intense experience is rather obvious, but what is the link between intensity and death within the framework of the film?[24] One may note that the corpse, found by the photographer at first in his studio as an image and then as an object in the park, is for him a meaningless object. Although he has reconstructed how the murder happened, he knows nothing else about it, about its reasons and consequences. For him it is just an instance of inexplicable (blind, abstract) violence. Moreover, even if confrontation with the corpse as the effect of an unexpected intervention of unfamiliar force seems to shake the photographer out of his usual "cool," for the viewer this is definitely not the first image of violence in the film, because what one may call low-level impersonal everyday violence is omnipresent in the world of *Blow-Up*. From the moment the photographer appears in his studio (having returned from the doss house) he is shown as an aggressive narcissist who treats everybody (mostly women, but this is the world of fashion photography) as an object which can be manipulated and exploited for his purposes or to fit the whim of the moment (the models, the woman from the park, the teenyboppers, etc.). Moreover, his role in the film is not to serve as some especially obnoxious case;[25] he is just a representative of his world, as we can gather by watching the behavior of the other people he meets and who belong to this milieu (the supermodel Verushka, Ron, the girl from the park, etc.). Perhaps the most illuminating example of this pattern of behavior can be seen at the Yardbirds concert where the photographer finds himself when he is trying to follow the girl from the park whom he saw in the street after her photographs were stolen from his studio. As usual the

---

[23] So, "realistically speaking," the dotted surface seems to be one of Bill's paintings rather than a carpet.
[24] Because Antonioni is not a Hollywood filmmaker and the photographer is not Hannibal Lecter, we can safely disregard the fin-de-siècle cliché that killing might be a source of intense aesthetic emotions.
[25] "Hemmings is an obnoxious human being, a predatory male who says he is sick of all the 'birds' and 'bitches' he comes in contact with." Brunette, *Antonioni*, 113.

photographer forgets his purpose in being there and "spontaneously" dives into the crowd to retrieve a piece of Jeff Beck's broken guitar.[26] But more important is what Beck demonstrates by breaking his guitar to pieces: gratuitous destruction (violence) which is taken for spontaneous behavior and which is therefore seen as self-affirming and even rebellious.[27] The logic behind this "habit" is obvious: in a world in which conflicts of meanings do not exist and everything is reconcilable, where everything can be replaced with anything else, the only measure of intensity is violence.[28] Therefore, when the photographer blows up the image from the park and gets to the point when the corpse disintegrates into an abstract pattern of dots, he reaches the level of the figuratively unrepresentable but omnipresent substance of his reality: the sheer substance of violence.

Thus we are presented with the last[29] and perhaps unexpected meaning of the title *Blow-Up*: the world of struggle was blown to bits by photography (which was only the first one of the modern techniques of "simulacra") and in this kind of pulverization conflict disappeared—it disintegrated into the easy-going life in which there is no contradiction between fashion house and doss house. This world, the world of mod London (but not everybody lives in this world), is smooth, modern, luxurious, free (there are no permanent rules), and "cool," but the flip side of this world is free-floating everyday violence which permeates everything. In a world in which there seems to be no place for it (which denies and disowns it), violence not only becomes omnipresent—it is no longer recognized as violence because it becomes *a way of life*. And if the corpse in the park (or rather its accidental photographic trace) is the privileged image in which such violence materializes visually, we can say that its vanishing from the park before it could be "properly" photographed is something more or something different than what it is usually taken to be by the critics: Antonioni's typical abandonment of the popular cinema narrative, done in order to frustrate the audience and make it think.[30] The disappearance of the dead body is in fact entirely consistent with the ontological status in the world of what the corpse

---

[26] The momentary intensity-elation of being the winner in this situation which is completely discontinuous with his preceding purpose (the girl) and the following one (taking Ron to the park to take a photo of the corpse).

[27] A clear parallel with the photographer's "I hate those bloody bitches"—the models are among his "instruments."

[28] This is visible even in the photographer's "social-realist" work: the photographs must be violent, that is, immediately shocking, because for him this is the only measure of their "truth."

[29] We have already mentioned blown-up photos, blown-up egos, and the atomic bomb.

[30] Like the abandonment of the search for Anna who disappeared in *L'avventura*.

comes to figure: it has to disappear because its presence has nothing to do with the particularity of the park[31] or the particularity of the photographed couple.[32] What it materializes is pure violence which is everywhere, which infects the entire reality presented to us in the film but remains invisible to its characters.

But this is perhaps not yet the whole story, because as the film seems to begin twice (the revelers, the doss house),[33] it also seems to have two endings: the disappearance of the corpse and the reappearance of the revelers. We have already mentioned the contradictory pair of interpretations of this celebrated second ending, but, whatever value we may attach to them, there is an important problem here. As a number of perspicacious critics have noted, if we take the revelers to stand for the society and its socially constructed values/meanings, they are completely unnecessary, because these thematics have already been fully explored in the film.[34] But does the scene really repeat the meanings we have already ingested, yet again hammering them into our heads? Only if we interpret the film in the aforementioned existential-epistemological way in which the critics usually juxtapose the disappearance of the corpse (reality is ungraspable) with the disappearance of the photographer in the last shot.

What if we connect the disappearance in the park to the reappearance which happens in the same place? Having seen that the body has disappeared, the photographer comes across the revelers who are playing tennis with an invisible ball. This can of course be taken as representing the conventional nature of social

---

[31] Some interpretations connect the meaning of the corpse with the park as the image of idyllic nature: "It is only later that he discovers, with the retrospective gaze of the artist interpreting his own work, that he has in fact portrayed not the embrace of lovers, but the death of an older man. In short, the fact of death which he had been seeking to evade. Had he seen Poussin or read Panofsky, he would have known that this disillusionment awaits all attempts at pastoral evasion: 'Et in Arcadia ego.' Death resides even in Arcady." Freccero, "*Blow-Up*," 120–1.

[32] It was a stroke of genius on Antonioni's part that he reduced the subplot of the couple to the stub we have in the final version of the film. In the original script the "murder plot" involved a more developed story of the triangle (the middle-aged man, the young woman and her young lover). Pomerance, *Michelangelo Red*, 262.

[33] Pomerance, *Michelangelo Red*, 239.

[34] "Much has been made of the clowns' thematic relevance, in that they provide a harbor of illusion for the hero after a fruitless voyage into reality. But precisely this thematic ground provides an even stronger objection to them ... Thematically I think that the film is stronger without them, that it makes its points more forcibly. Suppose the picture began with Hemmings coming out of the flophouse with the derelicts, conversing with them, then leaving them and getting into his Rolls. At once it seems more than Antonioni. And suppose it ended (where in fact I thought it was going to end) with the long shot of Hemmings walking away after he has discovered that the corpse has been removed. Everything that the subsequent scene supplies would already be there by implication— *everything*—and we would be spared the cloudy symbols of high romance. Again it would be more like Antonioni." Stanley Kauffmann, "A Year with *Blow-Up*: Some Notes," in *Focus on* Blow-Up, ed. Huss, 75.

reality (in order to play you have to agree to follow the convention, to pretend that the ball exists), but perhaps something else is operating here as well which has bearing on the meaning of the film. The photographer has a camera with him this time (he wanted to photograph the corpse) but it is of no use now: he can photograph "the society,"[35] but it is impossible to photograph the invisible ball which animates the players. One may quickly jump here to the conclusion that the ball represents desire, which has been shown in the film as the bane of the mod society, chasing after objects which elude them (Nepal, the career of a model, freedom in the form of tons of money[36]), but one has to note that these fantasy scenarios are the result of the already-functioning value system of the society, however mutable it may be. In other words, a fantasy scenario propelled by desire always manifests itself in the form of a definite object (e.g., Nepal) which makes sense for a group (e.g., one will be able to lead a balanced life there). This is not what is demonstrated by the game in the park: it is a game which does not make any sense even for its participants and it serves no other purpose than itself. In this sense perhaps it is no accident that the revelers look rather "otherworldly." Although critics try to locate them realistically and speak about revelers, clowns, students during Rag Week, commedia dell'arte, etc., their white (painted) faces have, in fact, replaced the pallor of the death mask of the "senseless" corpse in the park. But while the dead body was just some enigmatic weight one can do nothing with apart from photographing it (and even this has turned out to be impossible), the revelers are anything but dead; they are animated by an object which is invisible and which transcends the games of the society we have seen, the society whose idea of itself is "reveling," but which produced the corpse as its truth.[37] It is not accidental that the photographer is the privileged representative of such a society: it is a "disillusioned" society which believes only in what can be seen (and therefore photographed) and classifies any invisible object as "fiction" (a more learned way of putting it: social construction).[38] The revelers, however, do not represent this "truth"; in fact, they do not represent any truth at all. What they do is, by repeating this world (revelry doubled by

---

[35] He has done this in his professional life: the society's fantasies (fashion) and its "refuse" (the destitute).

[36] "I wish I had tons of money. Then I'll be free," says the photographer, who drives a Rolls-Royce—yet another example of the non-existence of contradiction.

[37] The mod society is of course in the pursuit of the idea of fun, but the fun we see in the film is a rather grim affair: the pleasure trip to the park ends with murder; the people in the club look like mannequins; at the pot party we find Ron on all fours with two joints in his mouth.

[38] For instance, the only visible aspect of love is sex, everything else is "discursive fiction."

revelry), become its spectral double (another reason for their "otherworldly" appearance), and therefore introduce within it a syncope, its difference from itself, a lack of consistency, a rift incarnated in the impossible object, which is invisible precisely from the point of view of socially constructed reality. They offer this *transcendent* object to the photographer in place of the dead body which disappeared as if to claim that a reality without transcendence is a corpse. Moreover, for the first time in his life the photographer is asked to verify the existence of something which cannot be seen and therefore photographed but which nonetheless animates free action. He has to relinquish the camera to pick up the ball, because he *is* the camera: as many critics have noted, his whole contact with the world is mediated by images, by the photographs he takes. After the photographer throws the ball back into the court, we no longer see the revellers but only his face which gradually lightens up (into a smile) as we hear the sound of the non-existent ball. It is emphatically not the moment he is *included* into the (social) illusion: we no longer see the revelers ("the society"), only him, and illusion is something he is a master of anyway. Moreover, he hates both the "bitches" who are used in creating it and the ones for whom it is created, so why would he smile? What he experiences, therefore, must be something of a different order: a moment of opening, of transcendence, his realization that there is another experience of freedom than the one which belongs to his world ("tons of money" and social constructs). For a moment what he sees is transfigured and this is precisely why we cannot see what he sees: for him the world remains the same but at the same time it becomes completely different.[39] But then the smile fades: he knows that he has to pick up the camera (return to his world) and, after picking it up, he fades from the image. Thus we are back at the beginning

---

[39] This transfiguration (things look different but the same), however, is inscribed into the film on the formal level as the lack of consistency of the look. As a number of formally minded critics noted, the reality represented in the film is visually constructed in such a way as to foreground a "pure look," that is, the look of the camera as different from the look of the main protagonist. Such self-reflexivity on the part of the camera is most clearly perceptible when the conventional expectations of the viewer are contradicted or frustrated as in the scene in which the photographer returns to the park in the morning to photograph the corpse which is no longer there: the photographer looks up at something beyond the frame—cut—the shot of moving branches and leaves against the sky, which looks like his point-of-view shot—the camera, without a cut, pans down on him standing motionlessly under the tree and looking ahead (Brunette, *Antonioni*, 123). This formalist approach, which emphasizes the self-reflexivity of Antonioni's film, is most interestingly presented by Lorenzo Cuccu, *Il discorso dello sguardo: Da "Blow Up" a "Identificazione di una donna"* (Pisa: ETS Editrice, 1990); Marie-Claire Ropars-Wuilleumier, "L'espace et le temps dans la narration des années 60: 'Blow up' ou le négatif du récit," in *Michelangelo Antonioni 1966/84*, ed. Lorenzo Cuccu (Rome: Ente Autonomo di Gestione per il Cinema, 1988); Sam Rohdie, *Antonioni* (London: British Film Institute, 1990).

of the film (the same lawn) and the fantasy of this world (the image of grass). For us, the grass is just the same but it is also different because we have learned something about it: the image is *potentially* productive. It contains an invisible inconsistency, which manifests itself in the strange feeling that the grass is both too green and not green enough. The ending is thus intentionally ambiguous but not in order to confuse the viewer. The photographer has learned something and so have we, but what will come out of this experience is not known.

6

Zabriskie Point (1970)

The first thing that is virtually always brought up when discussing Michelangelo Antonioni's *Zabriskie Point*—his second MGM film, which was released in the United States in February 1970—is not its dismal failure at the box office (which was after all not so unusual for an "artistic" film) but its almost unanimous denigration by American critics, including those, like Stanley Kauffmann, who had considered themselves Antonioni's champions up until that time. Such close agreement in the opinions of people with relatively different aesthetic convictions in itself indicates something problematic, especially if one compares it with their divergence of opinion about other "controversial" films of the period like *Bonnie and Clyde* (dir. Arthur Penn, 1967) or *Easy Rider* (dir. Dennis Hopper, 1969). To show how curious this critical reaction was, it is perhaps enough to mention the fact that practically everything in the film was denigrated by one critic or another, with one important exception: the brilliance of the visual "surface" of the film was often, if reluctantly, acknowledged. So, unless Antonioni's movie was worse than, for instance, the aforementioned titles (and comparison does not show that it was), the critical onslaught on *Zabriskie Point* seems to tell us even more about America (and its reflection in the critical establishment) in 1970 than Antonioni could show in the film itself.

Why was this film considered to be so terrible? Generally speaking, most of the criticism boiled down to two issues. Firstly, that Antonioni knew and understood nothing of the United States and his ignorance led to the construction a caricature of the country on screen; this view is exemplified by Pauline Kael's remark that "in *Zabriskie Point* … [Antonioni] has rigged an America that is *nothing but* a justification for violent destruction."[1] Secondly, that he prostrated

---

[1] Pauline Kael, "The Beauty of Destruction," *New Yorker*, February 21, 1970, 95; emphasis in the original.

himself before rebellious American youth, who were not worth the trouble; a rather florid example of which is the following:

> The lad ... is a lawless punk with no shadow of a claim to any opinion which should be taken seriously, for he has no formed identity, no social shape, no principle of existence (except freedom from); he has no problem and of course he cannot articulate. (Literally, I could barely understand a word he said. Spoken American language is really beyond a scandal!)[2]

Moreover, the above failures were usually presented as resulting from the weakness of the plot, which was said to be overly schematic because it was built on simplistic, black-and-white contrasts between the police and young radicals, corporate greed and utopian youth, Los Angeles and Death Valley, etc. In this respect Seymour Chatman's is a characteristic opinion: "Narrative so dominates one's experience of a fiction film as to control one's final reaction to it. Indeed, the more physically beautiful a weakly plotted and acted film is, the more pretentious it strikes us [sic]."[3] (This remark also conveniently includes another frequent accusation: that the principal actors, Mark Frechette and Daria Halprin, both non-professionals, acted poorly in the film.) There is, however, a certain problem here. It is all very well if a Hollywood production is accused of being weakly plotted, because Hollywood films are expected to be made according to a convention in which everything else in the film serves the purpose of forwarding the plot in one way or another. But all Antonioni's films are weakly plotted by American standards and in fact their interest lies precisely in an oblique relationship between their "weak" plots and Antonioni's formal manipulation of visual and aural elements in order to build up additional levels of meaning. And *Zabriskie Point* is no exception: if one looks and listens carefully, what may look like simplistic contrasts in the plot cease to be simplistic. These contrasts are engaged in a web of cross-reference which complicates matters significantly and allows what is typical for Antonioni to come to the fore: his poetics of the image (and sound) always has an analytical value which belies the simplistic analysis that contrasts a crude message with beautiful packaging.

Zabriskie Point unfolds in a number of locations which are not only linked or put into contrast by the plot, but are also differently rendered visual and auratic spaces. The film starts with an out-of-focus camera image accompanied

---

[2] Vernon Young, "Reflections on Two American Films," *The Hudson Review* 23, no. 3 (Autumn 1970), 538.
[3] Chatman, *Antonioni*, 167.

by percussive music mixed with electronically distorted voices out of which a variation on *cinéma vérité* emerges: in a large room a group of students of various ethnicities, though predominantly white, discuss a strike on a campus which is being organized and led by the Black Students Union (in the roles of the leaders of which certain Black Panthers activists, including Kathleen Cleaver, appear). The students discuss the strategy of the protest (how to defend themselves against the riot police) and, more importantly, the lack of white students' support for the strike (are the whites present in the room the only supporters of the Black protest?). In fact, most of the exchanges between the Black leaders and the white radicals present concern the "existential" difference between Black and white class and race consciousness, which is made explicit when one of the Black leaders addresses the whites:

> Y'all are dealing with things that are really irrelevant. ... You get busted for grass and this makes you a revolutionary. No, when the pigs are busting you on your head, they're kicking down your door, stopping you from living, when you can't get a job, can't go to school, can't eat, that's what makes you a revolutionary, dig? That's why black people are, like you say, in another bag.

The discussion gradually becomes more and more heated but also more and more chaotic. Yet it becomes refocused when one of the white participants asks a Black man, who is advocating armed struggle in anticipation of police violence, a fundamental question which takes us back to the aforementioned difference: "Are you willing to die?" To this the Black man answers, "Black people are dying. A lot of black people have died already in this country. Black people have earned this leadership in blood, Jack, we're not going to give it up." This is the weightiest and tensest moment in the discussion, and, moreover, it seems to arrive at a certain truth—historical evidence of the undeniable breach between the races. However, at this moment something happens which seems to deny this breach by turning it into farce—a young white man gets up and says: "Well, I'm willing to die, too. But not out of boredom." And he walks out. This man will turn out to be Mark, one of the two principal protagonists of the film, and what at first distinguishes him from the group is his pronouncement that, unlike other whites, he is willing to die *too* (like Black people). Yet because he is white, and therefore he has not experienced the discriminatory and violent treatment which is supposed to make one a true revolutionary, his assertion is not taken seriously; it is treated as a white man's "jive." "That bourgeois individualism that he's indulging in is gonna get him killed," says one of the Black leaders of the meeting, automatically assuming that the motive of a white man's will to act must be individualism, the American white man's anti-political mythology. And because Mark *is* going to die in *Zabriskie Point*, the struggle between historical and mythical determinism will from this moment become an important motif in the film.

After Mark (who is not yet identified by name) leaves the meeting, two other protagonists, each related to an important strand of the plot, are introduced. In the lobby of the Sunnydunes Development Co. building we encounter Daria, who does temporary secretarial work for the company. She is arguing with a willfully difficult security guard who denies her permission to visit the roof where she had forgotten a book during her lunch break. At this moment the top executive of the company, Lee Allen (Rod Taylor), gets out of a lift into the lobby and, attracted by the girl's beauty, is able to help her out by giving her permission. But apart from introducing protagonists essential for later narrative developments, the sequence also introduces an important motif which will be continued throughout the film. In the lobby, vision is, on the one hand, related to control: the security guard sits surrounded by CCTV screens (a novelty at that time) and this position of power seems to be the source of his haughtiness; yet the moment Allen appears the guard becomes all sycophancy and therefore we see whose power he represents by proxy. But this easy opposition between the observer who is in control (whether it be Allen or the guard) and the powerless observed is undermined by the space in which the scene takes place: the lobby is a hall of mirrors. It is not only the CCTV screens that "reflect" the reality of the offices and corridors: glass panels, polished marble, and other reflective surfaces of the lobby mirror people, objects, and their reflections into infinity.[4] The people who seem to observe, and thus to form an outside, are in fact a part of the spectacle.

The next sequence, in which we return to Mark, is crucial, because it establishes the main visual as well as conceptual framework of the film. It starts with the painted image of a Holstein cow, which looks like an advertisement, but begins to move leftward and turns out to be the painted side of a delivery truck. Surprisingly, what is revealed behind the truck is not a street view but a painted pastoral scene in which a farmer, mounted on his cart, is throwing food to a large

---

[4] Angelo Restivo, "Revisiting *Zabriskie Point*," in *Antonioni*, ed. Rascaroli and Rhodes, 89. This is noted by Restivo and related to Baudrillard's claim that "video, everywhere, serves only this end: it is a screen of ecstatic refraction … its goal is *to be hooked up to itself*" (*America*, trans. Chris Turner (London: Verso,1988), 37). I shall have more to say about Baudrillard and his use by Restivo later.

flock of pigs in a huge green pasture surrounded by grassy hills and overhung by a blue sky. In the painted distance we can see a train moving leftward, and when the camera, after a jump-cut to a closer view of the farmer and another cut, starts to pan right, we see more grass and pigs as well as a *trompe l'oeil* red wooden building, power lines, and utility poles running alongside it. When, after another cut, we finally get the chance to see where the mural ends and the real street continues (a shot in which the camera picks up Mark's red truck moving toward us), the real Los Angeles sky is simply a slightly faded continuation of the painted one and the power lines (or their shadows), which we may have taken to be a part of the mural, turn out to be the real power lines running alongside an LA street. But when Mark turns a corner, we seem to be offered a contrast rather than continuity: we see delivery trucks for Farmer John's Meats (one of the biggest pork producers in California[5]), so the bucolic surface of the mural seems to be contrasted with the violent reality (slaughter) behind it. Yet this effect of depth is destabilized again, because, as we see the delivery trucks, the camera flash-zooms in on a part of the mural located above the vehicles (a continuation of the part of the mural already seen) in which a clearly disadvantaged man (his clothes are torn and his physical appearance is rough in contrast to that of the painted farmers) is stealing a terrified pig. Therefore as soon as the distinction between illusion (pastoral) and reality (violence) is introduced, it is flattened out yet again, but because we start and finish with flatness, it seems as if depth were merely a virtual effect produced by depthless space.

It is also interesting that the flash-zoom is accompanied on the soundtrack by an electronic noise which continues as Mark's truck drives on, as if the visually perceived violence were picked up by the soundtrack and carried on even after the mural is no longer seen. For a short while the noise is toned down to the sound of engines when Mark and Morty (Bill Garaway; his roommate who is riding with him) pass two policemen on bikes, who are given the finger by Mark, but returns (made more industrial by what sounds like clashing metal) again during a famous sequence in which Mark is driving through an industrial part of LA full of huge and colorful billboards (Bethlehem Steel Corporation Los Angeles Plant, Ladewig Company Water Meter Valves, Danola Ham & Bacon, etc.) and then city traffic, moving against the out-of-focus industrial detritus in the background, all photographed through a telephoto lens to flatten the image as

---

[5] Pomerance, *Michelangelo Red*, 190.

much as possible. In this way the "pastoral" violence that appeared in the mural sequence, and that was picked up from it by the noisy soundtrack, is injected into the visual experience of the "real" (diegetic) LA. It is this violence which "flattens" the image, that is, which destabilizes the difference between illusion and reality. In the final part of this sequence Mark and Morty drive down a street still lined with billboards and tall utility poles, with the "industrial" soundtrack still blaring, and—presto!—after an intercut, which shows us the protagonists, the poles transform into the palm trees of Beverly Hills, and the distorted soundtrack is gone. We are back in "normal"-looking reality and among ordinary street sounds, but the very consistency of "normal" reality has been undermined for the viewer: is Sunset Boulevard reality or a pastoral illusion? Or a more unsettling question: does this difference have any meaning in LA?

This issue is also central to the Sunnydunes strand of the plot. Lee Allen is the chief executive of a company which wants to build and sell houses in the desert. In fact, after having seen the brutal treatment of the arrested students by the police, we are shown a commercial advertisement for those houses, in which figures who are literally plastic smile their plastic smiles; the females cook their plastic eggs-and-bacon in their plastic kitchens for the plastic junior and "that man of the house"; the males putt to their plastic hearts' content on the plastic "special practice putting green" (the model house comes fitted with the model family roles). This, of course, is too crude to be taken as a serious criticism of advertising or capitalism in general, and the joke status of the commercial is emphasized by a tongue-in-cheek quotation from Alfred Hitchcock. To the words, "Get out in the sun and water your own private garden," a plastic man sprinkles real water straight into the camera, like the shower in the famous scene in *Psycho* (1960; the plastic commercial *is*, in a sense, a horror movie).[6]

However, the superficially absurd commercial hides other and more interesting references. At first, what is being sold here looks like a pure escapist fantasy: "Why be caught up in the rat race of city life, when you can enjoy life the Sunnydunes way? ... So stop driving yourself crazy in that miserable crowded city. Move out today and start your life over with our Sunnydunes house in the sun." Yet the desert surely must offer something more than the sun, which is after all perhaps not so attractive to the inhabitants of sunny LA. And it does; it offers "the full relaxation of outdoor living": your own private pool, "emerald green

---

[6] That this quotation is not accidental is confirmed by the occurrence of at least two other references to Hitchcock in the film, which I mention further.

tennis lawns," "mountain water from oaken buckets," unpolluted air and some other conveniences, which can all be summarized by another phrase that can be found in the commercial: "your own private garden." However, the garden is not just a neutral object which might simply be more or less pleasurable—it gets morally, and ultimately also politically, qualified: "Become an independent man. Forge a life of your own, like the pioneers who molded the West." What we have here on offer is not just a house and a garden but, in an admittedly caricatured commercial form, (white) Americanness itself in the form of one of America's most abiding fantasies, which goes back at least to the times of J. Hector St. John de Crèvecœur and Thomas Jefferson. It is the pastoral fantasy of the American farm as a regenerative garden in which European immigrants can shed their former skin and become reborn out of the bounty of the virgin land, or, in the more Jeffersonian version, as the theory of native agricultural deliverance from moral and physical depredations of the city's wage-slavery.[7]

Jefferson's most famous expression of this fantasy, in which moral and political virtue go hand in hand, can be found in his *Notes on the State of Virginia* (1785):

> Those who labour in the earth are the chosen people of God, if ever he had a chosen people, whose breasts he has made his peculiar deposit for substantial and genuine virtue. It is the focus in which he keeps alive that sacred fire, which otherwise might escape from the face of the earth. Corruption of morals in the mass of cultivators is a phenomenon of which no age nor nation has furnished an example. It is the mark set on those, who not looking up to heaven, to their own soil and industry, as does the husbandman, for their subsistence, depend for it on the casualties and caprice of customers. Dependence begets subservience and venality, suffocates the germ of virtue, and prepares fit tools for the designs of ambition. ... The mobs of great cities add just so much to the support of pure government, as sores do to the strength of the human body. It is the manners and spirit of a people which preserve a republic in vigour. A degeneracy in these is a canker which soon eats to the heart of its laws and constitution.[8]

The American virtues—such as individualism, independence, confidence, and self-government—are explicitly linked by Jefferson to the renunciation of city life and strife for economic gain. His farmer lives a contented life because he does not feel the need to accumulate:

---

[7] The classic analysis of this fantasy is Leo Marx, *The Machine in the Garden: Technology and the Pastoral Ideal in America* (Oxford: Oxford University Press, 2000); first published in 1964.
[8] Thomas Jefferson, *The Essential Jefferson*, ed. Jean M. Yarbrough (Indianapolis: Hackett Publishing, 2006), 132–3.

The Virginia farmer on his family-sized farm would produce everything that his family needs and at most a little more. The goal is sufficiency, not economic growth—a virtual stasis that is a counterpart of the desired psychic balance or peace. (Notice that here "permanence of government" is one of Jefferson's chief concerns.) By equating desires with needs, turning his back on industry and trade, the husbandman would be free of the tyranny of the market. Here the absence of economic complexities makes credible the absence of their usual concomitant, a class structure. Jefferson grounds this happy classless state in the farmer's actual possession of land; in such a society all men would adopt an aloof patrician attitude toward acquisitive behavior.[9]

The crucial terms here are "stasis," "balance," and "peace." The pastoral ideal propagated by Jefferson is of a harmonious society, that is, a society bearing no contradiction (contradictory interests) within itself[10] and therefore free from all "unbalancing" factors. In other words, the peaceful state of such society implies that it remains in the state of stasis—it is a society existing outside of history. This is of course why Jefferson detests cities: industrialization (and with it wage labor) is the means by which history, in his times, encroaches upon American soil.

While within the visible distance many slaveholding farms existed in Virginia, and further north, as he knew from his own experience, grimy industrializing cities and struggling Yankee farmers, because Jefferson lived in the time of the open Frontier, he could imagine that the ideal pastoral republic was in the process of being created just beyond the horizon by the virtuous pioneers, people who were molding the West. That fantasy, updated and canonized by American Transcendentalism, continued uninterrupted throughout the nineteenth century, until the closing of the Frontier was announced in 1890, always at the cost of removing the pastoral scene out of sight and into the fantastic realm just beyond the horizon.[11]

---

[9] Marx, *The Machine in the Garden*, 127–8.

[10] In American circumstances free of feudal structures, Jefferson can imagine his farmers forming a classless society, but in Europe whence the genre was imported, the ideal pastoral society implied "a beautiful relation between rich and poor" (William Empson, *Some Versions of Pastoral* (New York: New Directions, 1974), 11).

[11] Just one quite humorous illustration of this rather serious problem: "One day in 1837, according to his journal, [Emerson] learns with 'sensible relief' that New England is destined to be the 'manufacturing country of America.' His logic is simple. Now, he explains, better-suited regions will provide food for the nation, and he no longer need feel obliged to sympathize with hard-pressed Yankee farmers" (Marx, *The Machine in the Garden*, 231). Evidently, the non-pastoral Yankee farmers did not pass the exacting Jeffersonian standard of virtue, non-acquisitiveness, and self-sufficiency.

But what happens to the fantasy when the horizon (like the Frontier) disappears? In other words, where exactly is the space that the Sunnydunes commercial advertises? In order to answer this question, it is enough to look at the name of the company: Sunnydunes Development—what it advertises is the development of LA by introducing an imaginary borderline between the Jeffersonian "miserable city" and the pastoral Sunnydunes houses in the sun. As LA is surrounded by desert, the Sunnydunes houses will be built on the outskirts of the existing city, and although the first few or even few dozen might at the beginning look "independent" of the city, the company, as we hear in Allen's office, is planning an investment of 200 million dollars at that moment and billions more in the future, so after a while the "independent" houses will simply constitute new LA suburbs stretching ever deeper into the desert. This means that from the very beginning the borderline (formerly the horizon) between the bad city and the good garden/farm gets folded back into the city and becomes a virtual (fantasy) limit that separates the city from itself. In other words, the city is the "miserable city," but at the same time it is "your own private garden," that is, the image of the city and the image of the garden are superimposed on each other without ever completely coinciding. The effect of such superimposition is perfectly captured by Antonioni in an aforementioned sequence: Beverly Hills is "real" but at the same time it looks like a mural painting of itself.[12]

This logic can also be illustrated in a different manner: precisely when there is nowhere to escape, the developer, in order to develop (to entice buyers), has to use the fantasy of the escape from development, so the difference between yes and no, the difference that distinguishes development from non-development (or city from nature), becomes a purely strategic difference internal to the development (city) itself. This "invagination" into the city space of the horizon, that is, the borderline between reality and fantasy space, is precisely the operation that opens the space to limitless development in all directions because in such space the "outer" horizon does not exist.[13] We see such horizon-less space when Mark steals a plane and takes a "scenic flight" over LA. Although the city is filmed from high altitude, the vanishing point against which he could situate himself (or we ourselves as viewers) is absent: the buildings stretch into the

---

[12] Pomerance, *Michelangelo Red*, 192.
[13] The concept of "sutured" and "non-sutured" space is analyzed in great detail and depth by Joan Copjec on the example of film noir in "Locked Room/Lonely Room: Private Space in Film Noir," in *Read My Desire: Lacan against the Historicists* (Cambridge, MA: The MIT Press, 1994), 163–200.

distance, gradually turning into a greenish blur, which in turn gradually takes on a bluish hue until it becomes the blue sky. Lee Allen presides over this virtual space which has no limit (one more house can always be imagined) and which offers no resistance (to development)—when one of the Sunnydunes executives speaks about reserving 40 million dollars for contingencies, Allen's reaction is: "Why tie up 40 million dollars for contingencies? I mean, what contingencies?"

But such limitless virtual space is far from offering more breathing space—it is, in fact, suffocating.[14] It produces the flattened, claustrophobic, hallucinatory unreality of the city experience rendered by Antonioni as Mark and Morty drive through LA. However, this claustrophobia is not just a matter of "feeling." As the strategic status of the difference between the inside (city) and the outside (nature) becomes the defining feature of such space, the "development" also comes to encompass other dimensions than land. One of the effects is that in the urban phantasmagoria images become imperative and the infiniteness of such space ensures that no one is exempted from their imperativeness, not an executive who manipulates the images for his own purposes, nor a radical who wants to destroy them. There are a number of examples of that in the film. Allen, driving to work, passes an American Airlines advertisement showing a watch on the wrist of an airline pilot, which makes Allen dutifully look at his own watch. When Mark finds himself in the town of Hawthorne, he wanders around, not knowing what to do, until a huge billboard advertising United Airlines appears behind his back saying "Let's get away from it all."[15] A few minutes later, he steals a small plane in order to do precisely that.[16]

However, there is a different kind of space in Antonioni's film, the desert, where Mark's and Daria's paths cross. Escaping from what happened on the campus, Mark takes a bus and goes to the end of the line, which turns out to be Hawthorne, where he steals a pink Cessna to perform a "scenic flight" over LA and then the desert. Daria's route is not so straightforward. She borrows an old Buick (without the owner's knowledge) and sets out on a voyage to Phoenix ("or rather, Carefree, a development-resort about thirty miles north of Phoenix"[17]),

---

[14] Copjec, "Locked Room/Lonely Room," 90–6.
[15] Of course, it is not accidental that the message Mark "obeys" is exactly the same we heard in the Sunnydunes commercial.
[16] These relations (and some others) between ads and protagonists are noted by Arrowsmith, *Antonioni*, 136–7. One of the accusations Chatman offers in his criticism of *Zabriskie Point* is that Angelenos do not even notice the billboards (*Antonioni*, 161), but this is precisely Antonioni's point: they do not notice, but just react to the messages without consciously registering them.
[17] Arrowsmith, *Antonioni*, 128–9.

where, in a villa at the edge of the desert, she is supposed to meet Lee Allen, her boss (and perhaps lover). But first she makes a detour. She wants to find the desert town of Ballister (though she does not even remember the name), in order to meet a friend, called Jimmy Patterson, because he had told her that it was "a fantastic place for meditation." Thus, we follow a girl dressed in a green designer tunic, the color of pastoral nature, wearing indigenous adornments ("a turquoise bracelet and rings, a Navaho turquoise necklace and a red-green Sioux bead belt"[18]), that is, we are given another example of a temporary escapee from the rush of the city, looking for contemplative circumstances in order to harmonize her life with her inner (natural) self. But what she finds in Ballister is very far from pastoral nature as a harmonious setting for meditation—it is a ghost town strewn with the material detritus of industrial civilization (the rusting body of a car, old containers, broken pieces of furniture, etc.). Yet Ballister has at least one of the features of the pastoral: it is static—the patrons of the bar Daria visits are worn-out old-timers looking stoically into the distance and doing nothing. All they can do in the ghost town is precisely "meditate," and this is perfectly shown by Antonioni in the figure of an old man in a cowboy hat who, throughout the Ballister episode, just sits at the bar next to a glass of beer, staring at the wall (that is, into himself) and smoking, completely oblivious to the reality round him—an American Buddha if ever there was one.

Who are these meditative old-timers and what are they doing in the ghost town? Although there are no "true" pioneers, only plastic (virtual) ones in phantasmagorical LA, because its smooth unresisting space does not demand (does not even allow) men whose individualism, independence, and endurance molded the West, they can be found, although in a hardly recognizable form, in Ballister, as represented, for instance, by toothless Johnny Wilson, "the middleweight champion of the world in 1920," whom Daria meets in the bar. But, despite appearances (the men sit listening to Patti Page's "The Tennessee Waltz," a nostalgic song about lost love), the town and its elderly inhabitants are not a nostalgic vignette of the passing old West of Jeffersonian self-sufficient and self-reliant men, and as such amenable to appropriation by the fantasy of the escape from "that miserable crowded city." In fact, Ballister demonstrates how the pastoral fantasy, realized as LA, precisely does *not* allow one to be an independent man and forge a life of one's own, because there is a source of the

---

[18] Ibid., 128.

stasis of the ghost town which is not fantastic at all. Balister's plight is strictly historical. Central to the development of LA as the city of omnipresent green vegetation and turquoise pools, which are crucial to its pastoral image, was the transfer to the LA area of large quantities of water from the lands surrounding it, the effect of which was that farms and orange groves, whose existence the water supported, withered and turned into desert.[19] Therefore, Ballister and its not-so-pastoral stasis are a residue of actual historical violence which was perpetrated so that the ahistorical pastoral city could come into existence. But the traces of the violence have been entirely erased from the virtual reality of the pastoral—one has to go into the desert, looking for peace, to find that the peace one encounters is man-made and, in fact, not peace at all. Therefore it is not surprising that the episode, which starts as a boring visit to a dusty museum of the old West, ends with violence, panic, and hasty departure. A group of boys, brought to Ballister from LA by Jimmy Paterson, who have just broken a window of the bar and infuriated its owner, menacingly surround Daria and demand "a piece of ass." When she takes it for a joke, they grab at her and try to tear her panties off, until she forces her way out of the group and runs away. At the place which is a trace of erased historical violence, Daria appropriately encounters violence which is seemingly inexplicable[20]—it materializes out of thin air for no reason and disappears accordingly (although its vague origin is LA).

The "gratuitous" violence in which the kids engage might remind us of the American critics' accusations about the absurdly violent police in the film. Although at first sight this connection does not seem to offer much, it is enough to see the violence against the background of the pastoral fantasy's denial of the historical dimension in order to arrive at an important point. The film shows us that, at least from one perspective, the ahistorical LA society is virtually classless, as everybody (rich and poor) is caught up in the pastoral fantasy of "beautiful relation" (the white workers whom Mark encounters in a shop in Hawthorne are as contemptuous of him as are the officers at the police station). There is, however, an exception: there are some people in LA whose very existence undermines this fantasy. These are, of course, the Black radicals we saw at the beginning of

---

[19] Pomerance, who relates the story in greater detail, quotes Carey McWilliams, who writes that "the Los Angeles basin of 1,400,000 acres of habitable land ... has only .06% of the natural stream flow of water in the state" (*Michelangelo Red*, 159). A part of the story, which also included land speculation, is presented in Roman Polański's *Chinatown* (1974).

[20] We are told that the kids are supposed to be "emotionally sick," but this is not much of an explanation in the first place, and additionally it is offered at one remove by the absent Jimmy Patterson through the mouth of the owner of the bar.

the film, whose claim has already been quoted: "A lot of black people have died already in this country. Black people have earned this leadership in blood, ... we're not going to give it up." They have earned the leadership in blood by dying as slaves, by being lynched under Jim Crow and now by participating in civil rights and Black liberation movements. In other words, it is the blood shed by Black Americans throughout American history that makes them unsusceptible to the ahistorical pastoral fantasy which is entirely white and which has fed on the blood. Firstly, the mythical image that the ante-bellum South had of itself was a version of this fantasy: the image of chivalrous and paternalistic slave-holding gentlemen-farmers courting sentimental ladies and loved by their devoted slaves who were not able to take care of themselves. Secondly, the Black presence in LA (and other urban areas) is the reminder of the fantasy's dismal historical post-bellum failure, that is, its economic impossibility. Blacks in American cities are mostly the descendants of the impoverished southern sharecroppers whose laboring in the earth definitely did not make them the chosen people of God, nor did it give them substantial and genuine virtue—just back-breaking labor and poverty. These were the people who, to improve their lot, escaped from the putative pastoral paradise to the slaughterhouses of Chicago and the "satanic mills" of northern industrial centers (Philadelphia, Detroit, Cleveland, New York).[21] So, when the Sunnydunes commercial advertises escape from the turmoil of the city, it seems that what is being escaped from might not be the rat race and pollution, primarily, but rather the militant upsurge in the city of the element that does not fit into the pastoral fantasy and therefore threatens to expose it for what it is: the violent collusion between the uniform and the business suit.

Although the Black political struggle against the pastoral fantasy that is defended by the police forces is explicitly featured only at the beginning of *Zabriskie Point*, it constitutes the backbone of the film, because it is intimately related to Mark's attitude throughout. In fact, when driving through LA, Mark and Morty pick up the political plot at exactly the moment it was broken off by Mark's exit from the meeting room shown at the beginning of the film. To Mark's jibe that "The day you don't count on losing is the day I'll join the movement," Morty answers: "What if joining isn't a matter of choice? For lots of people it's a matter of survival." Whom does he have in mind? Himself? Although we do

---

[21] Until 1910, more than 90 percent of the African-American population lived in the rural South.

not learn anything about Morty in the film, this is most unlikely. Probably, like the other white students we have seen, he has some kind of middle-class background, and we have just learned that Mark is probably a dropout from a rich family (Mark and Morty almost crash into Mark's sister's fancy convertible at a corner on Sunset Boulevard). Therefore we can only return to what was said at the students' meeting at the beginning of the film: people who do not have the choice are those who "can't get a job, can't go to school, can't eat," etc., that is, Black Americans. "That's what I mean," answers Mark to Morty's remark, "It's not a game." And the political plot develops precisely in this direction. Although a few busloads of white students and professors are arrested and roughed up by the police for protesting on campus, they are released after being booked, while the Black students barricaded in the campus library are treated to tear gas, approached like dangerous criminals (the police wield not truncheons but guns) and one of them is shot dead. Present at the scene and true to his word that for him, as for the Blacks, it is not a game, Mark pulls a gun out of his boot to shoot the police shooter, but somebody else does it first.

Why is Mark ready to kill the policeman? Because he "is a lawless punk with no shadow of a claim to any opinion which should be taken seriously, for he has no formed identity, no social shape, no principle of existence (except freedom from)"? This is not what we are shown in the film. Mark seems to have at least one principle of existence which is straightforwardly related to his attempt on the policeman's life. When Mark and a friend of his buy guns, they persuade the clerk not to check their criminal records before handing them the guns, by claiming that they live in "a neighborhood, that's, you know, borderline" (meaning the borderline of a black ghetto) and that they have to protect their women. But it seems that the place where Mark lives is not even "borderline," because the two times in the film when we see it, the only people around it are Black: once (when Mark is leaving to check what is happening on the campus) we see two Black kids on bikes in the foreground and more playing in the background, and the other time (when, from a shop in Hawthorne, Mark is calling Morty at their place) we see through the window behind Morty's back an elderly Black couple having a chat. Moreover, during one of the conversations between Mark and Daria in the desert later in the film, when she jokingly asks him to tell her the rest of his "criminal record" (he has just given her the reasons for his expulsion from college), he says: "Once I changed my color, but it didn't work, so I changed back." Daria treats it as a joke, which, on the surface, it is, but it also has a serious subtext which Daria is not in a position to understand knowing next to nothing about Mark. Identifying with the Black struggle, Mark seems to have an idea that a violent act, like killing a cop in retaliation for the killing of a Black student, would symbolically turn him into a Black irreversibly (i.e., he would get the same treatment as Blacks from the police), but because he failed to do it, he, in a sense, returned to being white. And his identification is only emphasized as it is given a historical parallel by his self-deprecating wry comment on Daria's remark that she heard on the radio that "the guy who killed the cop [on the campus] was white": "Ooh, white man taking up arms for the blacks, huh? Just like old John Brown."

This and the final death of Mark at the hands of the police—when he does change his color to Black, and properly, so to speak, that is, not by the retaliatory killing of a policeman, but by being treated exactly like the Black man who was shot unarmed on campus—bring us once more to one of the most oft-repeated accusations against the film: that the police violence presented in it is preposterously exaggerated, that is, "unrealistic."[22] Even leaving aside (for now) our former point about the film's destabilization of the very status of reality and therefore "objectivity," we may ask from whose perspective is the violence ("the gun happy attitude of the police in Antonioni's Los Angeles"[23]) exaggerated? Perhaps the introduction of a bit of historical context is in order here. Writing about James Baldwin's two great essays devoted to the question of race in the United States, which were published together in 1963 under the title *The Fire Next Time*, Ishmael Reed, another important Black writer and activist, notes that "'radical chic' was the expression introduced by the late Seymour Krim to chastise Baldwin for permitting *The Fire Next Time* to be published in *The New Yorker*, the epitome of uptown pretensions and snobbery."[24] Although for the white critical establishment the police violence in *Zabriskie Point* seemed crudely exaggerated, one does not have to look far to find views of police brutality not very different from what we see in the film—it is enough to pick up almost any book published in the 1960s by a Black author engaged in the struggle against racial prejudice, of which *The Autobiography of Malcolm X* is only perhaps the most famous example. Moreover, we are not dealing here with two different but equally valid perspectives between which one can choose as

---

[22] "[T]he evil police have been cast from the same mold as the old Hollywood Nazis," writes Kael in "The Beauty of Destruction," 96.
[23] Chatman, *Antonioni*, 162.
[24] Ishmael Reed, Preface to *Soul on Ice*, by Eldridge Cleaver (New York: Dell Publishing, 1999), 6.

one pleases: according to the white establishment (but not only establishment) the violence was negligible; according to Black radicals (but not only radicals) it was unbearable. If we want to take a *synoptic* view of the 1960s (and this is what the film was supposed to do, according to its critics, but failed dismally), we have to bear in mind that it was Black political activism and Black popular culture that created the political and cultural matrix of the decade.[25] This matrix was taken over by most whites (including those representing "uptown pretensions and snobbery") and variously adapted to their needs, but when these needs resulted in opinions, which denied their origin in the matrix, their truth value must be considered as disingenuous.[26]

But to return to the desert. As a product of virtual pastoral reality, Daria must run away from the encounter with its suppressed underside. But she does not turn back; she drives on into Death Valley, that is, the "real" desert, not the man-made one. Yet before we follow her to her meeting with Mark, something strange happens. In the last shot in which we see her car, which has been parked in front of the bar, driving off, the camera does not follow it but begins to approach one of the bar's windows, which has "pool room" painted on it and an Olympia beer neon sign. Through the window we can see the American Buddha, with his cigarette and beer glass, still sitting at the counter in the same place as previously doing nothing and staring into space to the melody of "The Tennessee Waltz." The camera moves closer and closer to the window and then penetrates through it as if it were a ghost, which is a more or less standard cinematic trick made possible by the zoom lens. But then the camera pulls back to where the window glass was a few seconds ago, but *it is not there*: the limit which used to divide the outer (the street/desert) from the inner (the room) has disappeared. At first the trick looks like a formal suggestion of the inner space in which the Buddha is submerged, oblivious to what happens around him (there is nobody else in the bar in this shot), but in the larger context of the film something else is also happening here.

After a cut we find ourselves, for the first time, in the real desert where Mark's and Daria's paths will cross. However, in the film the desert is not just

---

[25] Ibid., 10.
[26] One may be reminded that Pauline Kael made her name as a film critic by defending *Bonnie and Clyde* against accusations of being "a cliché-ridden fraud"—precisely her indictment of *Zabriskie Point*. "Bonnie and Clyde," in *Arthur Penn's* Bonnie and Clyde, ed. Lester D. Friedman (Cambridge: Cambridge University Press, 2000), 183; the review was originally published (where else but) in *The New Yorker*, October 21, 1967.

another geographical location continuous with the space of the city, in the way the developers conceive of it (their virtual space is infinite and homogeneous). Historicity suppressed as the ghost town constitutes a fault-line and by crossing it we enter a different spatial dimension. This is formally implied in the Buddha shot, as it technically consists of combining two crucial moments from the earlier part of the plot. We have already mentioned the flash-zoom-in on a bum stealing a pig painted in the pastoral mural on Farmer John's Meats building. We have also mentioned another pastoral image presented in the film, that is, the Sunnydunes commercial. But we have not noted that it includes a moment which corresponds to the pig-stealing in its otherwise harmonious "natural" imagery: within the plastic sunny Arcadia in which everybody is fit, smiling, content, and white, a small child, sitting in a pram next to his happy plastic mother in her "fully equipped Sunnydunes kitchen," is silently screaming his head off as if he were being flayed alive, and this is emphasized by the camera in exactly the opposite way than in the Farmer John's Meats mural: from the close-up on the face of the kid the camera flash-zooms out to include a table full of plastic (in)edibles. Therefore we have two "stains" which explode (or at least disturb) two explicit images of flat pastoral harmony offered to us, both implying a different space than the space of development. And the Buddha shot relates to both stains by bringing them together in the superimposition of the two movements of the camera just mentioned: according to Bob Rubin, Antonioni's assistant director on the film, the shot was done "with a forward zoom/reverse dolly combination."[27]

Having crossed the fault-line, we find ourselves in a different space. But what makes it different? The first hint can be seen just after the cut: a railway line that is completely straight and which Mark's airplane follows into the desert.[28] The desert we encounter in this part of the film is something different from Ballister. It is mostly Death Valley, which, as we learn from the information board at the eponymous Zabriskie Point (a viewing point in the desert) shown in the film, "is an area of ancient lake beds deposited five to ten million years ago. These beds have been tilted and pushed upward by earth forces, and eroded by wind and water." In other words, although Death

---

[27] Pomerance, *Michelangelo Red*, 188. Personal communication from Rubin is given as the source.
[28] The railway line and the train are images taken straight out of the meat factory mural. Mark does not have to go through the historical detour of Ballister because he bears this historical fault-line in himself: he has identified with the Black struggle, even if he perhaps does not know its historical, that is, anti-pastoral, stakes.

Valley is a natural phenomenon, it is the ruins of nature understood not only in the pastoral sense as an agricultural landscape of temperate climate, but even in the wild, "primeval" sense (virgin forests untouched by man, etc.). It is precisely by being such a ruin that the desert defies (by its age, its vastness, its emptiness, etc.) designs human imagination may have on it, and therefore confronting man with the *unknowable* (the opposite of the unresisting space of development). The chastising power of such confrontation is, in fact, a *locus classicus* of the American discourse that insists on the need to preserve the continent's remaining wilderness in its pristine state, which, not surprisingly, began to gain popularity the moment the Frontier was declared closed.[29] A metaphor that has been most frequently used for over a hundred years is that in the wilderness the human mind, which is cramped in congested city circumstances, *expands*. In the early days of the preservationist discourse this expansion was often given a religious coloration,[30] which is still continued, in a secularized manner, by the naturalist poetics of authenticity (finding one's true self in contact with the wilderness), but we do not need mystical props to see the mechanism of such expansion. In fact, there is a classic preservationist book written about a desert (Arches National Monument in Utah, now Arches National Park), first published in 1968, and therefore more or less contemporary with *Zabriskie Point*, which analyzes it rather well. Although Edward Abbey's *Desert Solitaire* might sometimes seem to lapse into the aforementioned poetics of authenticity, his description of the experience of the desert concedes nothing to it:

> [C]lean air to breathe … ; stillness, solitude and space; an unobstructed view every day and every night of sun, sky, stars, clouds, mountains, moon, cliffrock and canyons; a sense of time enough to let thought and feeling range from here *to the end of the world and back*; the discovery of something intimate—though impossible to name—in the remote.[31]

What allows the mind to expand ecstatically in the desert is the presence of the horizon (the end of the world) which allows thought and feeling to range and to

---

[29] The classic discussion of this topic is Roderick Frazier Nash, *The Wilderness and the American Mind* (New Haven: Yale University Press, 2014); first edition published in 1967.

[30] For instance, John Muir, the first "prophet" of American preservationism, writes: "I will confess that I take more intense delight from reading the power and goodness of God from 'the things which are made' [primeval nature] than from the Bible" (quoted in Nash, *The Wilderness*, 124).

[31] Edward Abbey, *Desert Solitaire* (Tuscon: The University of Arizona Press, 1988), 39; italics added.

return refreshed to itself. But whence the feeling of the presence of something intimate "in the remote," that is, in the horizon itself? This "something" intimate is, of course, the vanishing point on the horizon, the virtual (objectively non-existing) point toward which, from my point of view, all the lines recede and in which all of them converge. This is the point in which I, as a viewing subject (as the organizing principle of my viewing), am present in the landscape (in what I see) as an *unknown* quantity ("impossible to name")[32] and which, by splitting me between my place of observation and the horizon, makes me a desiring subject, that is, allows me to breathe in the entire space ranging "to the end of the world and back." And Abbey again hits the nail on the head when he speaks of this subject (himself), as "a man with small needs, infinite desires"[33]: only in the space bounded by the horizon can desires and vision range freely, while the invagination of the horizon results in derealization of the world and claustrophobia. That is why throughout the desert sequence of the film, communication routes (the railroad, roads) are mostly completely straight, the horizon is open, and the panoramic view converges to the vanishing point.[34] The desert's true beauty, therefore, lies in its indifference: it remains only itself, resistant to human symbolic designs on it. But such uselessness can, in fact, be very useful—it can help a man to purify his needs, leaving only "the naked self":[35] pure (infinite) desire. Yet this is only the desert's potential, the "reality

---

[32] Lacanian psychoanalysis calls this point object *a*.
[33] Abbey, *Desert Solitaire*, 41.
[34] Restivo, relying again on Baudrillard's *America*, writes that "Death Valley must be seen as a strict correlative to the refractive architecture of LA, with the 'synthesis' of the two being the desert house which is exploded at the film's end. For the desert—as a Deleuzian 'smooth space'—presents us with the same problems of vanishing points, perspective and figure-ground relations as do the 'striated,' or territorialized, spaces of Los Angeles" ("Zabriskie Point," 90–1). Although I have interpreted the city space in a similarly Baudrillardian manner (partially inspired by Restivo), I find, for reasons stated above, the collapsing of LA and the desert to be ungrounded in the experience of the film. Although Deleuze and Baudrillard each have their own vision of desert space, which serves their respective theories, and the latter's is even supposedly based on his own experiences of the very landscape shown in *Zabriskie Point* (the Mojave desert), what they say about the desert fits neither Antonioni's image nor the movie's plot. To give just one example, also used by Restivo: about driving through the desert Baudrillard writes, "Movement which moves through space of its own volition changes into absorption by space itself—end of resistance, end of scene of the journey as such." The journey aims for "the point of no return," when "there is no longer any reason for it to come to an end" (*America*, 10); thus, "the absorption by space itself" means that, in the experience of such "pure speed," it is the driver (as volitional subject) who vanishes. Applying this to *Zabriskie Point*, one wonders if some kind of mix up did not happen. One can obviously use Baudrillard's ideas in relation to, for example, *Easy Rider*, in which Billy and Wyatt seem to feel that they are themselves only when they are on their bikes, but pure speed is of no consequence for the desert experience in *Zabriskie Point*, even though the film uses a car and a plane.
[35] Abbey, *Desert Solitaire*, 6.

trip" one can experience by allowing the desert to work its ways, if one leaves one's pastoral preconceptions behind.

Mark and Daria both detour through the desert on their respective routes: Daria, as we have noted, in search of "nature"; Mark, because he "needed to get off the ground," that is, escape from the city and the police and decide what to do next, but also "to get high," to experience a boost of adrenaline to get him out of the state of confusion (as we have seen him do previously, e.g., driving through a crossing against the light). Daria has a predetermined itinerary (LA—Ballister—Phoenix), while Mark does not really know what to do. He does not seem to have a positive identity because he has shed his previous one (as a Beverly Hills kid) and identifies with people who still have to forge theirs (what it means to be an emancipated African American), while Daria is a self-assured "earth child" clad in green and wearing native American ornaments, bent on "being herself" (a static Arcadian ideal). Therefore it is not surprising that she immediately appropriates the desert as a home: "Don't you feel at home here?" she asks Mark, "It's peaceful." "It's dead," he answers, unconvinced. Against which she comes up with the concept of "a death game," whose point is to prove that the desert is not dead; that it is nature, full of various plants and creatures. This is of course true (any desert is an ecosystem) but beside the point, as Mark's impulse is directed precisely against domestication: not every space can or even should be made a home (not everything can or should serve self-realization). While Daria offers domestication as the universal solution to the world's problems ("There's a thousand sides, not just heroes and villains"), Mark rejects it as a part of the problem ("If you don't see them as villains, you can't get rid of them"), that is, when Daria domesticates by means of a multiplication of perspectives ("a thousand sides"), Mark resists by the establishment of the horizon of meaning ("When it gets down to it, you'd have to choose one side or the other"). Moreover, what is involved in Daria's domestication-by-naturalization impulse quickly comes to the fore: "It'd be nice if they could plant thoughts in our heads, so nobody would have bad memories ... only good things." It would be difficult to find a better metaphor for the wishful pastoral fantasizing that Daria represents perfectly: good thoughts, like domesticated garden plants, can cover the scars of personal history ("Yeah, to make you forget how terrible it really was," says Mark), turning one's mental life into a lush Arcadia. But, on the social/political level, a transplantation like that has already happened: the bad memory of desertified Ballister has been permanently excised from the pastoral phantasmagoria of LA, for which it never happened. In such a world "nothing is terrible," as Daria maintains, and insistence on contradictions is seen only as a failure of imagination.[36]

Daria's pastoral thinking is finally externalized in the film in her pot-induced sexual fantasy in which, while she and Mark are making love, their act is multiplied by a large number of other young people rolling in the sand ("There's a thousand sides"), taking on the hue of the earth, becoming one with it, and seemingly representing the life principle itself. It is as if all divisions have been overcome and the *undifferentiated* earth were making love to itself—the couples are only "strategically" differentiated: the partners, covered with sand, look almost the same.[37] Thus we find ourselves once again in the smooth, unresisting space of development not bounded by the horizon, but this time the lethal underpinnings of the fantasy are much more obvious: the only possibility to become one with the desert is to turn into dust, that is, to become dead (in order to survive in these circumstances one has to protect oneself by the inventions of civilization, such as a car or a plane).[38]

Daria's imaginary love-in is blended with the earth also in order to suggest a life-affirming, "natural," that is, innocent sexuality, but the film has already shown us that sexuality is particularly resistant to the pastoral vision. In fact, Daria's fantasy constitutes the fourth instance of its explicit appearance in the film. Mark's buzzing of her car may be considered just play, but it nonetheless includes the element of aggression: the man is the master of the situation and he uses his advantage mercilessly.[39] Another type of sexual relation presented in the film is more ominous: when the boss tells his secretary to go with him to a desert resort, you know what he expects her to do in the bosom of nature. And, finally, if one wants to find a believable image of innocent ("natural") sexuality in the film, one should not look for it in Daria's pastoral fantasy, but precisely

---

[36] "What do you mean, [they are on a] reality trip?" Daria asks Mark about his friends. "Oh, yeah, they can't imagine things," she answers herself.

[37] The difference between the sexes implies, of course, the individual's mortality, which is always a disturbing factor in the pastoral fantasy. To be more precise, there are not only couples but also trios engaged in making love.

[38] Mark does not only say that the desert is dead; he also speaks about its only possible human inhabitants. When Daria, having said that sometimes she feels like screaming, is yet reluctant to do it, Mark asks her: "Who [could hear you]? A ghost? A dead pioneer?"

[39] If one can say that domestication is Daria's stereotypically feminine reaction, Mark's modern Cessna buzzing Daria's ancient Buick presents a male pastoral stereotype: active domination of passive female earth. The absurd violence masquerading as play is emphasized by the reference to the scene in which Roger O. Thornhill is attacked by a crop-duster in *North by Northwest* (dir. Alfred Hitchcock, 1959).

where the pastoral shows its ugly lining: in the Ballister kids "spontaneous" harassment of the hippy protagonist.

However, in spite of the initial "domineering" impulse, Mark gradually comes under the sway of Daria's fantasy and of course by making love to her in the desert he takes a decisive step. His changing attitude is voiced explicitly after the love-making scene:

> Mark: I always knew it'd be like this.
> Daria: Us?
> Mark: The desert.[40]

Thus, in contradiction to what we heard from him earlier ("It's dead"), Mark is beginning to participate in the desert's domestication. And the scene that immediately follows such "home-making" is there precisely to show the incongruity between the home and the desert: a camper van with an overweight couple and their kid rolls into a parking space, and the absurdity of its presence in the middle of the desert is reinforced by the motorboat it is hauling and the ice-cream cone that the kid is licking. They are also very explicitly presented as an extension of the development impulse: the man speaks about building a drive-in at the place, which would bring lots of money, and their presence there is summed up on the soundtrack by the sound of jet-plane engines which we have heard previously accompanying some executives getting off their plane in Hawthorne. Moreover, the tourists and their mobile home are followed by their necessary accompaniment: a police car (meaningless development = meaningless violence) which stops at the parking place just as the tourists drive off and Mark and Daria appear. Thus, Mark, who is giving in to the imaginary plenitude of the pastoral-domestic fantasy, finds himself in a strange situation: on the one hand, he is reminded of his old desires, but, on the other, it seems as if, in the pastoral fantasy space, he has just stepped into by participating in Daria's home-making, his past wishes might immediately be realized and what he did not manage to do on the campus can be accomplished in the desert. But, of course, it cannot—the pastoral is an impotent fantasy, and Daria accordingly steps in between Mark and the policeman to prevent the former from shooting the latter. Although the pastoral fantasy tempts one by

---

[40] "I always knew it'd be like this" is one of the most often ridiculed moments in the film, but one wonders why. It does *not* refer to the love-making but to Mark's changing perception of the desert, therefore presenting us with a contradiction, not a plenitude.

seemingly materializing one's wishes, it is, in fact, an insurmountable obstacle to realizing them, just as buying the Sunnydunes house in the desert only prevents one from becoming an independent man and forging a life of one's own.[41]

In the film, Mark has been presented to us as split, as an unhappy consciousness divided between himself and a certain im/possibility ("to change his color") which makes him act. Now this split is confronted with a possibility of being healed by a fantasy of pastoral harmony with the earth (as the home), which as usual finally boils down to the fantasy of a successful sexual relationship (the love-in scene). For a while Mark is "naturally" overwhelmed by Daria and her beautiful body, in which the pastoral fantasy of peace and fulfillment seems to have materialized, to such an extent that he discards the gun and proceeds to commemorate the materialization in symbolic form by painting the plane together with Daria.[42] However, it is characteristic that what is supposed to be the message from the desert has nothing to do with it: the plane is mostly painted green (the color of pastoral, not desert nature[43]), and becomes an androgynous creature sporting female breasts painted on its wings, its fuselage transformed into a penis and the message "No words" written on it (the plenitude of enjoyment solidified in the androgynous creature allows for no words), as well as the pronouns she–he–it which are, as it were, encapsulated into one.[44] And finally this turns out to be the message of Daria, and not of Mark: he refuses to go for the fantasy of the plenitude of the successful relationship and self-realization ("You can just ditch

---

[41] The scene with the policeman (which is another reference to Hitchcock's *Psycho*) also interestingly "translates" the deficiency of the development space into the space of the desert. It is not only that with the policeman's appearance the horizon markedly closes in on him and Daria (it is mostly blocked by rock formations). Also, the camera pan which emulates the policeman's scanning of the horizon gets curtailed by a premature cut. After about 180 degrees, the shot ends, and in the next one we see the police car and then the policeman's head, which has turned 180 degrees without having seen about a half of what should have been the full 360-degree pan.

[42] Mark's (not entirely conscious?) reservations, however, come to the surface when he remarks about the painted plane: "They might not even think it's a plane—strange prehistoric bird spotted over Mojave desert with its genitals out." Yet we did see how the actual strange bird of sexuality with his genitals out behaved when Mark was buzzing Daria—nothing in the scene indicated peace and harmony.

[43] In fact, quite early the film offers a joking comment on the color green, which is throughout associated with Daria and the pastoral fantasy. When Daria turns off the motorway to look for Ballister, we see a huge billboard with an advertisement which shows a transparent bowl in which radishes and red onions are mixed with dollar bills, and a caption that says, "You are what you eat. Try our salads … Save with Desert Springs Savings and Loan." In the United States, green is also the color of money.

[44] They are encapsulated in the image of a bomb, but this is, of course, a "love-bomb" experienced at the moment of coming: the plane is an erect penis also bearing the inscription "No war."

[the plane] here and ride with me to Phoenix," says Daria[45]). Against his best interests ("I wanna take risks" he says), Mark chooses the unknowable (that is, his own split) and flies back to Hawthorne where the police are waiting. Probably taking him to be the killer of the policeman on the campus, they try to apprehend him, but when he resists, by attempting to maneuver the plane out of the police cars' way on the runway, he is simply shot without second thoughts on the part of the police. This is the moment he (symbolically) changes color, as he is no longer treated like a white member of the pastoral fantasy, and therefore presumed innocent, but as a Black stain on the fantasy, and therefore presumed guilty.

Daria carries on to Carefree, but, unlike Mark, completely unperturbed by their encounter and the desert. She is still someone who is not on a "reality trip," one who can easily imagine things: when she changes the channel on her car radio to some country-and-western station, suddenly a herd of trotting horses materializes on the other side of the road. Nor does the desert have any influence on the development space in which she lives: when Mick Jagger on her radio sings "when I'm hungry and thirsty too" ("You Got the Silver"), she reaches out for a red apple and starts chewing on it.[46]

Daria learns about Mark's death from the radio on her way, which makes her stop and consider returning to LA. But more important is the way her act of mourning Mark is presented: in fact, it is split into *three* actions. When she hears the news, she pulls over, gets out of the car, and among desert shrubs and cactuses gently sways along with them in the wind (she does not cry): it is not really Daria but the wind that mourns Mark here. Finally she decides to go on and after some time she arrives at the desert house where Allen's business dealings are taking place. Unnoticed, she passes some artificial looking ("plastic") women relaxing next to an artificial looking ("plastic") pool and enters a chamber in which mountain water is flowing down a solid rock wall (the house is an aerie built on a rock overlooking the desert). She wades through the "natural looking" water pooled at the bottom of the wall, lets the water flow down her face and green dress, and starts to sob. Again, it is not really Daria who is crying but the water itself that is mourning Mark. Then, after a cut, all the primary natural elements (but one) are cinematically brought together: in

---

[45] Additionally, what she proposes is a version of "the American dream"—the beginning of the New Life in the New World (or another state in this case).

[46] This is the second time she is eating an apple in the film. The first is when she is on her way to Ballister. Of course, this fits neatly my interpretation of Daria as Eve (a temptress) in relation to Mark.

a long shot (Daria's point-of-view) we see an enormous glass window behind which Allen and his guests (silently) discuss business, while the desert rocks that surround the house are reflected in the glass; this image is accompanied by the sound of the water trickling down the rock and the wind jangling the wind chimes that hang outside the window. Thus, on the flat virtual screen, which is nothing in itself (transparent glass), the businessmen's dealings and Daria's pastoral fantasy of desert as home mingle effortlessly and seamlessly, although the effect of this superimposition is quite oneiric (LA space was also presented as flat and phantasmagorical).

Obviously, there is a missing element in the natural imagery: fire. However, when we cut to a pan that allows the businessmen's faces to be seen in close-up, we notice an added element among them: a middle-aged native American maid who is serving drinks to the men. Moreover, when she puts down the drinks tray and starts to walk out of the shot, the focus is racked and Daria's reflection in the window is superimposed on the image of the maid. Because, as we have already noted, Daria's "earth-child" image is throughout the film emphasized by her green tunic and native American ornaments, it is not difficult to see what is being offered here: Daria is looking at the pastoral fantasy screen (natural imagery, which paradoxically seems to include the businessmen too[47]) in which she herself is present (she lives this fantasy) as an image that dissimulates a surplus element that is inconsistent with the rest of the image. It is also important to note that the inconsistent surplus element (which is potentially incendiary and therefore is a stand-in for the missing fire) does not look inconsistent to Daria at first sight—after all, why should a maid serving drinks be out of place at a business meeting? Moreover, the woman is relatively old and a servant, so she does not seem to bear much resemblance to the young, beautiful, and independent Daria. It is only the camera which, by the superimposition of images, seems to create the correspondence. Yet, having met Allen and been directed to her room by him, in the staircase Daria comes face to face with another native American, a

---

[47] In fact, there is no paradox here—it is just another and final example of how the claustrophobic, depthless development space operates. It is not the case that the Sunnydunes commercial constitutes a bright and happy but false screen/appearance that potential buyers believe, because it hides the reality of shady business deals and speculation. The screen covers nothing; it is transparent to potential buyers who of course do not believe that by buying the desert house they will become independent men and forge a life of their own. They know that they are being sold fiction (so the "natural" fiction and business intentions operate on the same surface), but in spite of that in the virtual space of development the fiction accomplishes its aims.

chambermaid, who is more or less her age, and this causes Daria to run back to her car and drive away in haste.

What is it that provokes such a strong emotional reaction? As the pastoral fantasy is Daria's way of life, within the fantasy she herself is a kind of native American (the child of the American earth—even the "howling wilderness" is imagined by her to be a home). But in Carefree she encounters the real children of the desert, and the real place assigned to them in the ahistorical pastoral fantasy. They are smoothly incorporated into it as servants of the people who produce the virtual space in which Daria lives: they provide literal service, like the maids, but also virtual service, like "ethnographic" entertainment, which produces the "native American" items that Daria wears. This incorporation, however, hides something much more sinister: as Ballister is a disavowed sign of the history expunged from the virtual space of LA, native Americans are the unacknowledged residue of the genocide which was committed in order that the virtual space of the ahistorical white pastoral fantasy of the garden could reign supreme on American soil. In other words, it was not only that in order that this fantasy, the fantasy of freedom and self-fulfillment, could be realized, somebody had to be enslaved; there were also others that had to be wiped out. Therefore Mark's lesson that there are not a thousand sides (different subjective opinions on one objective indivisible world, whose child each person is), but essentially just two (a conflict within the world masked by a fantasy which produces the image of the world itself as objective and indivisible) sinks in belatedly. Daria drives some distance, stops, gets out of the car, and, staring at the house, blows it up in her imagination (she still *can* "imagine things"). Although this is visually the most impressive sequence in the film, it is also one of those which met with most vituperative comments by critics: with consumer items ranging from folding chairs to books—and including staples of the 1960s American household, like Wonder Bread and Kellogg's cornflakes—the crude image of American materialism is supposed to be blown up here by uncomprehending Antonioni. However, within the context we have been outlining here, the meaning of the sequence is rather more complicated.

Although Daria might be shocked by recognizing that the pastoral fantasy of peaceful and fulfilling nature she lives has pure violence at its core, her "natural" reaction to the insight is *continuous* with the fantasy, that is, it introduces the last and missing natural element in her relation to Mark: fire. Daria became one with the earth in love-making, one with wind and then water in mourning Mark, and now one with fire (which is also Mark's element, considering his connection with violence and fire-arms) in the imaginary revenge. But is it revenge, one may ask? For an act of revenge, it is curiously non-violent[48]: before the house is blown up, we are shown its interiors, which are strangely lacking in human presence and although it explodes thirteen times (excluding the slow motion sequence), like New Year's Eve fireworks, one may suspect that the repetition takes place purely for the sake of intensification of the effect of something that could otherwise perhaps be seen as an ineffectual gesture. Moreover, the sequence which comes after the explosion, in which consumer items are blown up (plastic pool furniture with drinks, etc., a rack full of female clothes, a TV set, a refrigerator full of food, a bookcase full of books), is filmed in slow motion and in brilliant colors, so that the violence implied in the images is completely neutralized. Additionally, the exploding fragments are filmed against the blue sky, which, in conjunction with slow motion, takes on the appearance of hyperreal LA pool water, and creates a virtual environment in which lifeless items (consumer goods or their unrecognizable fragments) seem to turn into strange and colorful water creatures moving across the screen of their own volition. The effect is of utter weightlessness and grace. In other words, the fire element, which was supposed to destroy the pastoral fantasy, in fact seems to extend it, so that it reaches new heights: the consumer goods are transfigured and take on a fascinating *life* of their own. They become a second-level virtual nature which springs to life in front of our eyes, feeding, so to speak, on the original destructive impulse. This new "nature" in its Brownian motion is pure chaos and therefore presages the end of all meaning: each fragment is divorced from all the others (as well as from possible use) and thus constitutes a potential center of fascination as a totally decontextualized object. We have already seen that in the development space of LA the production of images has become more important than the production of goods, but the value of images was determined there by their symbolic context (pastoral fantasy) and therefore they were given some weight, while in the new blown-up dispensation of images their very weightlessness, the lack of connection with anything, is what counts, because only the weightless object without meaning has the power of fascinating completely.[49]

Therefore it does not seem accidental that the villa which is blown up is a modernist house in the functionalist style, a style in which all unnecessary

---

[48] Restivo, *Zabriskie Point*, 95.
[49] The only action which agrees with utter fascination is compulsive repetition—the thirteen explosions of the aerie are a premonition of that.

embellishments are prohibited. The explosion of the house establishes a space which is the exact opposite of the functionalist project: it produces fragments which are *pure* embellishments, embellishments only of themselves, not only without a house, but, by their power of fascination, excluding any reference to a possibility of even a virtual house, for instance, one created by the common white belief in the pastoral America. Hence the final scene, in which Daria drives toward the setting sun accompanied by a cheesy Roy Orbison song, an ending which was supposedly added against Antonioni's intentions,[50] does not really seem so out of place, and not only because it brings the fascination produced by the imagery of explosion to a more sober level. The final shot seems so meaningless not only because it is so hackneyed, but because we have seen it before: when Mark gets off the bus in Hawthorne, we see a billboard, taking up most of the screen, which shows, like the ending of the film, the sun setting behind desert mountains; it bears a caption: "Some things you can depend on. Bank of America." In the atomized world of meaningless fascination it is the only prospect that is left.

---

[50] Arrowsmith, *Antonioni*, 146, 186.

7

The Passenger (1975)

The Passenger is an untypical film for Michelangelo Antonioni in a number of ways. For the first time he was shooting a script written by someone else and a kind of thriller script to boot. Although Antonioni had adapted the original story by Mark Peploe to his purposes—so what the audience finally got was not a conventionally "thrilling" piece of cinema—in a commentary to the 2006 DVD release of the film Peploe reminds us that originally the thriller features of the script were much more pronounced. There is, however, another genre present in *The Passenger* too, which is just as obvious: although the film starts and ends with broken cars and general frustration, its main body takes us on the journey of a television reporter, David Locke (Jack Nicholson), who—having an accidental possibility to exchange his legal identity with David Robertson (Chuck Mulvehill), a man he meets by chance in an African village on the verge of a desert and who dies of heart failure the next day—grabs the opportunity and returns to Europe as someone else. Not knowing who Robertson was, he looks for clues in his pocket calendar notebook and sets out on a trip across the continent appearing at the meeting places he found in the notes. After visiting his own (Locke's) home in London (visiting London was also included in Robertson's own itinerary), he flies to Munich where it turns out that Robertson had been a gun runner. Because the next meeting place assigned him by Robertson's African client Achebe (Ambroise Bia; supposedly and ironically a leader of the rebels Locke failed to contact while in an unnamed African country shown to us at the beginning of the film) is Barcelona, Locke rents a car and drives there, after which he carries on to other meeting places.

Being on the road and traveling across a continent while learning who you are are of course the stuff of the American road movie. In *The Passenger*, however, we have an additional and possibly ironic twist to this genre, because what Locke is learning is in the first place not his own but somebody else's identity. Yet in the final analysis he does not only double for another—it is the convention itself which gets doubled: by learning about another's identity Locke of course also learns a lot about himself. This "overdose" of the road movie convention gets emphasized in other ways too, and sometimes to absurd degrees. In Spain, a country of small cars, where most of the driving is done, Locke rents a ridiculously American car, "un coche americano blanco," a giant white convertible straight out of Hollywood movies and, as if the car were not enough, the Locke character is acted by Jack Nicholson, most famous at that time (1975) for his role in *Easy Rider*, one of the most influential road movies of all time. Isn't this overkill of genre markers in a rather stark and restrained film like *The Passenger* somewhat suspicious?

Of course, the very title itself is an important signifier which can make us look for other markers of the road movie in the film. Yet, as we know, the work we are discussing was released with two titles of which only one has to do with driving. In the aforementioned commentary Peploe claims that the doubling of the title was purely coincidental: because a Polish film called *The Passenger* already existed (*Pasażerka*, dir. Andrzej Munk, 1963), the European title of release was changed to *Profession: Reporter*. Whether it is true or not, the very fact of the existence of these two versions throws into sharp relief a certain problem which the film seems to pose: each title puts a different emphasis on its meaning.[1] Because the film is a story of a man who happens to change his legal identity and carry on his life as somebody else, calling the film *The Passenger* emphasizes the "existential" edge of the plot about a man who, having become tired of his social identity (his job, his family, etc.), becomes a passenger of somebody else's life. On the other hand, *Profession: Reporter* emphasizes the central role of the man's profession and—if we take into consideration what kind of a reporter he is—also the matters which are the stuff of his reporting: postcolonial political violence in Africa or, more generally, in the "third world."

One would perhaps be justified in expecting that a film released in 1975 when the process of decolonization of Africa was far from finished, in which political violence featured rather strongly, and which was made by Antonioni after a documentary he had just done on revolutionary China, would have been received as (among other things) a kind of political gesture. But, in fact,

---

[1] In 1975, when the film was released, these two titles referred actually to two different *versions*: the American one was shorter because two scenes were cut from it: Locke visiting his flat in London and the "quarrel" with the Girl in the orange grove in Spain. I am using the American title throughout this text because the aforementioned full European DVD release from 2006 (Sony Pictures Home Entertainment) is called *The Passenger*.

its reception has always been strangely depoliticized and channeled mostly into either existential interpretations concentrating on identity problematics or into analyses of Antonioni's peculiar style, insisting on formalist games with the cinematic medium.

An excellent example of the former trend (and early reception of the film generally) is a part of Seymour Chatman book on Antonioni devoted to *The Passenger* in which he, for instance, claims:

> He is world-weary, like a romantic hero. Locke has seen enough of the world. Even the opportunities of another life shared with the likes of Maria Schneider cannot alter his basic melancholy. So he decides that nothing will and accepts his fate. For him death is liberation.[2]

It seems to me that something is fundamentally wrong with such an interpretation and for a number of reasons to which we will have to return. Just for now, one can say that—if one does not come to Antonioni's work already convinced that it is the cinema of depression and desperation (conforming to expectations as one of the sources of Locke's predicament is a motif which the film keeps returning to)—the main protagonist and especially the film are rather far from being melancholy. In fact the film is full of wry humor which works on many levels. There are humorous scenes played by Nicholson (e.g., apologizing to Jesus in the Munich church, attaching his false moustache to a lamp) and even by extras (e.g., a hotel porter stopping behind the door to overhear what Locke and the Girl are doing in the room). There are joking references to the conventions of American cinema (e.g., the white convertible mentioned above, but also the scene at Plaza de la Iglesia in San Ferdinando: we see a plaque on which "Plaza de la Iglesia" is inscribed, after which Locke says to the Girl: "Plaza de la Iglesia, this is it"). Moreover, the basis of the initial African sequence seems to be an ironic reversal of a Western racist attitude for which all Blacks look the same: Locke is able to get away with the exchange of identity, because he is in Africa where the natives do not seem to see much difference between one white man and another (he would not have been able to do it in a European hotel). Locke's first meeting with the Girl (Maria Schneider) might serve as yet another example: "Who are you?" she demands from Locke-turned-Robertson like the Caterpillar in *Alice in*

---

[2] Chatman, *Antonioni*, 188. What would make his potential life with Maria Schneider so exciting within the bounds of the plot of *The Passenger* is rather difficult to understand—unless, of course, one relates her image to *Last Tango in Paris* (dir. Bernardo Bertolucci, 1972), another famous film in which she features.

Wonderland,³ a book almost exclusively devoted to "identity problems," to which his answer is: "I used to be somebody else but I traded him in" ("'I can't explain *myself*, I'm afraid, Sir,' said Alice, 'because I'm not myself, you see'"⁴). In the light of the above, doesn't the melancholy existential plot perhaps begin to look like one belonging to the rabbit hole world of fancy and absurd (European) creatures addressed to good children and smelling of red herring?

As we watch the film, it becomes increasingly obvious that Locke's dissatisfaction has much more palpable and definite roots than general melancholy and this is even spelled out for us explicitly: the problem is that Locke is a liar and that he has gradually come to the realization that he is a liar even in spite of his efforts to tell the truth; that the (Western) idea of objectivity and detachment (he is called a detached and therefore penetrating reporter in his obituary in an English newspaper he finds in his flat in London) itself is a lie. In other words, there is nothing constitutionally wrong with the world, but there is the problem of vision (we are in the cinema after all). Moreover, if we insist on formation of and failure to achieve a new identity as being central to the film, perhaps the contortions of African countries on the way to producing for themselves new postcolonial *political* identities in which Western interests (old values and habits Locke dreams of leaving behind) would become subordinate to African ones can stand as the determining context to the existential peregrinations of one successful dealer in African truths.⁵ There is an obvious parallel between the political and existential plot in *The Passenger* but the former is the *source* of the letter: Locke does not become sick of his life because for no apparent reason he becomes "world-weary," but because of what he has seen and been doing in the "third word" throughout his professional career.⁶ We are approaching here a very old sentimentalist point everybody has heard proposing a remedy to evil in the world: "before you can change the world, you have to change yourself

---

³ In fact we are in the wonderland of Gaudi's Palau Güell and Locke, looking around, asks the Girl whether she thinks Gaudi was crazy (as mad as a March hare?).
⁴ *The Complete Illustrated Works of Lewis Carroll* (London: Chancellor Press, 1993), 47.
⁵ This is an important motif in the film. Achebe says: "Our main problem is the military assistance the government is getting from Europe" and the name of Patrice Lumumba appears on the cover of a French book Locke has with him in the African hotel. Lumumba was the first democratically elected prime minister of the Republic of Congo and was deposed by a military coup backed by Belgium, Great Britain, and the United States and executed by firing squad (which may have looked much the same as the scene of execution in *The Passenger*).
⁶ This includes his private life: we are shown that Locke's wife's estrangement is (at least partially) caused by what she thinks to be his "accepting too much" (e.g., not contradicting the African dictator's lies in the interview she witnesses).

first." Locke is not so naïve as to believe in this platitude but he is naïve enough: he knows he cannot change the world because he (we can assume) has tried to do it as a reporter, but he attempts to change at least himself. Yet this, of course, cannot happen—"the world" will sooner or later catch up with him.

The "formalist" approach to *The Passenger* may perhaps be traced to a number of comments Antonioni himself made about his film such as "I no longer want to employ the subjective camera" and "I have replaced my objectivity with that of the camera. … Actually, the liberty I have achieved in the making of this film is the liberty the character in the film tried to achieve by changing identity."[7] A good example of the way such hints can be developed in order to draw formalist conclusions concerning the camera work in Antonioni's film can be found in Sam Rohdie's analyses. For instance, writing about the famous seven-minute penultimate shot, he claims:

> Like Locke, the camera assumes a double position: it moves, it looks, as a subject, but at the same time it is an object of its own regard; it turns around the square and looks at itself turning. And just as the camera ends by registering its own movement, and the duration of its look, so too the audience finds itself in a similar position, looking at that movement of the camera, but catching, as it does so, its own reflection.[8]

Whether or not it is pertinent to the audience's position in the shot (I believe it isn't), Rohdie's is an interesting analysis because it nicely shifts the subject of doubling from the plot to the formal level of the film (according to all handbooks a modernist work should reflect its content in its form), but, I guess, one can legitimately ask a rather stupid question here: why is it all being done? Just to show how exquisitely sophisticated one's work can become, or, in other words, just to convince the audience (and the critics) how clever one is? I do not think that is enough to justify a very complicated seven-minute shot (it took eleven days to complete) in which the camera, commencing from the entrance to the hotel room in which Locke is lying on the bed (we can see him from his chest down), very slowly approaches the bars which separate the room from the square in front of the hotel, "miraculously" penetrates through them, and, making a loop around the square, returns to the bars (this time remaining outside) to peer

---

[7] Michelangelo Antonioni, *Interviews*, ed. Bert Cardullo (Jackson: University Press of Mississippi, 2008), 122, 123.
[8] Rohdie, *Antonioni*, 151.

into the room where Locke lies dead, having been shot by the African dictator's henchmen whose arrival in a car we have seen earlier in the same shot.

Interestingly, Rhodie also claims that in the penultimate shot:

> The camera glances by these events; none of them are central, nor given any weight, nor emphasized: the killers who come and go in the Citroen are of no more concern to the camera than the small boy who throws stones at the dog, or the old men who are talking. It is the same with the sound heard: a door opening and closing, a car backfiring (or is it a shot?), the sound of a trumpet, voices, a dog barking, the whistle of a train, a clock sounding. They just are and the camera does no more than register them.[9]

The shot is evidently a brilliant one and technically exquisite, the film's obvious *pièce de résistance* to marvel at—so we will have to return to it—but for the time being, and taking into consideration its sophistication and the suggested "coolness" or neutrality, perhaps we can ask: where can we find the exact opposite of the penultimate shot in the film? What is its "hottest" and roughest spot? I think there cannot be any doubt that it is the scene of the execution of an African, which—and this is *very* surprising—is hardly ever commented on in discussions devoted to *The Passenger*. Because we know from Antonioni himself that this sequence is actual footage of an execution, I would guess that the most likely explanation of this surprising silence is that those who have maintained it avoid this moment because they feel that Antonioni might be accused of exploiting tragic African political history or just the death of an unfortunate and unnamed human being. In other words, they assume that this sequence is more or less gratuitous and therefore turns the execution into something like a tourist attraction. But one can only assume that it is gratuitous if one takes the whole political plot as a pretext, a superficial "thriller-making" device, a classical MacGuffin, a red herring which, having won MGM's money, allows Antonioni to develop a "deeper" romantic-existential theme concerning the nature of the self, etc.[10]

My proposal is that the execution sequence is a centerpiece of the film and that an umbilical cord joins it with the penultimate shot which is treated by everybody as the most important one. Above all, even without knowing that

---

[9] Ibid., 147–8.
[10] Chatman, *Antonioni*, 194: "Thrillers depend on a sense that there is something to be saved … everything that Hitchcock means by the 'Macguffin.' Here, the cause—guns for rebels—is forgotten. Not only is the hero not saved, but the question of his salvation seems in some ways to be a red herring."

the sequence is a footage of a real execution, it is for the audience the most shocking and painful moment of the film and as such it immediately punctures the existentialist plot: what are the identity problems of a middle-aged middle-class man whose wife cheats on him, etc., in contrast with the mass political suffering of Africa? As I have tried to suggest above, it is, in fact, the existential plot which constitutes the MacGuffin of the film, in which political violence is present throughout, giving it its weight and *substance*, including the penultimate shot from which it is visually excised for reasons to which we will return.[11] In this context, it is not accidental that what the African dictator interviewed by Locke denies to political violence is precisely substance: "This [fighting with the United Liberation Front] is no longer a problem. Intellectuals and journalists like to make publicity out of it to give it some kind of political substance." Moreover, the execution sequence is also formally one of the models of the film. In *The Passenger* Antonioni repeatedly introduces new locations in the same way: first, the camera picks up some people (often at work or play), then pans to show us the landscape or cityscape, and only after this proceeds to find a protagonist for us.[12] The beginning of the execution sequence is constructed in the same way: local bystanders—a shot of the sea or lake on the shore of which the execution is taking place—and then the convict being led to his death.

If the execution scene is a seed out of which one formal model used in the film develops, one can of course ask what the sources of the most brilliant, penultimate shot are on the technical level. In fact there are at least three scenes which can be considered precursors of the penultimate shot. In chronological order, the first one is the shot in which Locke exchanges his shirt for Robertson's: in one continuous shot we see Locke in his checked shirt in close-up raising his eyes to the ceiling, the camera tilts up following his eyes and shows us the ceiling fan, then it pans across the ceiling and down one of the walls to show us Locke's back (he has moved) in Robertson's blue shirt. The exchange of the shirts off screen lasts less than ten seconds, which is utterly "unrealistic," but what is more important, these few seconds Locke is off screen are precisely the time when he becomes "transformed," that is, when he decides to "become" Robertson and this is of course the most crucial moment of the film, at least

---

[11] On the level of the plot, the execution might have been the point which became the last straw for Locke and triggered his "sickness." In fact, this is what Antonioni himself suggests (*Interviews*, 118).

[12] Workers repairing the pavement in Bloomsbury—The Brunswick Centre—Locke walks into the frame; travelers at the Munich airport—a pan of the airport hall—Locke at the Avis desk; the roof of Umbraculo in Barcelona—children playing—Locke on a bench; etc.

until the penultimate shot. Thus, the moment of the most radical discontinuity is rendered here by the perfectly continuous work of the camera. The second shot is a 180-degree pan which is the subjective shot of what Locke's wife, Rachel (Jenny Runacre), sees (we see her and then the camera identifies with her gaze as she looks around, turning about 180 degrees to return to her looking at the scene) while Locke is interviewing the African dictator. Although the shot is subjective (what a character sees), its intention is "objective"—Rachel is criticizing Locke for "accepting too much" and the scene (as it is related by her to Martin Knight (Ian Hendry)) is supposed to show the discrepancy between the dictator's words ("There is no fighting any more. ... We are a unified nation") and the "objective truth" of his heavily guarded mansion. An interesting point is that Rachel's subjective shot is introduced by the question put by Knight (Locke's TV producer): "Did you love him?" (they are in Knight's studio reminiscing about Locke) to which she answers coldly, "Yes, I think so. Just didn't make each other very happy," which sounds like going through the motions of a social convention rather than truth. So, although there is "objective" evil in the world, there is also the evil eye (Rachel's) that looks and accuses—not the dictator primarily, but Locke who after all asks the dictator a few unpleasant questions. The third and most revealing scene takes place during another interview, this time with an African witch doctor (James Campbell). Locke has problems with understanding how a man who spent several years in France and Yugoslavia can be a guardian of "savage" tribal customs—"Don't they strike you as false now and wrong perhaps for the tribe?" Locke asks. To which he get this answer: "Mr Locke, there are perfectly satisfactory answers to all your questions. But I don't think you understand how little you can learn from them. Your questions are much more revealing about yourself than my answer would be about me." At first this seems to dovetail pretty neatly into one of the motifs present in the film from the very beginning in Africa when Locke, conversing with Robertson, claimed that the West cannot understand Africa because we apply our own cognitive habits to a reality which does not fit them and hence we get a distorted image leading to distorted relations with that continent.[13] Yet what is going on in the scene is something much more interesting. When Locke tries to defend himself by saying: "I meant them [his questions] quite sincerely," the witch

---

[13] Locke himself "comments" on this kind of "culturalism" by wearing a sarcastic grin while he listens to himself explaining these things to Robertson on tape.

doctor says: "Mr Locke, we can have a conversation but only if it's not just what *you* think is sincere, but also what I believe to be honest." After which he turns the camera 180 degrees to face Locke, adding: "Now we can have an interview. You can ask me the same questions as before." At first what he has said sounds like a pleonasm. But it is not; thinking is not the same as believing and what is sincere is not exactly what is honest. If we remind ourselves that "sincere" comes from Latin *sincerus*, meaning clear, pure, transparent, and that "honest" derives from Latin *honos* or *honor*, meaning honor, we can see that sincerity is on the side of "objectivity," detachment, and truth, while honesty on the side of taking a stance, engagement, and struggle; and the distance between thinking (in the West tantamount to detachment) and believing only reinforces this difference.[14] What kind of "truth" is the witch doctor trying to elicit from the uncomprehending Locke (we see him looking confusedly into his own camera)? Why does he make him look at himself? Perhaps to make him see that his sincerity is just a species of colonialist condescension/violence; in other words, to make him see that he is faking. And it seems that the witch doctor finally succeeds, because the self-reflexivity he proposes—of turning Locke's "camera" on himself—is the beginning of Locke's "sickness." Individual psychological penetration is of no importance here, only Locke's "political psychology" is of interest: he finally realizes that the very notion of "objectivity" in his political analyses has always worked on the side of the exploiter; that his attitude has been the same as the one the African dictator's ambassador in London displays to Rachel when commenting on the struggling rebels: "They're very troublesome people. Very unintelligent." After all, doesn't Locke ask the witch doctor precisely why he remains so unintelligent and sticks to African customs when the West has so much to offer? But we already know from the film what kind of assistance it offers: there is no soap in Africa, but there are plenty of guns. Moreover, the placing of the witch doctor in a political rather than purely "cultural" context is unmistakable: we cut to the sequence in which he features after Locke, speaking to the Girl, comments on one of the notes in Robertson's notebook: "I think this Daisy[15] is a man," that is, somebody involved in the armed struggle against

---

[14] "Which Tribe Do You Belong To?" asks the title of a book (by Alberto Moravia) which we see in Locke's flat in London while he withdraws money and papers out of his "treasure box." As a reporter he believed in his detachment—as a purveyor of the objective truth he could not belong to any struggle.

[15] In Robertson's notebook there are meeting dates and places but his business partners are given female names for secrecy purposes.

dictatorship whom Locke (as Robertson) is supposed to meet in Osuna at the Hotel de la Gloria (and where he meets his death instead).[16]

But what does it all have to do with the penultimate shot from which we started? The prevalent world-weary-man interpretation sees Locke's journey through Spain as a story of dissipation and defeat. Yet what is the point of appending to this scenario a shot which, in fact, cancels the intended melancholy with its brilliance and intensity of vision? In order to make some sense of this discrepancy, I think we can take our cue from an element which, at first sight rather inexplicably, appears in two last shots: a driving-school car. It drives into the frame at the beginning of the penultimate shot, disappears for a while, makes a U-turn off screen, and reappears again, only to drive off once more; then, after the camera moves through the bars outside the room, we see it again for some time, and after this, in the final shot, it drives away "into the sunset" for good.

The presence of a driving school in a film whose main genre affiliation is the road movie can hardly be accidental. But our principal driver has failed (after all, even while driving, he has only been a passenger of somebody else's fate) and at the end of the penultimate shot lies dead, so what is being taught here and to whom? If the driver failed, he probably had not learned his lesson well enough. But what was it? If the penultimate shot is a lesson it is obviously a lesson in looking—it is a very long shot in which hardly anything is said and the uttered words are not of much consequence. Moreover, in the shot the camera abandons Locke and, exasperated with his experience of the world, leaves him to his own visual devices, so to speak.

Throughout the film Locke is repeatedly asked to agree that what he sees is beautiful. Looking at the desert in Africa, Robertson addresses him: "Beautiful, don't you think so?" Locke answers: "Beautiful? I don't know" (which is a polite form of denial) and proceeds to a "humanitarian" cliché that he prefers men to landscapes[17] (a cliché which will be tested the following day and found wanting). Later, in a funicular which is transporting him over Barcelona harbor, a Spaniard tells Locke: "Es bonito, verdad? Is beautiful!" to which he does not give any answer. And finally, when the white convertible breaks down in southern Spanish wasteland overgrown with shrubs, it is the Girl who asks: "Isn't it beautiful here?" to which Locke half-heartedly answers: "Yes, it's very beautiful." That Locke is unconvinced is made clear at the Hotel de la Gloria in

---

[16] Achebe, a leader of the struggle, asks Locke to give his regards to Daisy.
[17] "There are men who live in the desert," counters Robertson, bringing together beauty of the world and the political struggle he serves.

Osuna where the Girl unexpectedly appears (she was supposed to go to Almería to wait for him) and where he tells her a story about a blind man who regained his sight when he was nearly forty (Locke is thirty-seven):

> At first he was elated, really high. Faces, colours, landscapes. But then everything began to change. The world was much poorer than he imagined. No one had ever told him how much dirt there was. How much ugliness. He noticed ugliness everywhere. … He began to live in darkness. He never left his room. After three years he killed himself.

For obvious reasons this story has become the *pièce de résistance* of the melancholy interpretation. Moreover, it even seems to be emphasized by a purely cinematic gesture which follows the story. Locke and the Girl lie on the bed while he is telling her about the blind man; after he finishes, the Girl gets depressed, throws herself into Locke's arms and, while she almost starts to sob, the camera slowly moves up the wall, following a hanging electric cord, and comes to rest on a rather kitschy picture of a landscape which seems to be a kind of ironic comment on people's need to sentimentalize and beautify the ugly objectivity of the world. But perhaps things are not so obvious.

The first question we have to ask here is: how does the story about the blind man relate to what we have seen in the film? What is the ugliness Locke speaks about in his allegory? As we already noted, the landscapes in *The Passenger* are consistently presented as beautiful. Although the beauty might be unconventional (it includes both African desert and the dusty "wasteland" of southern Spain), Locke is explicitly confronted with injunctions to acknowledge its power.[18] If there is so much beauty in the world, what is the dirt that smears it

---

[18] The European cityscape is more ambiguous. Although *The Passenger* is famous for its architectural focus, the well-known buildings that feature in it are presented in a rather ironic light. The first identifiable building we are shown is the Brunswick Centre in London, a controversial piece of functionalist architecture, which does not seem to be contextualized by Antonioni in any way (unless it is to remind us of the African buildings we have seen, which were similarly whitish, simple, and functional). Irony becomes most obvious when Locke finds himself in Munich in a typically ornate baroque church, dripping gold and flying cupids, which is turned in the film into the site of an exchange of money and military documentation and therefore gets incorporated into the plot about political struggle and suffering (religion has served colonialism in all kind of ways). Moreover, when the camera finally focuses on the interior of the church (after everybody but Locke is gone), it slowly glides down the altar (Locke's POV shot), which is, in a sense, the wrong direction, because what the altar presents is an apotheosis, a formal "Gloria" of a saint, so it is supposed to make an impression of the saint ascending upward to heaven. We get the same movement of the camera when we find ourselves with Locke in Gaudí's Palau Güell: the main party room is shown starting from the ceiling, the frame gliding down the walls and the staircase where we see some descending German (!) tourists (we hear them on the soundtrack)—it is Locke's POV shot as well. (The saint's Gloria in the Munich church is noted and commented upon by Arrowsmith, *Antonioni*, 157.)

and makes it so ugly? Within the framework of the film there is only one possible answer, which, by the way, we have already suggested: it is political violence that is ugliness incarnate. The ugliness, however, inheres not only in violent acts (as exemplified by the execution scene, which is the "ugliest" and most excruciating one in the film); it also resides in the eye of the beholder who paints the world ugly with his own filth. What exemplifies such filth is not only the greed and hunger for power in the eye of the African dictator (and his former colonial rulers) but also Locke's "objectivity and detachment" which find their ugly truth in "intelligent" moderation between extremes.

In order to cleanse one's vision, a lesson in looking is in order, and this is not only indicated by (the rather humorous) presence of the driving school in the two last shots. In the final part of *The Passenger*, which takes place in Osuna, we are gradually invited to detach our vision from Locke's. When Locke arrives at the Hotel de la Gloria and enters his room, he sees the Girl looking out onto the square in front of the hotel and, without looking out himself, asks her: "What can you see?" She answers: "A little boy and an old woman. They are having an argument about which way to go." The important thing here is that as viewers we are, in a sense, in Locke's position: although we see him in an American shot, we also see what he sees—the Girl's back, as she is looking out, is reflected for us in the wardrobe mirror. Moreover, we do not see what the Girl is describing to Locke either, so we only get her rendering in words of what she sees. In the next shot, Locke lies down on the bed and in the following one the Girl looks out again, but this time we see what is happening on the square over her shoulder. "What can you see now?" Locke asks her and this time we get her description superimposed on what we can also see ourselves through the barred window: "A man scratching his shoulder. A kid throwing stones. And dust. It's very dusty here." What is also important is that what we can see through the windowpane looks almost as if we were watching a black-and-white TV screen: the colors are so subdued that they become almost different shades of gray. The virtual lack of color and the subject of dust is an overture which leads us to the aforementioned sequence in which the blind man story is told, after which Locke asks the girl to leave and finally he himself walks to the French door, opens it, and looks out through the bars onto the square. What is interesting, this last shot before the penultimate one is technically very similar to the shirt-exchange "transformatory" shot in Africa: Locke opens the door and the camera looks onto the square across his shoulder (a repetition of the shot in which the Girl was looking out but without the "redundant" verbal rendering of what is seen); the shoulder gradually disappears as the camera gets closer to the bars, so the shot seems to be a subjective one from Locke's point of view. Then the camera slowly tilts upward and pans to the left back into the room where after a while Locke's back enters the frame. The stages are clearly marked: the description of the world (just words, no vision), then vision made redundant (gray) with words,[19] then the silent but "colored" shot of the square in which the camera, at first simulating Locke's point of view, detaches itself from his subjective perspective (non-subjective "spiritual" transformation). Then, and after a cut, the penultimate shot begins in which we finally get through the bars and onto the square, that is, out of the private room and onto the scene of the social.

We already quoted Rohdie emphasizing the detachment of the camera: "The camera glances by these events; none of them are central, nor given any weight, nor emphasized … They just are and the camera does no more than register

---

[19] This point of view is associated with the Girl, which at first sight may appear strange, because she is usually interpreted as an "enlivening" factor in the melancholy plot. However, if one looks closer at the way she is presented in the film, matters cease to be so obvious. When we see the Girl for the first time, she is reading a book sitting on a bench at the Brunswick Centre. She is wearing a green shirt and, having put the book down, stretches herself in the sun among foliage. This way she is associated with the lush green and brown image of rich Europe as "a green bower" (Arrowsmith, *Antonioni*, 159), with comfortable, regressive, middle-class safety exemplified especially by Lansdowne Crescent (in London's Notting Hill, where Locke used to live) and Munich, and contrasted with the stark imagery and colors of Africa and southern Spain. In this particular scene the greenery is perhaps also contrasted with the functional sparseness of the Brunswick as radically different from "nature-inspired" Gaudi buildings in Barcelona where we meet her again. There, on the roof of the Casa Milà, the Girl and Locke witness a seemingly gratuitous and inconsequential quarrel between an unknown couple. This quarrel, however, takes us forward to another "green" scene in the south of Spain. In the lush vegetation of an orange grove in the middle of sun-scorched wasteland, Locke (wearing a green polo shirt) wakes up to find that he cannot leave behind his old self ("the only one I know"), which results in a quarrel with the Girl (holding in her hand an orange she has just picked up from a tree) who, claiming that she is "not interested in giving up," leaves him (but only for a while). The scene would fall neatly into the tired old man/fresh young girl cliché, if it were not for the context in which it is inserted. First of all, there is another woman in the film who is not interested in giving up and this is Locke's estranged wife, who chases them (on one level the representative of Locke's old identity which does not want to die). Moreover, the scenes in the grove and of the reconciliation between the Girl and Locke are followed by a scene taking place in the kitschy, over-adorned, and almost entirely green interior of a posh restaurant where Locke, observing through the window an attractive woman in a bikini, is asked by the Girl a perennial female question, "What are you thinking?" To which he gives a perennial male answer, "Nothing," while it is rather obvious what his thoughts were: Locke is getting tired of the Girl and looking around for some other "entertainment." What we see here, therefore, is not just Locke who is back to his old self, but also a boring middle-class couple having their meal in a rather tasteless place for the rich British or German tourists (it is definitely a "green bower restaurant") with the Girl as a younger version of irritating Rachel. What is more, this vision is finally clinched by the way the appearance of the Girl in Osuna is staged: we first see her reflecting in the mirror. Within the film, the meaning of this kind of appearance has already been established—there are only two people who are shown this way: Martin Knight in Barcelona and Rachel Locke in Almería, both belonging to the spurned numbing comfortable bower, both pursuing Locke and both unwelcome.

them." This is, I believe, both right and wrong. It is true that the camera gets through the bars and enters the square to show us the ordinary world in which it emphasizes nothing, but the effect it creates in the viewer is not the detachment (and the doubling) Rohdie argues for. The penultimate shot shows us ordinary sights and sounds but because it is so long and hardly anything extraordinary happens in it (the murder takes place "behind" the camera), we have plenty of time to concentrate on what is shown to us. In fact, we "overinvest" our "visual energy" in it, trying to find something "important" (in the Hollywood sense: important for the development of the plot, whether amorous or thrilling) and this effort on our part is continuously inspired by the brilliant and defamiliarizing form of this shot (if the camera did not behave in an extraordinary way, many viewers would probably very quickly lose interest in looking for clues). The extraordinary length and form of the shot shake us out of our habitual visual slumber, creating an impression that anything we see in it can be of crucial importance—this gradually produces an incredible *intensity* of vision[20]: the most ordinary, even ugly (in the conventional sense) world finally appears to us in all its glory. In this way, the penultimate shot pulls us out of the melancholy allegory into the overwhelming visual experience of the world. And I use the world "glory" advisedly: another thing we learn in the social arena in front of the Hotel de la Gloria is that the only true transcendence is not vertical (an ascending saint in Munich, contradicted by the "descending" movement of the camera) but a horizontal release into an intensified visual (perhaps even visionary) experience.

It has always puzzled me that one can see as melancholy a film which culminates in such visual brilliance. In fact, one can claim that what Antonioni aimed at in the penultimate shot is a level of intensity which could match the "ugliest" sequence of *The Passenger*, the execution. Not in order to moderate or deny it in any way but quite the opposite—the close relationship between the ugliest and most beautiful moments of the film establishes the necessary stereoscopy of vision: the ugliness in the world is undeniable, even omnipresent, but only intensity of vision puts it into perspective because it allows for engagement in the world for the sake of the world itself and not for the sake of one's self-interest. Only for those who see its beauty is the world worth fighting for, while detachment spreads pestilence and is, in fact, a way of participation in ugliness.

---

[20] One can even say that Antonioni "cheats" a bit in this respect by throwing in a few splashes of bright red clothes into the shot.

In this sense, the penultimate shot can be conceived as the summary of the film on both anecdotal and formal level. Antonioni himself declared sometime after he made *The Passenger* that "[i]t's a resume of the whole film, not just a conclusion."[21] But we can also suggest that it brings together at least the three source scenes we mentioned: (1) the exchange of shirts in Africa (spiritual transformation), (2) Rachel's subjective 180-degree shot (Africa in its ugly aspect), and (3) the witch doctor scene (sincerity vs. honesty)—(1) in order to become someone else (2) you have to look around and see what is ugly (3) but also see the world in all its brilliance which is only possible from an engaged position.

The final shot clinches the lesson in looking in an interesting way: after the police and the strangers are gone, evening stillness returns to Osuna under a quiet sky painted pinkish by the setting sun. Firstly, the color palette of the final shot is different from the prevalent contrasts used throughout the film: the cold white, blue and dirty-sand-yellow of Africa and Southern Spain juxtaposed against the warm greens and browns characteristic of the European "bower" (London and Munich especially).[22] The last shot uses blues, yellows, oranges, greens, browns toned down by the evening and juxtaposed with the flaming pink of the sunset, in which electric lights glimmer in almost Christmas fashion enhanced by the colorful stained glass of the Hotel de la Gloria. At first sight we seem to be returning here to the kitschy landscape which we saw hanging in Locke's room in the hotel, which we took for an ironic comment on the blind man story or perhaps for an illustration of escapist vision. But it turns out now that there was no irony at all in the *landschaft*, that it was the camera's "premonition" of what would happen in the last shot, because, in spite of presenting us with the proverbially kitschy sunset landscape, the last shot is altogether beautiful, exuding a newly achieved serenity, a necessary aftermath of transforming intensification experienced in the penultimate shot. In this light, it is not surprising that the last shot begins with the retirement of the driving school car (after the day's lesson something has been learned) which switches its headlights on and drives away for the day's rest. But the humorous reference to the end of the lesson does not seem to be its only role—when the headlights are switched on something "miraculous" happens again: their ghostly reflection appears superimposed like new stars on the evening sky. This effect is probably

---

[21] Antonioni, *Interviews*, 166.
[22] Arrowsmith, *Antonioni*, 159.

caused by the strong light on the set, which, reflected from the lens, is reflected yet again by the filter placed in front of the lens, so that the reflection goes back into the lens and gets recorded on the film stock.[23] There is no better way to show that what is happening here is the consolidation of a new vision, the appearance of a new "filter" which allows for a new way of looking and of seeing the world in new colors.

Moreover, this new beginning is humorously, but also touchingly, emphasized on the level of the anecdote. When the driving school car has gone, we witness a quarrel between the hotel owner and his wife, after which the man walks away into the sunset lighting a cigarette, while the woman turns on the lights in the hall, peers after him around the corner of the hotel, and returns to the doorway to sit down on the steps to knit and probably wait for his return. Although we do not hear clearly what they are quarrelling about, we can assume that it has to do with the events of the day, that is, the wife, thinking that it may still be dangerous outside, is trying to prevent her husband from going out for a walk or to meet his friends and have a few pints. On the one hand, it is an unimportant ordinary event, but at the same time it is, of course, one of the most "mythical" and "archetypal" situations: a man leaves the safety of his home and profession and sets out into the dangerous world to find himself and prove his mettle—which is also a repetition of the plot we have just witnessed.[24] What is more, the ending perversely returns us yet again to the conventions of American cinema: everybody knows who rides off into the sunset at the end of a Hollywood movie. In this way, the last shot also becomes symbolic of the whole wonderful enterprise called *The Passenger*: the most un-Hollywood-like lesson on looking which is accomplished by prizing open the spiritually and visually restrictive ruling cinematic conventions, paid for and brought to your local cinema by Metro-Goldwyn-Mayer.

---

[23] Grzegorz Królikiewicz, *Anty-Faust. Próba analizy filmu Michelangelo Antonioniego "Zawód reporter"* (Łódź: Studio Filmowe N, 1996), 97.
[24] Ibid., 100–3.

Bibliography

Abbey, Edward. *Desert Solitaire*. Tuscon: The University of Arizona Press, 1988. First published 1968 by McGraw-Hill.
Affron, Mirella Joan. "Text and Memory in *Eclipse*." *Literature/Film Quarterly* 9, no. 3 (1981): 139–51.
Amberg, George. "But Eros Is Sick." In *L'Avventura: A Film by Michelangelo Antonioni*, edited by George Amberg and Robert Hughes, 243–51.
Amberg, George and Robert Hughes, eds. *L'Avventura: A Film by Michelangelo Antonioni*. New York: Grove Press, 1969.
Antonioni, Michelangelo. *The Architecture of Vision: Writings and Interviews on Cinema*. Ed. Carlo Di Carlo and Giorgio Tinazzi. American Edition by Marga Cottino-Jones. Chicago: Chicago University Press, 2007.
Antonioni, Michelangelo. *Interviews*. Ed. Bert Cardullo. Jackson: University Press of Mississippi, 2008.
Antonioni, Michelangelo. "A Talk with Michelangelo Antonioni on His Work: Students and Faculty at the Centro Sperimentale di Cinematografia in Rome." In *L'Avventura: A Film by Michelangelo Antonioni*, edited by George Amberg and Robert Hughes, 211–34.
Arrowsmith, William. *Antonioni: The Poet of Images*. Ed. Ted Perry. New York: Oxford University Press, 1995.
Baudelaire, Charles. *Paris Spleen*. Trans. Louise Varèse. New York: New Directions, 1970.
Baudrillard, Jean. *America*. Trans. Chris Turner. London: Verso, 1988.
Baudrillard, Jean. *Symbolic Exchange and Death*. Trans. Ian Hamilton Grant. London: Sage, 1993.
Benjamin, Walter. *The Origin of German Tragic Drama*. Trans. John Osborne. London: New Left Books, 1977.
Berger, John. *About Looking*. New York: Pantheon Books, 1980.
Bergman, Ingmar. *Interviews*. Ed. Raphael Shargel. Jackson: University Press of Mississippi, 2007.
Bergson, Henri. *Laughter: An Essay on the Meaning of the Comic*. Trans. Cloudesley Brereton and Fred Rothwell. Copenhagen and Los Angeles: Green Integer Books, 1999.
Blunt, Anthony. *Sicilian Baroque*. London: Weidenfeld & Nicolson, 1968.
Bourdieu, Pierre. *Masculine Domination*. Trans. Richard Nice. Oxford: Polity Press, 2001.

Brunette, Peter. *The Films of Michelangelo Antonioni*. Cambridge: Cambridge University Press, 1998.

Brunette, Peter. *Roberto Rossellini*. Berkeley: University of California Press, 1996.

Buck-Morss, Susan. *The Dialectics of Seeing: Walter Benjamin and the Arcades Project*. Cambridge, MA: The MIT Press, 1991.

Buck-Morss, Susan. "The Flaneur, the Sandwichman and the Whore: The Politics of Loitering." *New German Critique*, no. 39, Second Special Issue on Walter Benjamin (Autumn 1986): 99–140.

Burch, Noël. *Theory of Film Practice*. Trans. Helen R. Lane. Princeton: Princeton University Press, 1973.

Carroll, Lewis. *The Complete Illustrated Works of Lewis Carroll*. London: Chancellor Press, 1993.

Chatman, Seymour. "All the Adventures." In *L'avventura*, edited by Seymour Chatman and Guido Fink, 3–15.

Chatman, Seymour. *Antonioni or, the Surface of the World*. Berkeley: University of California Press, 1985.

Chatman, Seymour. "Notes on the Continuity Script." In *L'avventura*, edited by Seymour Chatman and Guido Fink, 161–3.

Chatman, Seymour and Guido Fink, eds. *L'avventura*. New Brunswick, NJ: Rutgers University Press, 1989.

Chiaretti, Tomasso. "The Adventure of *L'Avventura*." In *L'Avventura*, edited by George Amberg and Robert Hughes, 185–208.

Copjec, Joan. *Read My Desire: Lacan against the Historicists*. Cambridge, MA: The MIT Press, 1994.

Cuccu, Lorenzo. *Il discorso dello sguardo: Da "Blow Up" a "Identificazione di una donna"*. Pisa: ETS Editrice, 1990.

Dalle Vacche, Angela. *Cinema and Painting: How Art Is Used in Film*. Austin: University of Texas Press, 1996.

Empson, William. *Some Versions of Pastoral*. New York: New Directions, 1974.

Fernandez, Dominique. "The Poet of Matriarchy." In *L'Avventura*, edited by George Amberg and Robert Hughes, 252–4.

Freccero, John. "*Blow-Up*: From the Word to the Image." In *Focus on* Blow-Up, edited by Roy Huss, 116–28.

Friedman, Lester D., ed. *Arthur Penn's* Bonnie and Clyde. Cambridge: Cambridge University Press, 2000.

Galt, Rosalind. "On *L'avventura* and the Picturesque." In *Antonioni: Centenary Essays*, edited by Laura Rascaroli and John David Rhodes, 134–53.

Ginsborg, Paul. *A History of Contemporary Italy: Society and Politics 1943–1988*. London: Penguin, 1990.

Grøtta, Marit. *Baudelaire's Media Aesthetics: The Gaze of the Flâneur and 19th-Century Media*. London: Bloomsbury, 2015.

Haaland, Torunn. "*Flânerie*: Spatial Practices and Nomadic Thought in Antonioni's *La note*." *Italica* 90, no. 4 (Winter 2013): 596–619.
Hale, Sheila. *Titian: His Life*. New York: HarperCollins, 2012.
Huss, Roy, ed. *Focus on* Blow-Up. Englewood Cliffs, NJ: Prentice-Hall, 1971.
Jefferson, Thomas. *The Essential Jefferson*. Ed. Jean M. Yarbrough. Indianapolis: Hackett Publishing, 2006.
Kael, Pauline. "The Beauty of Destruction." *New Yorker*, February 21, 1970.
Kael, Pauline. "Bonnie and Clyde." *New Yorker*, October 21, 1967.
Kauffmann, Stanley, "A Year with *Blow-Up*: Some Notes." In *Focus on* Blow-Up, edited by Roy Huss, 70–7.
Kirk, Terry. *The Architecture of Modern Italy, Volume II: Visions of Utopia, 1900–Present*. New York: Princeton Architectural Press, 2005.
Królikiewicz, Grzegorz. *Anty-Faust. Próba analizy filmu Michelangelo Antonioniego "Zawód reporter."* Łódź: Studio Filmowe N, 1996.
Lacan, Jacques. *The Seminar of Jacques Lacan, Book VIII: Transference*. Ed. Jacques-Alain Miller. Trans. Bruce Fink. Cambridge: Polity Press, 2015.
Lacan, Jacques. *The Seminar of Jacques Lacan, Book XI: The Four Fundamental Concepts of Psychoanalysis*. Ed. Jacques-Alain Miller. Trans. Alan Sheridan. New York: W. W. Norton, 1981.
Luzzi, Joseph. *A Cinema of Poetry: Aesthetics of the Italian Art Film*. Baltimore: The Johns Hopkins University Press, 2014.
Marx, Leo. *The Machine in the Garden: Technology and the Pastoral Ideal in America*. Oxford: Oxford University Press, 2000. First published 1964.
Miller Lane, Barbara. "Modern Architecture and Politics in Germany, 1918–1945." In *Housing and Dwelling: Perspectives on Modern Domestic Architecture*, edited by Barbara Miller Lane, 259–68. Oxon: Routledge, 2007.
Musil, Robert. *The Man without Qualities*. Trans. Sophie Wilkins. New York: Vintage, 1996.
Nash, Roderick Frazier. *The Wilderness and the American Mind*. New Haven: Yale University Press, 2014. First published 1967.
Paci, Enzo. "Uomini, scimmie e cose." In *L'Europeo*, edited by Roberto Leydi. (Milan), April 22, 1962.
Pasolini, Pier Paolo. "The Cinema of Poetry." In *Movies and Methods, Volume I*, edited by Bill Nichols, 542–58. Berkeley: University of California Press, 1976.
Pasolini, Pier Paolo. "Il vuoto del potere in Italia." *Corriere della sera*, February 1, 1975.
Perez, Gilberto. *The Material Ghost: Films and Their Medium*. Baltimore: The Johns Hopkins University Press, 1998.
Pomerance, Murray. *Michelangelo Red Antonioni Blue: Eight Reflections on Cinema*. Berkeley: University of California Press, 2011.
Rascaroli, Laura and John David Rhodes, eds. *Antonioni: Centenary Essays*. Basingstoke: BFI/Palgrave Macmillan, 2011.

Rascaroli, Laura and John David Rhodes, "Interstitial, Pretentious, Dead: Antonioni at 100." In *Antonioni: Centenary Essays*, edited by Laura Rascaroli and John David Rhodes, 1–17.

Reed, Ishmael. Preface to *Soul on Ice*, by Eldridge Cleaver, 1–11. New York: Dell Publishing, 1999.

Restivo, Angelo. *The Cinema of Economic Miracles: Visuality and Modernisation in the Italian Art Film*. Durham, NC: Duke University Press, 2002.

Restivo, Angelo. "Revisiting *Zabriskie Point*." In *Antonioni: Centenary Essays*, edited by Laura Rascaroli and John David Rhodes, 82–97.

Rohdie, Sam. *Antonioni*. London: British Film Institute, 1990.

Ropars-Wuilleumier, Marie-Claire. "L'espace et le temps dans la narration des années 60: 'Blow up' ou le négatif du récit." In *Michelangelo Antonioni 1966/84*, edited by Lorenzo Cuccu, 206–32. Rome: Ente Autonomo di Gestione per il Cinema, 1988.

Rowe, Colin. "James Stirling: A Highly Personal and Very Disjointed Memoir." In *James Stirling: Buildings and Projects*, edited by Peter Arnell and Ted Bickford, 10–27. New York: Rizzoli Publications, 1984.

Simon, John. "Thoughts on *L'avventura*." In *L'avventura*, edited by George Amberg and Robert Hughes, 267–72.

Sitney, P. Adams. *Vital Crises in Italian Cinema: Iconography, Stylistics, Politics*. Oxford: Oxford University Press, 2013. First published 1995 by University of Texas Press.

Sontag, Susan. *On Photography*. London: Penguin, 1979.

Young, Vernon. "Reflections on Two American Films." *The Hudson Review* 23, no. 3 (Autumn 1970): 533–9.

Žižek, Slavoj. *Enjoy Your Symptom! Jacques Lacan in Hollywood and Out*. Routledge: London, 1992.

Zupančič, Alenka. *The Shortest Shadow: Nietzsche's Philosophy of the Two*. Cambridge, MA: The MIT Press, 2003.

The Internet

Pasolini, Pier Paolo. "Disappearance of Fireflies." Trans. Christopher Mott. Accessed September 24, 2019. http://www.diagonalthoughts.com/?p=2107.

Rosenfeld, David Saul. "Michelangelo Antonioni's *L'eclisse*: A Broken Piece of Wood, a Matchbook, a Woman, a Man." Accessed June 8, 2019. http://www.davidsaulrosenfeld.com/.

Scalia, Rossella. "Schisina Ghost Villages, Sicily." Accessed February 19, 2018. https://vimeo.com/126946161.

Filmography

Films directed by Michelangelo Antonioni:

L'avventura (1960)
Production: A Cino del Duca, co-production: Cinematographische Europee (Rome) and Société Cinématographique Lyre (Paris); story: Antonioni; script: Antonioni, Elio Bartolini, Tonino Guerra; photography: Aldo Scavarda; music: Giovanni Fusco; editing: Eraldo da Roma. Cast: Gabriele Ferzetti, Monica Vitti, Lea Massari, Dominique Blanchard, Renzo Ricci, James Addams, Dorothy De Poliolo, Giovanni Petrucci. 145 mins.

La notte (1961)
Production: Emanuele Casutto for Nepi-Film (Rome), Silva Film (Rome), and Sofitedip (Paris); story: Antonioni; script: Antonioni, Ennio Flaiano, Tonino Guerra; photography: Gianni di Venanzo; music: Giorgio Gaslini; editing: Eraldo da Roma; cast: Marcello Mastroanni, Jeanne Moreau, Monica Vitti, Bernhard Wicki, Maria Pia Luzi, Gitt Magrini, Vincenzo Corbella. 122 mins.

L'eclisse (1962)
Production: Robert and Raymond Hakim for Interopa Film, Cineriz (Rome), and Paris Film Production (Paris); story: Antonioni and Tonino Guerra; script: Antonioni, Tonino Guerra, Elio Bartolini, Ottiero Ottieri; photography: Gianni di Venanzo; music: Giovanni Fusco; editing: Eraldo da Roma; cast: Monica Vitti, Alain Delon, Lilla Brignone, Francisco Rabal. 125 mins.

Il deserto rosso/Red Desert (1964)
Production: Antonio Cervi for Film Duemila, Cinematographica Federiz (Rome), and Francoriz (Paris); story: Antonioni and Tonino Guerra; script: Antonioni and Tonino Guerra; photography: Carlo di Palma; music: Giovanni Fusco, electronic music: Vittorio Gelmetti; editing: Eraldo da Roma; cast: Monica Vitti, Richard Harris, Carlo de Pra, Aldo Grotti, Valerio Bartoleschi. 120 mins (UK and US 116 mins).

Blow-Up (1966)
Production: Bridge Films (Carlo Ponti) for Matro-Goldwyn-Mayer; story: based on "Las babas del diablo" by Julio Cortàzar; script: Antonioni and Tonino Guerra; photography: Carlo di Palma; music: Herbert Hancock, The Yardbirds; editing: Frank Clarke; cast: David Hemmings, Vanessa Redgrave, Sarah Miles, Peter Bowles, Verushka. 111 mins.

Zabriskie Point (1970)
Production: Carlo Ponti for MGM; script: Antonioni, Fred Gardner, Sam Shepard, Tonino Guerra, and Clare Peploe; photography: Alfio Conti; music: Pink Floyd, The Rolling Stones, The Youngbloods, The Greateful Dead; editing: Franco Arcalli; cast: Mark Frechette, Daria Halprin, Rod Taylor. 110 mins.

Professione: Reporter/The Passenger (1975)
Production: Carlo Ponti for MGM, co-production: Compagnia Cinematografica Champion (Rome), Les Films Concordia (Paris), and CIPI Cinematográfica (Madrid); story: Mark Peploe; script: Mark Peploe, Peter Wollen, and Antonioni; photography: LucianoTovoli; editing: Franco Arcalli and Antonioni; cast: Jack Nicholson, Maria Schneider, Jenny Runacre, Ian Hendry. European version 127 mins, English-language version 122 mins.

Stromboli, terra di Dio/Stromboli, Land of God (1949), dir. Roberto Rossellini
Production: Berit Film (Roberto Rossellini and Ingrid Bergman) and RKO; story: Rossellini; script: Rossellini, Gian Paolo Callegari, Renzo Cesana, Art Cohn, Sergio Amidei; photography: Otello Martelli; music: Renzo Rossellini; editing: Jolanda Benvenuti and Roland Gross (for the American version); cast: Ingrid Bergman, Mario Vitale, Renzo Cesana, Mario Sponza, and the people of Stromboli. 105 mins (81 mins in the American version).

DVDs/Blu-rays

L'avventura. DVD. New York: The Criterion Collection, 2001.
La notte. DVD. London: Eureka Entertainment, 2008.
L'eclisse. DVD. New York: The Criterion Collection, 2005.
Red Desert (*Il deserto rosso*). DVD/Blu-ray. London: British Film Institute, 2011.
Blow-Up. DVD. Burbank, CA: Turner Entertainment/Warner Home Video, 2004.
Zabriskie Point. DVD. Burbank, CA: Turner Entertainment/Warner Home Video, 2009.
The Passenger. DVD. Culver City, CA: Sony Pictures Home Entertainment, 2006.
Stromboli, Land of God (*Stromboli, terra di Dio*). Blu-ray. London: British Film Institute, 2015.

Index

Abbey, Edward 150, 151
Adorno, Theodor W. 41, 49
Alice in Wonderland (Lewis Carroll) 163–4
alienation 11–13, 43, 75, 96
allegory 59, 102, 174
antagonism (political) 46, 97, 120, 158
anxiety 52, 53, 54, 68, 90, 94, 101, 103, 108, 109, 110
architecture 25, 28–9, 38, 43–5, 69–70, 75 n.5, 151 n.34, 171 n.18
authenticity 150

Baudelaire, Charles 56 n.44–5
Baudrillard, Jean 99 n.18, 138 n.4, 151 n.34
Bauhaus 69
Beck, Jeff 127
Benjamin, Walter 56 n.44, 102
Berger, John 122 n.17
Bergman, Ingmar 1, 2, 3, 8
Bergman, Ingrid 3 n.4, 15
Bergson, Henri 23
beyond 101, 104–5, 106–7, 109, 112. *See also* transcendence
Black struggle 135, 144–6, 147
boom (Italian economic/building) 7, 13, 25, 27, 28, 33, 45, 56, 58 n.49, 59, 74, 75 n.5, 85
Bourdieu, Pierre 53 n.36
Broch, Hermann 51

Cannes Film Festival statement 11, 13–14, 19. *See also* Eros *and* malady of sentiments
capital 7, 8, 24, 45, 57, 66, 67, 69, 70
  and writing 50
Cassa per il Mezzogiorno 31, 32
Chinatown (Roman Polański) 144 n. 19
Christian Democrats (Democrazia Cristiana) 27, 31, 45, 79, 112
Cleaver, Kathleen 135
cognitive habits 168

Cold War 50 n.26, 85
colonialism 78, 79 n.13, 85, 86
comism, 20–1, 22, 23, 33–4. *See also* humor
commodity 50, 52, 53, 55, 58, 59, 60, 68
consumerism 45, 97, 98, 99, 113
creative disintegration 9
Crèvecœur, J. Hector St. John de 139
The Crew (Michelangelo Antonioni) 9
The Cry (Michelangelo Antonioni) 5–6

death drive 101
decolonization 162
depression 94, 100
desert 138, 141, 142, 155, 157, 158, 170, 171
  as home 152–4, 157
  man-made 143–4
  space of 148–52
Desert Solitaire (Edward Abbey) 150–1
desire 104, 129, 151
detachment 164, 169, 172, 174. *See also* objectivity
development (real estate) 141, 142, 150, 153, 154, 157 n.47, 159
double (*doppelgänger*) 37, 47, 51 n.28
dystopia 93

economic miracle (Italian) 75, 94, 99, 107, 112
8½ (Federico Fellini) 34 n.64
enjoyment (*jouissance*) 23, 26, 32, 34, 36, 44, 48, 49, 57, 58, 66, 69, 96, 100, 101, 104, 107, 111, 155
  and architecture in *L'avventura* 28–30, 32–3
  and architecture in *La notte* 44–5
  of capital 45, 46 n.14, 70
  comic side of 23
  consumer 99, 101
  feminine 33
  patriarchal 32, 35, 36, 37, 38, 39, 47

Ente Nazionale Idrocarburi (ENI) 94–5
Ente per la Riforma Agraria in Sicilia (ERAS) 31, 32
epiphany 81, 86, 87
epistemological uncertainty 117, 123
Eros (sickness of) 11, 13, 14, 33, 42. *See also* Cannes Film Festival statement; malady of sentiments
Espozicione Universale Roma (EUR) 74, 75, 79, 81
eternal-feminine 54, 67
excitation 103, 108, 109, 112. *See also* enjoyment

fantasy 37, 39, 73, 76, 79–80, 109, 113, 129, 131, 141
   male 33, 51, 53
   of nature in *Blow-Up* 116, 118–19
   of nature in *L'eclisse* 79–84
   of nature in *Red Desert* 95–8, 100, 105, 106, 110, 113
   pastoral in *Zabriskie Point* 139–40, 141, 143, 144, 145, 149, 152, 153, 154–5, 156, 157, 158, 159
   and Afro-Americans 144–5
   and native Americans 157–8
   two modalities of in *L'eclisse* 77–9, 80
Fascism 27, 75 n. 5, 79, 99 n. 19
Fellini, Federico 3
femininity 53 n. 36. *See also* eternal-feminine
filth 93, 99, 100, 102, 103, 104, 107, 112, 113, 171–2. *See also* pollution
flânerie 56, 60
fragmentation 72, 97, 122–3
Frontier 140, 141, 150
future 49–50, 59, 65, 66, 67, 68, 112

Gaudí, Antoni 164 n.4, 171 n.18, 173 n.19
gaze 39, 73–4
genocide 158
Geworfenheit 14
The Girl Friends (Michelangelo Antonioni) 4
glory 173 n. 19, 174
Gropius, Walter 69

Hands over the City (Francesco Rosi) 31 n.52
Hemingway, Ernest 46 n.11, 78–9, 81
horizon 140, 141, 150, 151, 152. *See also* Frontier
humor 155 n. 43, 163–4, 172, 175, 176. *See also* comism
hyperreality 97, 159
hyperspace 59

Identification of a Woman (Michelangelo Antonioni) 9
identity 56, 59, 164
illusion 117, 120, 121, 130, 137, 138
impulse 118–19
intensity 126–7

Jagger, Mick 156
Jefferson, Thomas 139–40
Journey to Italy (Roberto Rossellini) 3 n.4

Kierkegaard, Søren 19 n. 22

Lacan, Jacques 101, 105 n.30, 151
The Lady without Camellias (Michelangelo Antonioni) 4–5
Last Tango in Paris (Bernardo Bertolucci) 163 n. 2
look 73–4, 100, 103, 105, 130 n. 39
looking (lesson in) 170, 172, 174–5

malady of sentiments (*malattia dei sentimenti*) 42, 53, 85
market 99, 100
Mattei, Enrico 95, 107
melancholy 103, 163, 164, 170, 171, 174
   the discourse of 102
melodrama 55, 56, 62, 63–5, 67
Metropolis (Fritz Lang) 93
miracle (Italian economic) 75, 94, 95, 99, 107, 112
Munk, Andrzej 162
Musil, Robert 49
The Mystery of Oberwald (Michelangelo Antonioni) 9

neorealism (Italian) 3
neutralization of the political 120–1

North by Northwest (Alfred Hitchcock) 153
Notes on the State of Virginia (Thomas Jefferson) 139

objectivity 164, 169, 171, 172
  as violence 169
out-of-focus shots 107, 111–12, 134, 137

panopticism 57, 58, 59, 69
Pasolini, Pier Paolo 1–2, 7, 98 n.15, 99 n.19
pastoral 77, 137, 139–40, 141, 143, 144
patriarchy 7, 15, 23, 25, 27, 29, 38, 53, 55, 62, 67, 68
  and architecture/real estate 32–3
  and feminine enjoyment 33–4
  submission to in *L'avventura* 39
  two modalities of in *L'avventura* 20–2
  withdrawal from in *L'avventura* 17–20
Pavese, Cesare 4
periphery 60, 66
phantasmagoria 51, 67, 142, 152, 157
  and commodity 52, 53
photography 121–2
Pirelli skyscraper 43, 57, 69
plastic 98, 113
pollution 95. *See also* filth
preservationism 150
Psycho (Alfred Hitchcock) 138, 155 n. 41

real estate 24, 31, 32–3
reconciliability 12, 127
Reed, Ishmael 147
reification 85, 86, 90
road movie 161–2, 170
Rohe, Ludwig Mies van der 69
Roman Charity (Cimon and Pero) 34–5, 39

sacrifice 26, 46, 63, 64, 65
St Peter's basilica 27, 33, 39
Sicilian Baroque 25, 28
"The Snows of Kilimanjaro" (Ernest Hemingway) 78–9, 8 n.18
social cement 97
social construction of meaning 128–9
Sontag, Susan 122 n.17
spectrality 50, 68, 130
  spectral materiality 7, 8
  spectral woman in *La notte* 51–4

stasis 140, 143, 144
Story of the Love Affair (Michelangelo Antonioni) 4–5
Stromboli, Land of God (Roberto Rossellini) 14–16, 18, 20, 21, 23, 28 n. 45
sublimity 86, 106
symbol 102, 103

Taut, Bruno 69
Tender Is the Night (F. Scott Fitzgerald) 19 n.22
transcendence 65, 68, 69, 102, 103, 130, 174
Transcendentalism 140

unknowable 150, 156
unrepresentable 48, 86, 90, 127
utopia 8, 60, 65–6, 67, 68, 69, 72, 90, 91, 105 n.31, 112, 113

The Vanquished (Michelangelo Antonioni) 4 n.6
Vatican 33
violence 9, 60, 79, 85, 126, 127, 128, 137, 138, 144, 154, 158, 162, 172
  police in *Zabriskie Point* 147–8
  as political substance 167
  unrepresentable 86
virtuality 66, 67, 81, 90, 91, 141, 143, 159
  two modalities of in *L'eclisse* 86–6
  virtual space in *Zabriskie Point* 141, 143
vision
  cleansing of 172
  intensity of 170, 174
  stereoscopy of 174
visionary moment/experience 81–2, 65–6, 174
Visconti, Luchino 1, 3

wilderness 150
writing
  mechanization of 50, 57
  as vocation 66

Yardbirds 126

Žižek, Slavoj 16

www.ingramcontent.com/pod-product-compliance
Lightning Source LLC
Chambersburg PA
CBHW052046300426
44117CB00012B/1993